Coming Full Circle

ALSO BY WANDA LLOYD

The Edge of Change: Women in the 21st Century Press
(CO-EDITOR, 2009)

COMING
FULL
CIRCLE

From Jim Crow to Journalism

WANDA SMALLS LLOYD

Foreword by Tina McElroy Ansa

NewSouth Books

Montgomery

NewSouth Books
105 S. Court Street
Montgomery, AL 36104

LIBRARY OF CONGRESS CATALOGING-IN-PUBLICATION DATA
Names: Lloyd, Wanda S., author. Title: Coming full circle : from Jim Crow to
journalism / Wanda Smalls Lloyd ; foreword by Tina McElroy Ansa.
Description: Montgomery : NewSouth Books, 2020. | Identifiers: LCCN
2019043238 (print) | LCCN 2019043239 (ebook) | ISBN 9781588384072
(hardback) | ISBN 9781588384089 (ebook)
Subjects: LCSH: Lloyd, Wanda S. | Journalists—United States—Biography. |
African American women journalists—Biography. | African American
newspaper editors—Biography.
Classification: LCC PN4874.L565 A3 2020 (print) | LCC PN4874.L565 (ebook)
| DDC 070.92 [B]—dc23
LC record available at https://lccn.loc.gov/2019043238
LC ebook record available at https://lccn.loc.gov/2019043239

Design by Randall Williams
Printed in the United States of America by Sheridan

NEWSOUTH BOOKS: Suzanne La Rosa, publisher; Randall Williams, editor-in-chief;
Lisa Emerson, accounting manager; Lisa Harrison, publicist; Matthew Byrne,
production manager; Beth Marino, senior publicity/marketing manager; Kelly Snyder
and Isabella Barrera, editorial and publicity assistants; Laura Murray, cover designer.

The Black Belt, defined by its dark, rich soil, stretches across central Alabama. It was the heart of the cotton belt. It was and is a place of great beauty, of extreme wealth and grinding poverty, of pain and joy. Here we take our stand, listening to the past, looking to the future.

To Willie Lloyd, my rock.

To Shelby Lloyd, my sunshine.

"If they don't give you a seat at the table, bring a folding chair."

— SHIRLEY CHISHOLM

Contents

Foreword

TINA MCELROY ANSA

Just to tell you what kind of woman Wanda Smalls Lloyd is: The moment she informed me she had decided to focus and write the memoir we had talked about for years I began composing this foreword. I was just that certain that she would complete her goal. And more importantly, I knew Wanda had a story to tell. I've known that for decades.

Her past and journey held an important story. And luckily for us readers, she had the tools to tell it. As those who know her can attest, as usual, she did not fail to deliver.

The wonderful thing about a truly fine memoir is the boxes of memories it also opens up in the author. It should open up doors to the writer's past; windows into her house; closets into his own memories. Just as one turns the pages of a memoir of merit, one carefully pulls open the dusty drawers of one's own faintly familiar chest or desk.

Writing one's first book—I mean hunkering down in your soul and deciding this is the thing you are going to accomplish—changes you. Digging deeply into your past takes distance and closeness, objectivity and understanding, vulnerability and guts. For some, it is too deep and unsettling a plunge. That plunge is the very thing that gives this memoir meat.

The examination of self can be a daunting task. However, miraculous things happen when you write from your heart as well as your head. This insightful heartfelt memoir is such a lovely example of just that. Lifetime journalist Wanda Lloyd set out, she thought, to write a standard career autobiography: African American girl from the segregated South follows her dream to learn the craft and end up in an executive corner office overlooking the Potomac River at *USA Today* and in the editor's chair of the daily newspaper in Alabama's capital city. Yet what she has written is no "Up from Segregation" story. This is a life—curious, sharp, circuitous, full of epiphanies and lessons learned. Nuanced. Personal. Revealing. So familiar to some readers; a revelation to others.

I always thought of my friend as invincible. Fearless. Formidable. Words I dared not use on myself seemed to fit her perfectly. And of course, not one of us living is totally all that. We are human, flawed, confused, vulnerable, smart, scared, scarred, brave, triumphant. Wanda shows in *Coming Full Circle* how one can be all those things and live a wonderful life.

It is one of the elements that I especially love about this volume of memoir: the way in which the author is so open and transparent about her life, her feelings, her weaknesses as well as her myriad accomplishments, and yes, even her fears. In fact, this book is itself a little like the author. (And isn't that the best kind?) Formal, precise, edited, spell-checked, correct, beautifully written on first glance. Then, as we delve a bit more into this story, we see the rich, fecund, little-mined vein beneath.

In the author's own words, as she completed the volume, "Now, it's a whole other book, Tina. A different deeper story than I even realized myself."

It has been a fascinating discovery to watch unfold.

I MET WANDA ON the first fall day as freshmen at Spelman College more than fifty years ago. We both came to the college's Atlanta campus from the south: me from Macon in the middle of the state and Wanda from Savannah on the coast. In true Wanda style, by the time I arrived in our second-floor dorm room overlooking a huge leafy oak tree, she had moved in, unpacked, and already purchased and installed red-and-black checkered curtains and bedspreads for us both. So began our journey/friendship.

We were completely different in many ways—temperament, temperature, taste, timing. Wanda made her bed each morning upon rising. I figured, why bother? She completed her assignments as soon as they were given. I was up all night just before they were due. She slept with the window open. I couldn't stand the draft.

However, on one thing we agreed: We both knew we wanted a life of words, writing for a living.

Truth be told, despite our differences, in the quiet moments we did influence each other. Although the rest of us English majors in our freshman dorm teased her for duty to learning while we wasted hours playing bid whist on my bed, the sight of Wanda bent over her electric typewriter the first day of the assignment was an image the influence of which was inestimable. Even after we parted as roommates our sophomore year, Wanda continued to influence me. She is one of the reasons that I became a journalist. Junior year, she marched into my dorm room and shamed me into joining the school newspaper of which she would become the editor. "You call yourself a writer and you don't even write for the *Spelman Spotlight!*" Then, the next year, she insisted that I take the few classes offered in the fledgling journalism department at Clark College across the street.

She tends to do that.

I've known Wanda through our college years, through our first jobs in publishing, through moves and marriage and motherhood. And somehow I always knew she would write this memoir. Wanda is memorable. Ask any of the many colleagues, students, and green reporters who have been touched and changed by her knowledge and experience and wisdom.

I have always been impressed with Wanda. She is deeply moral and deeply honest. In fact, waaayyy honest. I learned early on in our relationship not to ask her a question if I did not want a straight-no-chaser answer. But after fifty years of friendship and life, I know that I can trust her word. That's a lot of years to witness someone you know and admire achieve, explore, stumble, get up, pivot, start over, and succeed again. And in all that time keep to her cultural/historical/family and moral center.

Wanda is a font of memories that not only show what she did, but more importantly, how she did it. It is in just those moments that *Coming Full Circle* teaches readers, young and, well, seasoned, how to be fighters.

The writer weaves and bobs through her life, then, turns back and flips on us, giving us seemingly innocent information about herself, or a colleague, a mentor, her mother—the glamorous globe-trotting Gloria—only to circle back to an epiphany we did not see coming.

I saw Wanda work hard to dig deep into her seven decades on this earth.

I'm proud to know Wanda, and I'm even more pleased that you, the reader, will get to know her, too.

––––––––––––

Tina McElroy Ansa is the award-winning author of five novels, including Baby of the Family, Ugly Ways *and* The Hand I Fan With. *She writes from her home on St. Simons Island, Georgia.*

Preface

I grew up in Savannah, just off the coast of Georgia at a time when there were two societies—one black and one white. For every accommodation that existed for white people, there was a separate yet unequal accommodation for colored people or Negroes, as we were called at the time. It was long after I became an adult and moved away before I learned just how different those societies were. Ironically, a white author named John Berendt blew the cover off Savannah's white society for me in 1994 when his *Midnight in the Garden of Good and Evil* bounded onto the *New York Times* bestseller list and stayed there for a record-breaking four years. The book became a popular movie in 1997.

Midnight—or "The Book" (with "The" pronounced "Thee") as people in Savannah still refer to Berendt's work—used a variety of eccentric personalities to tell the story of a local murder and the several court trials of suspect Jim Williams, a white male socialite who was ultimately acquitted. While that book's intrigue kept readers glued to the pages, the real story for some of us was how, in decades past, certain people in Savannah had advantages of wealth, protected neighborhoods with amenities, better quality schools, grand cultural venues, and high-society balls that celebrated life's milestones. As African Americans, we had our own cultural opportunities—albeit less grand—but the white world we read about in "The Book" was one most of us didn't know about, didn't think about, and probably didn't care about.

As African Americans, we lived in an isolated world, in communities where our neighbors included those who were college-educated and those who never graduated from high school. We lived together in a supportive way, in neighborhoods where some households were led by women who were educators and some by men who wore uniforms to work. Ours was a community whose teachers had superior expectations for our academic success even though they were forced to teach us in substandard facilities with hand-me-down books and furniture carted over from white schools, cementing in our minds the fact that we were considered second-class citizens.

When I consider it, I am shaken by the reality that although I was born eighty-four years after slavery was legally abolished, the nation of my youth was still in a state of racial brokenness. My generation came of age when Negro men and women could still be killed for merely disobeying a white person's orders, or a black man for looking at a white woman a certain way. Public lynchings often followed court proceedings that already were a white male supremacy system of justice, or injustice. Lynchings waned after the 1920s, the decade of my parents' births, and the 1930s, but they did occur in the 1950s and '60s and were regularly chronicled in *Jet* magazine, the national newsweekly for and about black people that came in the mail to our homes. It was in *Jet* that we first saw the horrific photo of the body of Emmett Till, the black Chicago youth who was mutilated and killed by white men while he was visiting relatives in Mississippi—the *Jet* headline read, "Negro Boy Was Killed for 'Wolf Whistle.'"

After the era of physical lynchings, social lynchings continued for decades. These denied civil rights to African Americans by suppressing opportunities for education, employment, housing, transportation, and many more areas rigidly controlled by the laws and customs of Jim Crow segregation. Members of my own family suffered the indignities of segregation. Others joined the NAACP and became part of the solution, as exhibited by the collection of loving cups engraved with my late grandfather's name displayed on the living room mantel in my grandmother's house.

In Savannah, I grew up in a solidly middle class, well-educated family. If you want to read a "poor me" story, this is not the place. Mine is not a rags-to-riches story. Yet among African Americans, there was no distinction between class or income during Jim Crow years. We endured the city's separate and subpar facilities. Between us, African Americans had great respect for each other. But laws dictated that white people would consider us second-class citizens no matter who we were.

I stepped into adulthood crossing the bridge between full segregation and the civil rights movement. As a child I attended some of the movement's mass meetings at churches in Savannah. Later, as a student at Spelman College, I saw and heard Dr. Martin Luther King Jr. speak at a standing-room-only and spiritually rousing evening service at Mount Moriah Baptist Church, across the street from Morehouse College. The civil rights movement left me appreciative of the right to worship God without fear of reprisal and to vote without fear of sanction, and grateful for the five freedoms in the First Amendment. I have enjoyed the benefits of freedom of the press and have celebrated that I could go to any school or work in any place where I am qualified to be.

When I turned eighteen, I couldn't wait to register, and I have never *not* voted in a statewide or national election in the eight states in which I have lived and worked since then. Too many people—black and white— were hosed down, attacked by dogs, beaten or shot for me to understand why any citizen would miss an opportunity to submit a ballot for political representation.

AFTER HIGH SCHOOL, I was ready to get away from Savannah. On a Monday morning, the day after graduation, I tossed a packed suitcase into the trunk of my Uncle James's Cadillac Fleetwood before he returned home to New York City.

"I'm going home with you," I told him.

Like most graduates, we had received only diploma covers during the ceremony, and we would have to go to the school the next day to pick up our diplomas. "Drive me to the school," I said. "Park out front. Keep the motor running."

Somehow, I made it into journalism despite growing up in a place where I didn't have African American or female role models in the profession. In our community, television news and mainstream newspaper ranks were filled with white men. I read the black press and our local daily newspapers, but still, my world was small. I was familiar with John H. Johnson, the African

American man who used a small loan from his mother when he founded *Ebony* and *Jet* magazines, national publications based in Chicago. But as a child I didn't yet know about the accomplishments of journalists like Ethel Lois Payne, who was known as "the first lady of the black press" and later became a correspondent for CBS News, Ida B. Wells, who in the 1890s documented and investigated lynchings in the United States, or Tuskegee Airman Chuck Stone, who started his career at the black weekly *New York Age* and then worked as a columnist for the mainstream *Philadelphia Daily News*. There were no lessons in our public schools about the many pioneering journalists in the black press. As an African American and female, I knew journalism was different for us. But I wonder how many, like me, knew just how different.

Ultimately, I rose to a place in my career where I was able to address the lack of diversity and to help make the path easier for women and people of color to make their own difference through the stories they would tell or the newsrooms they would run. My journey is outlined here, with hopes that younger generations of women, African Americans, and others will be inspired to knock down walls and push through glass ceilings.

In the twenty-first century, in some ways, life is so much better. Middle-income black families live in neighborhoods side by side with diverse populations of people. For the most part, children of different races play together, adults work together, and there is no legal separation. Still, we have seen many signs of racial regression, especially under the administration of the forty-fifth president. In some circles it is still difficult and rare to have open and meaningful conversations about race and racist behavior across racial and cultural lines. Despite the election of the first African American president in 2008, the administration that followed Barack Obama's came in with an agenda seemingly based on political division and the rancor of racism.

IT TOOK MORE THAN twenty years to get as far away from Savannah's systemic oppression as I could, and it took about the same additional time to figure out how to return and help make my hometown better.

In 1996, I was leaving *USA Today* and the Washington, D.C., area, heading for my next newspaper in South Carolina. I said at my going-away party at *USA Today*: "I am not in the South, but the South is still in me."

I was about to begin a reverse journey that took another seventeen years to complete. I returned to Savannah in 2013 as an associate professor and chair of the Department of Journalism and Mass Communications at Savannah State University.

That's when I realized that life is all about coming full circle.

ACKNOWLEDGMENTS

I owe much to so many.

I write to honor Mrs. Ella P. Law, my high school journalism teacher who saw in me not only a passion for writing, but also my ability to be a newsroom leader. After a year in her journalism class in the eleventh grade, Mrs. Law appointed me to be editor-in-chief of the *Beach Beacon* at the all-black Alfred Ely Beach High School in Savannah, Georgia. And I write to honor Alan Bussell, a white journalist who left his newspaper job in Memphis, Tennessee, to teach journalism at Clark College, an HBCU in Atlanta, Georgia. He took a fledgling program and created a generation of young journalists who went to work at notable mainstream media companies.

I honor the women in my family. Although none were writers, they were instrumental in my development as a journalist by always telling life stories. Their oral history lessons bolstered my capacity for writing success. I hope I do them justice with this memoir. My maternal grandmother, Oper Lee Watson Walker, set high standards for me to become a proper young lady and responsible adult. My mother's sister, Catherine Walker Williams, with her husband, Osie, took me in at my request when I was eight years old. Aunt Catherine, with her Spelman College undergraduate degree in English and her master's degree in reading, taught me to read at an early age. She built a library in a closet at home and stocked it with books and encyclopedias to ensure I could constantly have my head in a book. My mother, Gloria Walker, set out on her own career path far away from me, but she was the corporate role model I needed when my career began to blossom as an executive. She gave me insight into what it was like to be a black woman working in a world of mostly white men.

I am grateful that my mother demanded that I mail frequent handwritten letters to her. As much as I hated it at the time, I am thankful that she used a red pen to correct my spelling and grammar and sent the letters back to me. She was dismayed that I was not required to take Latin, as she had in high school, but she taught me from her remembered lessons about root words, to help me better understand language. These lessons made me a better editor and writer.

I honor my friend, Stacy Hawkins Adams, a student I "adopted" (or maybe she adopted me) as a mentee when I visited her Jackson State University campus in Mississippi. Stacy thrived in journalism before she transitioned to writing novels. At some point, the mentee became my mentor. Stacy is one of many young people I have adopted throughout my career. When they are ready to fly, I always encourage them to inspire and to bring someone else along. She did that for me in completing this book.

I write to honor friends and colleagues across the nation—classmates from high school and Spelman College, people from newspapers and universities where I worked, and in the associations and churches where I have been a member—so many who followed the journey of my writing through my blog, social media posts, newspaper commentaries, and magazine articles. The constant feedback and comments of "I can't wait to read your book" kept me writing. I appreciate the students at Savannah State University who listened with great interest to my career adventures and encouraged me to write some of my stories to help inspire people of their generation.

I am humbled and grateful that NewSouth Books of Montgomery, Alabama, agreed to take me on as a project, thankful that Suzanne La Rosa patiently guided me through the business aspects of publishing. "Make every word count," she told me in our first conversation. I wrote it down and taped it above my computer, a daily reminder. And I am thankful for Randall Williams, the former journalist who is a masterful literary editor-in-chief. He held me accountable for every point of style, every word, every fact, every historical reference.

My first conversations about writing this memoir were with my friend Tina McElroy Ansa, my freshman-year college roommate and Georgia neighbor just a couple of hours down the road. Tina patiently listened to me talk about my desire to document my journey, especially for young African American women and others who might benefit from reading about my experiences. As a novelist, journalist, publisher, magazine writer, filmmaker, network television commentator and writing coach, Tina has been with me on this journey since our first day at Spelman. As different as we acknowledge that we are in personality, we are bonded through our love for the power of words. Along the way of this book, Tina held my heart in her hands and gently led me through the process, and she didn't give up on me when life got in the way of writing.

And most of all I write to honor my family. My husband, Willie Lloyd, has believed in me and supported every step of my career, sometimes giving up his own dreams so I could follow mine. Through more than four decades of marriage, he never complained about our moves to new cities and having to restart his own life with new employment and new friendships. He constantly pushed me to step into the spotlight while he walked in my shadow.

And I write to honor Shelby Lloyd, my daughter and my best friend. She is the one person who can make me smile and cry at the same time—mostly tears of joy. She has been patient with my career travel, my calls from work to say "I'll see you in thirty minutes" when it was sometimes a couple of hours before I arrived home because there was always one more story to edit, one more reporter who needed my time, one more reader calling to complain about coverage. Shelby endured the moves and school changes, the constant phone calls from aspiring journalists who needed a sympathetic ear on my days off and the interruptions in our conversations when we were out in public and young people stopped to ask for impromptu advice.

At some point, I realized that Shelby was listening to my conversations, doomed to repeat them when she, herself, became a mentor to young businesswomen. As I was writing this book, Shelby was anxious to read some of the essays and chapters, and she gave me quick and valuable feedback. It has been through the lens of Shelby's perspective, perched on the upper cusp of the millennial generation, that I realize how important it is to share my story.

Coming Full Circle

Prologue: A Seat at the Table

"Ooooh-ooo-wee, Sister *Lloyd*," a deacon said one Sunday morning as we passed each other in the hallway near the office at Mt. Zion Baptist Church in Arlington, Virginia. "I saw you on TV the other day, Sister Lloyd."

Sister is the title used in the Baptist church to denote that we are all family in the eyes of God. I slowed my walk through the crowded hallway that was boisterous with people laughing and hugging and children racing about between Sunday School and the 11 a.m. worship service.

"Good morning, Deacon. What do you mean?"

"I saw you on C-SPAN sitting at the head of that big table at *USA Today* and running the meeting with *aaaall* those white folks around you."

The deacon went on to describe in detail the conference room where the editors were working—an expansive table with seats for about twenty people, a wall of TVs tuned to different news programs, and another wall adorned with the front pages of the past few days. All the details were provided because he wanted me to know that he was really watching closely.

"Sister Lloyd," he said, "*you were in charge.*"

C-SPAN, the public-service cable TV network, chronicles public and governmental affairs in the nation's capital. In hot, steamy August, when Congress and much of the government shuts down for vacation, C-SPAN fills its programming void by visiting Washington-area news organizations like *USA Today*, which then was located in suburban Rosslyn, on the banks of the Potomac River in Arlington County, Virginia.

I was Senior Editor/Days and Administration at the time. The innocuous title, not of my choosing, nevertheless put me in a seat of influence at the newspaper, where I had quickly climbed the newsroom ladder after joining the staff in 1986 as a deputy managing editor.

The "administration" part of my title gave me responsibility for oversight of newsroom training and performance improvement, financial budgets, staff and internship recruiting, relationships with readers and journalism associations, and just about anything else that came along as a short- or long-term project. The "days" part of my job meant I was in charge of planning each edition from morning until evening, when other editors would take over what we call "getting the paper out the door."

I led two of the three daily news meetings that C-SPAN occasionally filmed, one broadcast of which the deacon had seen. My job was to make sure potential Page One stories and photographs were well into the planning process for the next edition. Occupying a seat at that table at *USA Today* let editors share story ideas that might make it to the next day's front page or other section fronts. There is no greater recognition for a reporter than to have his or her stories appear on Page One.

I HAD COME TO *USA Today* after eleven years in editing roles at the *Washington Post*—decidedly one of the best newspapers in the nation—and three other newspapers. For much of my last few years at the *Post*, I was deputy Washington editor for the news service— we called it LAT-WP—that was jointly owned by the *Post* and the *Los Angeles Times*. That role put me in a position to sit in on two of the daily newsroom meetings where the venerable editor Ben Bradlee was flanked at the table by representatives from the various newsroom staffs—sports, features, business, photography and the metro/local, national and international news teams. Those editors had a seat at the table, to share their best offerings of stories for the next day's newspapers. They all had a position of influence in a competitive atmosphere where they jockeyed for story and photo positions on Page One.

When I attended news meetings at the *Post*, I occupied a seat along the wall, ready to take notes and return to the news service area to put together my own "budget" of stories that would be available to the hundreds of LAT-WP clients worldwide.

I was in the room, but I was not yet at the table.

After those years at the *Washington Post*, where few people seemed to care about helping me advance my career, I then found myself at *USA Today* in a place where—once I exhibited more self-confidence and a desire to learn—I had the comfort of a team of colleagues who were supportive and encouraged me to stretch my leadership goals. Okay, perhaps some were just glad that someone else was willing to gather information about stories and put story budgets together. But I reveled in the added responsibility. My desire to learn grew every day, and my job expanded until one day I indeed was seated at the table.

At first I felt out of place. I was still relatively new to the newspaper, I didn't know my colleagues well, and I had to gain self-confidence about my knowledge of the stories I would be pitching. Second, I was still suffering from a place of inferiority around white people because I had come out of years of Jim Crow existence in the South. It made a difference, I think, growing up in an all-black environment instead of in a place of racial balance and inclusion. That was my own albatross—the emotional burden of generations of African Americans who were told to be silent in the presence of white people, who were told we could only go to schools with other blacks, or that we had to enter public buildings through back doors, or use "colored" water fountains or restrooms.

I carried this burden for a long time after I entered the working world. And now here I was, about fifteen years into my career, taking a seat at the table and being given the opportunity to lead in a bicultural society. I had to learn to be assertive and to assume high-level professional responsibilities, and to do all that amidst people who, I thought, were judging me from their white perspectives. When I joined the *USA Today* staff in 1986, I learned to prepare so I was confident in my knowledge every time I walked into a meeting. Every mistake I made was a lesson, and I was determined never to repeat mistakes. In fact, I worked hard at being over-prepared.

THE TIMING OF THAT Sunday morning encounter with the deacon was in the early 1990s. Very few people of color, especially women, were then in positions of influence in mainstream media newsrooms, not at newspapers and not in radio or television news. Very few of us had seats at the table.

The American Society of News Editors (ASNE), on whose board I served for six years, conducted an annual count of newsroom workers. ASNE didn't start counting women leaders until well into the 2000s, so there are no numbers for the period when I was senior editor at *USA Today*—seated at the table and leading those daily news meetings. But in 1990, the ASNE survey documented that minorities made up 7.8 percent of total newsroom staffs across the United States; one can assume that the number of women newsroom leaders, regardless of race, was similarly far below parity. In any case, when I retired from daily newspapers in 2013, ASNE counted only four African American women leading the newsrooms of the then more than one thousand U.S. dailies; my departure left the number at three.

Occupying a seat at the table gives one power and prestige, and a great deal of satisfaction comes to those who earn that responsibility. As leaders, we have a mandate to speak up and speak out. Sometimes young professionals—especially women—are shy about speaking up. I used to be one of them. But getting to the table after years of hard work is validation that we have much to contribute.

Having a seat at the table should include appreciating the platform to speak up in areas of coverage that are important to editors who are given those opportunities. It doesn't mean editors should unnecessarily ram certain stories into the newspaper or on TV, but in my case it gave me a chance to remind editors day after day that stories should reflect our readership, taking us beyond stories mainly of interest to white or male readers to those inviting all readers no matter their race, gender, age, geographic location, topics of interest, or political leanings.

Also, it was important for me to build a pipeline by looking around the newsroom, then with a staff of more than four hundred journalists, to see where we needed to add additional diverse people, and by helping to groom or encourage some toward taking their own seats at the table where news decisions are made.

I enjoyed my seat at the table. And because I had found people willing to bring me along, I soon took on the responsibility to support other young editors, especially young women and people of color. At the *Washington Post*, the news meetings had been culturally lonely for me. At *USA Today*,

I found it rewarding to be in a position to help build a diverse pipeline for leadership.

The dearth of women leaders in newsrooms is still a problem, as documented in Michelle Weldon's March 2017 article, "Making History: Why We Need More Women Leaders in Journalism," for *The Movement Blog* on the website of the nonprofit women's leadership organization, Take the Lead. Weldon wrote:

> Generations after women journalists have supposedly freed themselves from the mandatory "pink ghetto" of exclusively writing about topics of food, family, furniture, fun and fitness, the media landscape is still uneven. And it matters because who reports and edits the news gets to pick what information and news people watch, read and listen to, and what shapes their view of the world.

That is what having a seat at the table means to people who have influence over news decisions.

ON THE DAY THE deacon stopped me in the hallway at Mt. Zion Church, I saw the pride in his eyes at seeing this black woman—someone he actually knew—on C-SPAN in a position of power and authority. It warmed my heart that he was proud for me. No matter how much I hear from colleagues and friends of other races that they think I'm doing a good job—no matter what the task—it means so much more to get that kind of affirmation from one of my own people, the kind this deacon was offering me that Sunday morning. I live for validation from people who may have walked my journey, lived a life similar to mine, suffered oppression and the indignities of civil wrongs—and overcome.

On that day at Mt. Zion, I represented members of my extended family who pushed me beyond the expected reality for a black girl who grew up during the era of Jim Crow laws, the teachers in my segregated schools in Savannah who challenged me beyond the resources we were given, members of Second African Baptist Church in Savannah who taught me Bible stories in Sunday School and gave me Easter speeches to memorize and recite as my first lessons in public speaking. I represented the neighbor ladies who told stories on the front porch of my grandmother's house while swatting flies, fanning the summer heat, and drinking fresh-squeezed, ice-cold lemonade out of Mason jars. They encouraged me to make good grades and they scrutinized my report cards to reinforce their interest in my well-being. I represented the legacy of Spelman College (an HBCU) in Atlanta, an institution that gave leadership opportunities to generations of African American women, including two generations in my own family before me.

"You'll be great, baby," they would tell me, building my confidence along the way. That was my validation then, and on that Sunday morning in the church hallway it was as if the deacon was saying, "Well done. You have a seat at the table. Now use it to do some good."

USA Today was the first of many seats at the table for me—plenty of opportunities to do some good.

1. The Beginning

My mother, Gloria Marie Walker, was born in 1929 in her parents' house on West 41st Street in Savannah, Georgia. I was born in 1949 in Columbus, Ohio, but I was brought to the house in Savannah when I was six weeks old and it is where I spent much of my childhood. For reasons I will explain, it would take me years to call Gloria "Mother." In my young and confused mind, I thought for a long time that my grandmother was my mother, and that Gloria, as I called her in my early years, was my sister. Gloria was stunningly attractive, energetic, smart, and a lot of fun. I thought she was the ideal big sister.

Gloria and others in the family, and a few close family friends, referred to my maternal grandmother as "Mother" or "Mudear." So I mostly called my grandmother "Mother" as well. My earliest memories are in her home, which was built in the late 1920s with green-stained cedar shingles and with a metal green-and-white-striped awning across the broad front porch. A much-used wooden swing was suspended by metal chains from the porch ceiling. The swing would become the place where, as a child, I would make an important family decision.

I spent summer afternoons on that porch, reading books, singing songs, and playing with neighborhood friends. The two porch stoops held large cement pots of overgrown flowers that my grandmother misted on hot days to give a cooling effect when rare breezes stirred. On oppressively hot days when there was no breeze, we used cardboard fans—the kind common in churches and funeral homes—to cool ourselves, taking advantage of the shade provided by the porch awning and the lush greenery surrounding us. In the evening, those same fans were used to swat gnats and mosquitoes that buzzed around our heads and drew blood from our extremities. A mosquito buzzing around my ear today evokes the same dread it did so many decades ago.

MY MOTHER'S PARENTS WERE James Madison and Oper Lee Walker. For the times, and for an African American family, the Walkers were likely pretty well off. My grandfather, an insurance district manager with the Atlanta Life Insurance Company, moved his family to Savannah in the late 1920s.

My grandfather's career took him on the road a lot as he traveled throughout southeast Georgia and north Florida to hire and train insurance agents for Atlanta Life Insurance Company. He was well known in the Savannah community, working with the NAACP and becoming a deacon and superintendent of the Sunday School at Second African Baptist Church. He died when I was a year old.

My grandmother was one of two children of the Watsons, a family of sharecroppers in north Georgia. My grandmother and her sister, Eliza Marie, from whom my mother Gloria received her middle name, attended Spelman Normal School around the 1900s. The Watson sisters told me stories about how their father worked hard at farming to pay the ten dollars a month to keep both of his daughters in school at Spelman, which later became Spelman College.

"Auntie," my grandmother's sister, had a long career as a teacher in Canton, a city in Cherokee County in north Georgia. Auntie married James Allen Burge, an educator who became a school principal. Burge Street in Canton is named for the man I called "Uncle J. A."

My grandmother was also an educator, but what she taught was cosmetology and business. She learned her trade at Spelman and in Savannah she became Madam J. M. Walker—no relation to Madam C. J. Walker of St. Louis, the first black female self-made millionaire. According to the book *Madam C. J. Walker's Secrets to Success* by A'Lelia Bundles, the "Madam" title was adopted by black cosmetologists from women pioneers of the French beauty industry.

My grandmother used "J. M." in her professional name because she wanted to ensure the respect of white people on whom she relied for getting products and services for her business. "I don't want them to call me by my first name," she said. Even when she shopped downtown on Saturdays, white people working in the stores always referred to her as Mrs. Walker, a rare honor during an era in the South when white people often called black women "girl" or "gal."

She taught cosmetology to adults in night school at Beach-Cuyler School. When she opened her business on West Broad Street, she was president of the company and my grandfather was vice president. She named the business Boyce's School of Beauty Culture, giving it the middle name of her first-born child, Catherine Boyce Walker.

Growing up in the beauty school in the 1950s, I recall Boyce's as a bustling place, especially on Saturdays when working women took the time to indulge in beauty services. In the building's large front room, sinks for washing hair were mounted along a wall and huge floor-standing hair dryers were placed behind chairs along another wall. Each hairstyling station held an electric element designed to heat heavy irons for straightening and curling to tame black women's thick hair. The sizzle and smell of hot combs, curling irons, and burning hair permeated the place, along with music and gossip. Women came in looking bedraggled after a hard week of work. They left as visions of loveliness.

Some women were bold enough for the strong chemicals that colored their locks. Many older women left the shop with what was called a rinse, which left their thinning hair slightly blue or purple, a process I never appreciated as a beauty service. But the older women liked their rinses. "Who wants purple hair?" I would sometimes ask my grandmother. I never got a clear answer.

For years after her death when I would visit Savannah and run into women who were beauticians, some would give our family's Madam Walker credit for teaching them beauty culture and training them to successfully run their own businesses.

Like Madam C. J. Walker, my grandmother made the pomades used in her beauty school. At home the kitchen often smelled of the mixtures she created and put into small jars. She then affixed labels and took the jars to

Boyce's for use by her students and to sell to customers. I believe the difference between my grandmother and Madam C. J. Walker was that my grandmother never attempted to mass-produce her products, thus vastly limiting her income potential.

To this day, people ask me if my grandmother was *the* Madam Walker. "No," I say sadly, "my grandmother was never wealthy."

WEST BROAD STREET (NOW Martin Luther King Jr. Boulevard) was *the* corridor of commerce for the African American community. The street ran alongside a neighborhood called Frogtown, after the croaking creatures that emerged after heavy rains, where former slaves had settled after the Civil War. The area adjacent to Frogtown became a thriving black business district.

The segregated Star and Dunbar movie theaters, black-owned Savannah Pharmacy, barbers, beauty shops, funeral homes, and churches were established on West Broad Street. Black doctors and lawyers had offices on the street. The Wage Earner's Bank, built in 1914 as the second-largest black bank in the country, was located there, as were shoe repair shops, clothing stores, and hardware and general stores. Many of these businesses were owned by blacks, and other shops were owned by Jewish families who were apparently kind to black patrons, perhaps bespeaking the Jews' own unkind snubs by Savannah's white upper-crust society.

Businesses on West Broad Street were places where black people could spend their money with dignity, which was not always the case on Broughton Street, the busy promenade where blacks often were often not allowed to work behind the counter, or try on hats before they bought them, or have change put in our hands instead of dropped on the counter. On Broughton Street, black people couldn't eat at lunch counters or expect respect for the dollars we spent. West Broad Street was thus our world.

Meanwhile, the center of life for me was the big green house where the 41st Street Community Club was formed on the front porch in the early 1950s by a group of neighbor ladies who wanted to assure the continued safety and beauty of the neighborhood. This was the house where my grandmother took in boarders—insurance agents like my late grandfather—who were in Savannah on business at a time before local hotels opened their doors to the green money of black customers. These men would call ahead and ask if they could spend a few nights in her house. She would offer them a key, a bed and the opportunity to share our only bathroom—clean and simple with a toilet, pedestal sink, a wall-mounted medicine cabinet, and a claw-foot tub; there was never a shower. My grandmother would get up early and prepare a full breakfast of bacon or sausage, grits, toast, coffee, and fresh-squeezed orange juice before the salesman would depart to board the nearest city bus. She was running an early version of a bed and breakfast. It amazes me to think about it today, how safe we felt with strangers having a key and staying overnight in our home, just yards away from where we were sleeping in our own beds.

This was the house where Aunt Catherine was married in the living room in 1945, and where, as a child on pre-air-conditioning hot muggy nights I would nestle beside my grandmother on a daybed on the screened-in side porch. The house where I learned to serve my grandmother's bridge parties and garden club meetings and helped her by mixing tiny green mint candies with peanuts, making tea sandwiches, and filled the punch bowl with frappé—a chilled party drink made of ginger ale and colorful floating scoops of ice cream or sherbet.

I learned a lot from my grandmother and her friends about how to be a lady. "Mother" was stylish and formal. When we went out she wore gloves, a leather handbag and matching shoes, and on Sundays, always a stunning hat for church. She was an expert seamstress with an eye for color and design. She made almost all her church outfits. It was my pleasure as a little girl to go with her downtown on Saturdays to Hogan's Department Store that had a big selection of fabrics. She would pick out the cloth for her spring or winter wardrobe, and she and I would go through displays of sewing patterns and select the styles she would create. She made one-piece sheath dresses with jackets in complementing colors and contrasting fabrics. She made most of my clothes, too. I learned to sew through years of passing pinking shears, pin cushions, and zippers to my grandmother and threading needles when her eyesight started to fail and arthritis stiffened her fingers. "You'll be tall," she predicted, "and you'll need to learn how to sew so you can make clothes with sleeves long enough for your long arms."

At home, she was a gardener who took pride in growing gardenias, roses, gladioli, lilies, coleus, and caladiums. She was a member (probably a founder) of the Jonquil Garden Club, an organization that began in the mid 1950s and is active today. Jonquils are clusters of small fragrant yellow flowers with leaves in the shape of cylinders. *All* of the flowers my grandmother used came from her own yard or from the large pots on her front porch. I regularly saw blue ribbons come back into the house after garden club events. (In 1962 for the golden anniversary of Girl Scouting, the local council held two gardening contests for Girl Scouts in Savannah—one contest for white Girl Scouts and one for black Girl Scouts. The charge was to make a garden display with golden flowers. I was a member of the all-black scout troop that met at the St. Matthews Episcopal Church on West Broad Street. A small team of judges came to our house to look at my garden of dark yellow jonquils. My little garden won first place among the black Girl Scouts in Savannah.)

GLORIA, THE YOUNGEST OF James and Oper Lee Walker's four children, was pampered and spoiled by her oldest sibling, Catherine, her senior by seventeen years, and by two brothers, James Jr. and Watson.

James Jr., the second child, never went to college. Described as rambunctious, never taking school or himself seriously, he knocked around in Savannah for a while as a young man, driving taxis, working for his father at the insurance company and dipping his toes into various entrepreneurial ventures, without much success. He was a handsome man, with dark wavy hair, a thick mustache, and he had a warm and broad smile that could light up the world. His handsomeness no doubt paid off with the ladies because he was married five times.

Uncle Watson, the third child in the Walker family, went to Nashville for college and medical school, and then mustered into the U.S. Army in World War II where he served in Germany. By the early 1950s, he and his wife, Juanita, were settled in Columbus, Ohio, where he broke racial barriers as a surgeon and became a civil rights hero. As a school board member for sixteen years and twice-elected board chair, Uncle Watson led the Columbus public school system through desegregation.

Because she was born the day after Christmas, my mother was given the name Gloria to celebrate the joy of the holiday season. Her brothers would tease her about being born so close to Christmas. They would scheme to cheat their baby sister out of two complete presents by wrapping up a pair of shoes in two boxes, giving her one shoe on Christmas Day and the matching shoe the next day for her birthday. Sometimes it was shoes, sometimes it was pajamas—whatever they could think of that came in pairs.

Catherine was away in school when Gloria was born. When the family had moved from Atlanta to Savannah in 1929, Catherine was a high school student at Spelman, the school for girls who came from black families that wanted a first-rate, gender-segregated education for their daughters. Catherine moved out of the Atlanta family house and onto Spelman's campus, where she lived until she graduated from college in 1936. When Catherine rejoined the family in Savannah, she took on a surrogate-mother role for my mother.

Gloria was educated in public schools in Savannah, but at some point she was sent away to Boylan Haven School, a boarding school for black girls in Jacksonville, Florida. Like many non-public schools for black children in the South, this one was started by well-intentioned Christian white women from New England—"Up North," as we called it—who saw fit to bring the model of their own cultured education south for promising African American girls from families who were willing and had the financial capacity to let their daughters go to school away from home.

Gloria was one of those privileged few black girls from Savannah who had the benefit of this private school education for a while. My grandmother was a busy businesswoman, and Gloria's three siblings were grown or gone from the house, perhaps leaving a void for ensuring she was safely cared for in her early teen years. My grandmother, being the proper woman she was, probably would not have considered having what was called many years later a "latchkey child." Sending her youngest child off to boarding school was likely the tolerable solution.

Perhaps because of her experience around the white Christian women at Boylan Haven School, in adulthood Gloria spoke not with the Southern drawl of many of her friends who also grew up in Savannah, but she somehow acquired a proper, accent-less tone that belied discerning what part of the country she called home. And I never heard her use traditional Southern colloquialisms like "y'all" or "fixin' to" or "ain't" like so many of us spoke growing up in the South.

Like her own mother, Gloria had style and flair. When I see photos of movie stars who were popular in the 1940s and 1950s they remind me of my mother, always neatly buttoned down in suits or form-fitting dresses, wearing high chunky-heeled shoes and sometimes hats. Gloria matured in the era of stars like Lauren Bacall, Diahann Carroll, Elizabeth Taylor, Katharine Hepburn, Dorothy Dandridge, Joan Crawford, Eartha Kitt, and Lena Horne, and she carried herself as if she were one of those celebrities. She adored the finer things in life.

From my earliest years, I still imagine the rustle of my mother's full taffeta skirt with a freshly starched crinoline slip underneath, and the clicking of her high-heeled shoes as she quickly made her way across the slick linoleum floors in my grandmother's house where the three of us lived. Tall, light brown-skinned with a slender figure, Gloria had soft and fine, naturally dark-red hair. I was lulled by the waft of my mother's floral cologne scent as she readied herself to go out with friends. She was young, just nineteen years older than me and probably still anxious to enjoy nights on the town, whatever that meant in the early-1950s Savannah for a young African American woman who was divorced.

Perhaps Gloria tried to emulate some of the stars from her day in their movie images. Like many young women of her time, she smoked cigarettes— Winstons, I think—which she held in a dainty way that revealed the proper young woman she was. She collected some awesome mid-century ashtrays to go along with her smoking habit. I recall from my younger years that, like many of her friends, she was hardly ever without a cigarette. It was a lifestyle that probably led to the cancer that decades later spread through her lungs and suffocated the life from her.

As I GREW UP, there was hardly any mention of my biological father, John Henry Smalls, yet I hardly ever questioned why I was only close to my mother's family. The Walkers surrounded me with love, they inspired me to always perform the best that I could, and they exposed me to an array of cultural opportunities. One time I asked if I had another family and my grandmother, not happy with the man my mother chose to marry, said proudly, "We Walkers have our own pot to pee in. We don't need them." Even then I saw that as a mean-spirited comment, but my mother's family was my village and I was treated like the family princess. The status of my father and his family never came up again. As a young adult, when I finally met my father, and later his brother, I got a somewhat different side of the story. I learned that John Henry Smalls had attended high school with my mother and served in the U.S. Navy during World War II. Like many young men of that era, he left home before finishing high school, but he returned from the war and completed work for his high school diploma. He attended Howard University in Washington, D.C., and Howard's law school. I never found out if he graduated from law school, passed the bar, or ever practiced law. His details were scant and I didn't insist on getting the full story.

Gloria Walker and John Smalls were married for a short time. Based on my mother's age—she was nineteen when I was born—and the fact that she did not complete college after starting at Fisk University in Nashville and transferring to Howard University for a short time, they were likely unprepared for an unexpected pregnancy or marriage. The brief time my parents lived together was in my grandmother's house on West 41st Street.

Years later my grandmother would tell me that the bedroom furniture I used until I was an adult was purchased by my parents for their room in her house. That was the first "proof" I had that my parents were ever married. I later found evidence of their marriage through Census records, and I found their divorce decree among my mother's papers after she passed away.

I don't remember the day Gloria left me behind to seek what became a successful career, but I know I was five or younger because I remember her coming back to Savannah in July 1954 for my big sixth birthday party that was held on the manicured lawn of the empty lot next to my grandmother's house. I wore a short-sleeved red dotted Swiss dress that day. We played "pin the tail on the donkey" blindfolded and the many presents I received were displayed on the bed in the front bedroom of my grandmother's house, the room where my mother was born.

2. An Only Child

As an only child with no cousins in Savannah and no knowledge of my biological father or his family, I was always in search of playmates. The children in our neighborhood knew our limits: Never leave the block without adult supervision. Ride your bicycle on the sidewalk, not in the street. Never cross the street without an adult to help you look both ways. Never go inside a neighbor's house without telling a parent exactly where you are. Come home by the time the streetlights turn on. Those were our rules and we never challenged them.

Our games were simple. We played hopscotch with chalk outlines of boxes on the sidewalk, jumped ropes and skated, and the little girls played hand games and sang "Little Sally Walker" while dancing in a circle. I often played "house" seated at a child-sized card table and chair in my grandmother's covered driveway and pretended to eat mud pies and drink tea from the little play tea set I got one Christmas. Sometimes I would sneak a few leaves from my grandmother's lush garden. That antic caught up with me when I woke up one night crying out with pain in my mouth, and my hands and face were a swollen mess of hives and rash.

"Oh, Lord, look at this baby," my grandmother shouted. She yelled out to my mother, "Call 'Crackpot!'" That was her nickname for Dr. Sykes, the black family doctor who made house calls even in the middle of the night. Dr. Sykes came quickly and asked me questions about what I had done all day. I had to admit that a friend and I used our hands to tear up a large plant leaf in our game of playing house.

"What did the plant look like?" the doctor asked. I described its deep-green, heart-shaped leaves. "Humph. You 'ate' an elephant ear," he said. It turned out that the plants called elephant ears are known to cause allergic reactions in people who touch them or ingest them raw. The same plants are popular for eating in some Asian cultures, but they are always cooked, which eliminates their toxicity.

Dr. Sykes left behind some medicine to take away my symptoms. The next day my grandmother put on her gardening clothes—a long-sleeved collared shirt buttoned up to the neck, garden gloves, and a big straw hat to shield her face from the sun. She told me to stay in the house as she went outside and pulled up every bulbous plant like the one I had enjoyed at play. No more elephant ears were available for make-believe house or tea parties.

Some sixty years later when my husband and I moved to Savannah, we bought a house with elephant ears growing in the yard. A few days after we took possession of the house, on a hot summer day, I put on a long-sleeved shirt, long pants, boots, thick garden gloves, and a sun hat for the arduous task of pulling the plants up and bagging them for trash pickup.

"Why did you take up those nice plants?" my husband asked. "I liked them." I told him my childhood story.

I WAS NEVER EXACTLY clear why in 1956 Uncle Watson needed to send for my mother—who had moved to Fort Dix, New Jersey, for a job, leaving me in Savannah in the care of my grandmother. In Columbus, Uncle Watson and Aunt Juanita had four children, my cousins, three boys and a girl, ages three through seven, who needed care for a couple of years. One version of the story was that Aunt Juanita went back to school in her native St. Louis to complete her nursing education that had been interrupted when Uncle Watson was stationed in Germany and while they built their family. There was also the theory that they were separated when she left her family behind in Columbus. As adults used to tell us, "That's grown folks' business." I never pressed for more of an answer.

Whatever the reason, in 1956 after my mother was situated at Uncle Watson's, my grandmother and I took a long train ride—in Jim Crow segregated cars until we crossed the Mason Dixon Line—to Columbus, where I went from being an only child to a child with four "siblings."

Only-child syndrome is a label given to people who were raised without any siblings. Only children can be challenging. Characteristics of only-child syndrome include selfishness, an inability to share, and difficulty making friends. We only children are protective of our personal space and possessions. My personal space included time to sit alone and think, to read, and to do creative things. As an only child, I was an introvert for many years, even into adulthood. I was too young at the time to understand these only-child shortcomings. I learned more about them a generation later when my husband and I raised an only child. Was God forcing payback on my own only-child selfishness? A dose of comeuppance, perhaps?

Living with cousins was an intrusion in my only-child life. When I arrived in Columbus, I found them close and supportive of each other, and the three boys were, well, rambunctious. There was always noise in the house. These cousins came into my life with nicknames: Watson Jr., was "Squirt"; Charles, pudgy as a kid, was "Fatso"; James, named after our grandfather and uncle, was "Pee-bomb"; and Wilhelmina, the baby of the family, was "Nellybelle."

"What's your nickname?" I was asked shortly after I arrived in Columbus.

"I don't have a nickname. My name is Wanda," was my simple reply. I wanted to be called only by my given name.

Many in my generation express nostalgia for the days when neighbors, friends, and church members felt the right, and maybe the responsibility, to discipline neighborhood children when they caught them acting out.

Like the day when there was a fight among my cousins and me on the way home from school. Whatever the reason for the fight, we had the good fortune—or misfortune—to fight in front of a house where a neighbor recognized my cousins. She had telephoned our house before we got home. My grandmother took the call. She was calm, quietly telling us she knew about the fight. But that wasn't the end of it. When Uncle Watson came home that evening, he meted out his version of corporal punishment, lining us up in the basement, slapping his belt in his hand as we were told to face the wall and lean in.

Such incidents were rare, but in them Uncle Watson, a surgeon, would remind us of his professional title. After a few slaps on our buttocks, he would ask, referring, of course, to his medical degree: "Do you know what my MD stands for?"

"No, Daddy, what does it stand for?" we always responded.

"My MD means 'Mean Daddy,'" he would bellow as he ascended the basement steps, leaving us raw, embarrassed, and scared to move.

Uncle Watson was a taskmaster. He didn't take mess off his kids (except for sweet Wilhelmina, the baby). He drilled into us the need to do our best in school, to be honest at all times, and to love God. He required us to read the Bible and learn Bible verses, which we had to recite by heart just before each Sunday dinner. He didn't tolerate disrespect, bad behavior, or incorrect grammar. Despite his strong hand of discipline and the spankings, in my adult years I loved him dearly. When I was engaged to be married in 1975 I asked Uncle Watson to travel to Savannah and stand in as father of the bride. He said "yes" before I could finish asking him.

We don't see much of that adult-in-the-community discipline anymore because some young parents may call the police if anyone else puts hands on their children, or even if we are caught telling them to stop bad behavior. It can be dangerous now to intervene. For that matter, corporal punishment, even by the parents of a child, is less frequent or even taboo. Exercising it can result in social worker or even law enforcement involvement.

A similar cultural change can be seen in children's toys. For Christmas that year one of my gifts under the tree was a child-size iron and ironing board set (I'm not sure why, because to this day ironing is one of my least favorite household chores). The little iron was a low-power toy with a real electric cord that would get lukewarm for my pretend ironing. Today's Consumer Product Safety Commission would never approve of a toy like that.

That toy, by the way, figured in the kind of incident that led me to regret having to take on "siblings" in Columbus. One day, after some disagreement with my cousins, one of the boys got a pair of scissors and cut the cord on my little iron.

AFTER ALMOST A YEAR in Columbus, at the end of the school year, Uncle Watson loaded us all into his station wagon and drove us to Savannah to stay for the summer while he prepared to move the family into a bigger house before school restarted in the fall in Ohio.

I was happy to be back on my old turf, living in my grandmother's big green cedar-shingled house even though I still had cousins to deal with. But this was *my* house, the place I had lived since I was a baby, where until 1956 I was living life as an only child. I liked it that way.

The big green house was next door to a vacant lot my grandmother had owned before deeding it to Aunt Catherine and her husband, Uncle Osie Williams. In Southern communities it was common then for families to subdivide property if for no other reason than to keep younger generations close by, which would come in handy when the elders needed support in their aging years.

On their lot, Aunt Catherine and Uncle Osie were building a new pink-brick house that was somewhat of a mismatch on the street of mostly small, one-story wood-framed houses built in the 1920s and 1930s. A large picture window was situated between two front entrances, a main entrance into the living room and another into the laundry room and kitchen. From the street, it appeared to be a tall one-story house. But if you stood off to the side near the kitchen, you looked up at windows on a second story, something few in the neighborhood were used to seeing.

Aunt Catherine, after many years teaching sixth grade at West Savannah School, was about to begin her first year teaching special education at Tompkins Elementary on Savannah's West Side. Uncle Osie was a mortician and funeral director who had established a funeral home in 1948. Shortly thereafter, he took on as a business partner George Williams, the husband of Aunt Catherine's good friend, Celestine. The partners were not brothers, as many people in Savannah assumed. They just happened to have the same last name. Together, they owned and ran Williams & Williams Funeral Home on Gwinnett Street, on Savannah's East Side.

At the end of the summer, I knew I didn't want to return to Ohio, a place with harsh winters, to a house full of cousins and headed by a man who did not spare the rod. But the August 1957 day came when my mother, grandmother, uncle and four young cousins were piling into a station wagon. My packed clothes were in one of the suitcases tied atop the car.

I was expected to climb in alongside my cousins for the ride back to

Columbus, a long trip on mostly two-lane state roads. There were no interstates. Today we might break up such a trip because we can check into any hotel and use any facilities along the way. That was not the case in 1957.

The journey was through north Georgia, east Tennessee, Kentucky, and into north central Ohio. Not an ideal trip for a black family traveling through Appalachia in the 1950s, but it was a route that many of my family members had probably followed generations earlier when most of my maternal grandfather's eight siblings migrated to Cleveland.

So IN THE BIG green house, at the end of the summer on the day of packing up for the trip back to Ohio, Aunt Catherine and Uncle Osie were standing around watching all the loading and trying to keep children from running into the street as adults tended to more pressing matters.

I stood on the sidewalk amidst the cacophony of laughter, childhood shrieks, the tooting of horns from cars with waving neighbors passing by, and my grandmother's admonitions to "keep it down" or "don't run" while the car packing continued. I was silent, thinking, hoping for a plan that would keep me from having to get in that car for the long trip back to Ohio.

I walked over to Aunt Catherine and Uncle Osie.

"Can we talk on the porch?" I asked, taking each by the hand and leading them up the steps to the porch of my grandmother's house.

Aunt Catherine was short, maybe five feet four inches, fair in complexion, and a bit pudgy. Her husband was tall, even lighter in complexion, and he always wore the uniform of undertakers a black suit seven days a week. Based on height, they seemed a mismatch, but they were a team in business and in love. Also, theirs was a childless marriage.

We three sat in the porch swing, suspended from ceiling hooks by stout chains that sounded a metallic scrape with every back and forth motion. I tucked my eight-year-old body between the two adults, poised for a grown-up conversation.

"You don't have any children, do you?" Of course I knew the answer before I asked the question.

"No, we don't," Aunt Catherine responded in her soft Southern tone. "God hasn't blessed us with children."

We were keeping an eye on the car being loaded at the curb, with my four cousins still running around. It seemed nobody noticed the three of us up on the porch, hidden behind the leafy plants rooted in huge cement pots, carrying on our adult conversation in the swing.

Uncle Osie confirmed his wife's response, looking down at the children and at that moment probably relieved that God had not blessed them with so much childhood energy.

"Would you *like* to have a child?" I asked, pumping my little legs so the swing would sway ever so slightly.

"You want to live with us?" Aunt Catherine asked, tears welling up in her eyes. "We've thought about asking your mother to let us take care of you. We just weren't sure she would agree . . ."

That was all I needed to hear. I cut her off, jumping down from the swing and grabbing their hands, leading them down the porch steps. "Let's go tell them," I said, eagerly pulling them along, not risking the chance they would change their minds. "I want to live with you. You can be my new parents."

"Glooo-ria," Aunt Catherine called to my mother in a sing-song voice, interrupting my mother's packing duties. "Wanda wants to stay here with us," nodding down at me, indicating that I had asked for this change of plan.

My mother and my grandmother stopped packing the car and glanced at me for a moment, and then they resumed the packing, basically ignoring what they just heard. Soon everything from the curb was finally inside the car or tied on top, the suitcase with my clothes somewhere in the packed mix.

"Get in," my mother said, indicating an open back door for my four cousins and me to pile into the station wagon.

"I think she's serious," Aunt Catherine said.

After some adult whispering out of my earshot, and when all my cousins and the traveling adults were in the car, the family drove away, leaving me behind, waving at my departing kinfolk, including my mother.

I took Aunt Catherine and Uncle Osie by the hand and led them into the pretty but not yet completed pink-brick house for a tour of where we would live.

After the tour, just as we were walking out of the unfinished house, the Ohio-bound station wagon pulled back up to the curb. Uncle Watson and my mother had driven around the neighborhood, thinking they would circle back after a while to find an emotionally overwrought child standing at the curb in a state of panic because her mother, uncle, and cousins had left her. They had come back thinking they would pick up the obstinate child who said she didn't want to go back to Ohio.

But they didn't find that.

"She is serious," Uncle Osie told my mother. "She wants to stay with us—forever."

After some more adult conversations on the sideline, someone retrieved my clothes from the car. There were hugs and kisses and then I was left standing at the curb with my new "family."

I was again an only child.

3. The Family I Created

The best part of my growing-up years began on Columbus Day, October 12, 1957. I was in the third grade and my family—a family I had created—moved into a brand-new pink-brick house on West 41st Street in Savannah. I had created the family two months earlier when I was eight years old and bold enough to demand to change my family structure so I could live with two people who would give me the only-child love I believed I deserved. It was one of the best decisions of my life.

As Uncle Watson's station wagon drove out of sight toward Ohio without me in it, I took my new parents by the hand and led them into the pink house. It was a typical mid-century dwelling with a large galley kitchen with a dishwasher and a garbage disposal—appliances unheard of in our black neighborhood in the 1950s—and central heat! Every room also had a window air conditioning unit, making it the first air-conditioned house on the block. The focal point of the living room was a fireplace, trimmed floor to ceiling with the same pink brick as on the outside walls. The fireplace was just for show; an electric log insert was added for effect.

The dining room's large picture window looked out onto 41st Street. A few years later, after he suffered a debilitating stroke, Osie Williams would sit in a recliner in front of that picture window—partially paralyzed and speechless—waving to passersby with his one good hand and sometimes motioning them to come inside to visit with him. Many obliged, including some he didn't know. It was a friendly and trusting era.

A crystal chandelier hung from the center of the dining room ceiling. I would come to despise that chandelier because it became my chore to clean it a couple of times a year by taking each crystal piece off and dipping it into a tub of water with bleach, and then put it all back together. It was an all-day chore that kept me in the house on a Saturday instead of playing outside with friends. Yet, that chore would become one of my many lessons on the details of keeping a clean house, free of dust and grime.

The three bedrooms were served by a single bathroom with a typical fifties-style pink-and-gray tiled floor and half walls, pink fixtures and wooden cabinets painted pink. The large screened-in back porch would later be enclosed for me to use as a playroom, study space and in my teen years a place for my friends to hang out and dance to my records. Our music was bolstered by the sounds we heard on black AM radio stations.

The house had a second floor with a wood-paneled office area (we called it the "study"), a bathroom with a walk-in shower, and a floored attic for storage. In the study there was a walk-in closet, built not for clothes, but lined with bookshelves for Aunt Catherine's many schoolbooks and teacher files.

I led my aunt and uncle down the hall on the first floor and picked out my bedroom. The room had four windows and was intended to be a sitting room or den. I claimed the space as mine.

"Every room I've ever slept in has been pink," I said. "I want blue walls." I was too young to know then that pink was traditionally for girls and blue was for boys. I just knew I didn't want to wake up to pink walls ever again.

My mother and my grandmother had always been mother figures in my life. I wasn't looking for a new person to call "Mother" or "Mom." Aunt Catherine knew she would always be Aunt Catherine to me.

"Uncle Osie, may I call you 'Daddy?'" I asked. He pulled me into his strong tall frame and hugged me as hard as I had ever been hugged. At that moment, I had a new family, a new home, and, finally, some peace and quiet. It never bothered me that I called one parent "Aunt" and the other one "Daddy." This was *my* family and I used the names I wanted to use.

We three lived in my grandmother's big green house from that August day until Columbus Day in October 1957 when we moved into the completed pink brick house and I took possession of my blue bedroom.

THOUGH I HAD REARRANGED my family by self-selecting new parents, a year later my grandmother returned from Ohio and was ever-present in her green house next door. It may not have been a conventional domestic situation, but it was mine, and I never thought it remarkable. The main thing is that I was happy growing up in it.

Other extended family members on my mother's side were also significant fixtures in my life.

James Jr., the second Walker sibling after Catherine, was married five times. Uncle James and a business partner once owned a gas station (and this part was never clear to me) and I was told they were violating a law about how gas was being sold. This was perhaps in the 1940s during World War II when gasoline shortages forced rationing. It took some fancy footwork and legal maneuvering on the part of my grandfather who was somehow able to keep his older son out of jail.

Taxi companies were racially segregated in the South during the Jim Crow years. Uncle James was a driver for the all-black Milton Cab Company when I was a child, and he would sometimes "babysit" me in the afternoon by driving me around town on the front seat of his taxi. He had lost one of his early wives in childbirth and he never had children despite the number of times he was married. Uncle James's last marriage, to a lovely woman named Lillian who already had an adult daughter, was a true love story. In fact, my mother told me that when Uncle James died at home in his bed, "he had a smile on his face," indicating that his heart gave out during a moment of intimacy.

James and Lillian moved north together and worked as a pair, becoming a housekeeper and driver for wealthy white families in New Jersey and New York City. They were an attractive couple, he looking every bit like my handsome grandfather in the pictures I saw, and she was always well-dressed with a smiling face and kind to everyone she knew.

They acquired a tiny one-bedroom unit in a co-op building in East Elmhurst in Queens. When I visited them in the summer, I would sleep on the pullout sofa in the living room. Uncle James constantly gave me life lessons, and he required me to write them letters and share grades from my school report cards. When I was in college he gave me my first lesson in highway driving on the New Jersey Turnpike, an experience that scared me to death. I was already driving, but there were no superhighways in Savannah at the time, just city streets and country roads.

"Drive on the right and pass on the left," he taught me, the first time I heard that phrase.

When I got my first full-time job out of college, Uncle James gave me a lesson in saving money.

"Put aside a dime out of every dollar you make, and someday you will be able to retire." It took a while to get on the path of saving at that rate, but I have always had a savings account or some other mechanism controlling my spending and putting money aside. He was right. When the time came to retire, I had a plan and it worked.

When I graduated from Spelman in 1971, Uncle James and Aunt Lillian drove down from New York to Savannah to pick up my grandmother and Aunt Catherine for the trip to Atlanta to see me graduate. My mother flew in from Dallas. Uncle James always had a nice car, Cadillacs usually, purchased inexpensively or gifted from some of his wealthy white bosses, and he took the time in Savannah to clean his car. On the way to Atlanta, with the four of them in Uncle James's freshly shiny black Cadillac, they were stopped on a two-lane road in some small Georgia town. He never had trouble driving nice cars in New York, but in small-town Georgia he was "driving while black" in a luxury car. No charges were filed, and there was no anger in Uncle James's voice when they arrived at the hotel in Atlanta.

Uncle James died before I was married. Shortly after our daughter, Shelby, was born, Aunt Lillian called to say she wanted to hold the baby. She took a train ride from New York to Washington with what we call a grandmother clock—a wall version of a grandfather clock—on her lap. The clock had belonged to Uncle James, and she brought it as a gift for our baby. Shelby still has that clock.

Uncle Watson was the twinkle in my grandmother's eye. Over the years, he only returned to Savannah for short visits, often flying in for an overnight stay. Perhaps he was eschewing the thought of returning to the racially oppressive South, as many African Americans did during the Jim Crow years, or maybe his family and medical practice kept him too busy. But he made it a point to call his mother "long distance" every Sunday afternoon. My grandmother looked forward to his monthly letters—usually a one-pager written in the typical chicken scratch doctors' handwriting, always with a check enclosed. My grandmother had two Sunday indulgences after church—watching the Ed Sullivan Show on TV at night and talking to her beloved Watson on the phone.

Uncle Watson, a surgeon, was denied employment at segregated hospitals when he arrived in Columbus in 1948. He heroically served as president of the public school board there for twenty years, and he cautiously began to challenge discriminatory assumptions in the school system. He often told the story about how he managed to get lights for the all-black East High School during a closed-door board meeting. As described by Gregory S. Jacobs in *Getting Around Brown: Desegregation, Development, and the Columbus Public Schools*, Watson Walker described his action in this way:

> "I knew this was one of the things the black community was incensed about. They had been working on it for years and had been rebuffed at every turn. The only reason [white board members] didn't want lights for East was that the white schools preferred to play East at daytime because they figured if they came out in the East end at nighttime they were going to get beat up. These were prevalent racial attitudes that had to be erased.
>
> "I have asked the question, 'How many schools with football fields do you have that are not lighted?' Everything got quiet. Of course, I was playing the part of not knowing that I was asking a racially loaded question. They finally said, 'One,' and I said, 'Which one?' And everybody got quiet again. The attitude they had was, 'Is he crazy? Does he know the answer to this or is he pulling our leg?' And I had this angelic face and they couldn't tell what was going on. They finally said, 'East High'."

In addition to his medical practice Uncle Watson was chief of surgery at the Ohio State Penitentiary and he was known as one of the best amateur golfers in the city. Ironically, the four children of the history-making former school board leader were not direct beneficiaries of the later integrated public schools. Uncle Watson and Aunt Juanita sent their children to be educated at Columbus Academy, one of the city's most prestigious private schools.

4. My Village

In her children's picture book, *It Takes a Village*, former Secretary of State Hillary Rodham Clinton wrote, "Every child needs a champion. Or Two. Or Three. Or more." My own upbringing was the epitome of the maxim that inspired the title of Clinton's book: "It takes a village to raise a child."

In Savannah, my village was family, neighbors, church, teachers, and school friends within a Jim Crow world. Dr. Jamison, a black dentist, took care of our teeth; my family deposited money in black-owned Carver State Bank, established in 1927; all of the teachers in our schools were black; if we got sick in the middle of the night, Dr. Sykes, a black physician, readily made house calls; when we needed a plumber or an electrician, black tradesmen came to our house to fix things. And like our own family business, a funeral home, when someone in our community died, black funeral directors would handle the arrangements and burials—in segregated cemeteries. I'm not saying that was a bad thing. It just was what it was.

In fact, Laurel Grove South, the historic cemetery where my grandparents and my mother are buried, is still the black side of the city-owned burial ground, with its modest headstones and, in many cases, crumbling infrastructure. Laurel Grove North, the white side, is more elaborate with towering memorials and sturdy, grand ironwork. My husband and I already have deeds with our names for the family plot in Laurel Grove South.

Growing up in a restrictive, segregated society meant we were not able to go to certain places or travel in certain ways like white people. Yet despite the restrictions forced upon us, I felt the love of my village, which shielded me from most of the indignities and injustices of our legally segregated society. I mostly didn't feel the oppression until I was an older teenager.

Neighbors on West 41st Street in Savannah were a huge part of my village. Most of the families were traditional—mother, father, children, and sometimes a grandmother or a great aunt. In many cases the women were homemakers, yet a few were teachers like Aunt Catherine. That doesn't mean the men were not educated. Quite the contrary. Many African Americans in our neighborhood—male and female—were graduates of Savannah State College (now University; an HBCU). Due to discrimination and perhaps the propensity of the white community at the time to tamp down professional dreams and economic success of black men, many households consisted of a professional wife and a laborer husband. The well-educated black women usually taught school. While some black men who were college-educated became postal workers or preachers, many black men found good jobs working in the local factories that refined sugar or manufactured paper.

Most of the small houses on our block were built so closely together that you could walk between two of them and reach out and touch both. The Blackshears on one side of my grandmother's house had a girl about my age living with them. She was Mrs. Blackshear's younger sister. On the other side were the Colberts. She was a widowed hairdresser who served customers in her house. The Williams family (no relation) on the other side of the Colberts had grandchildren my age and we played together after homework was done until their parents picked them up.

Across the street Mrs. Hurley would walk down the block every day—on hot days with an open umbrella, a parasol, to shield her face from the sun. She was always neatly dressed, usually wearing a shirtwaist dress, thick stockings, chunky-heeled shoes, white gloves, round wire-rimmed glasses, and a small hat. Mrs. Hurley and her adult daughter, "Miss Odessa," never owned a car. Next door to them was another Walker family (no relation to us). One of the sons, "Monkey," went to high school with my mother. I never knew the origin of his nickname and I never learned his real first name.

Directly across the street from us were the Gartrells, who lived in a small house full of beautiful children with "good hair." My grandmother used to tell me Mrs. Gartrell was proud of her childrens' beauty, and that she would line her girls up and give them lessons on how to fling their bouncy hair, something most black girls like me could not do. (The Urban Dictionary states that "most people who use the term 'good hair' would never admit the inferiority complex from which it came." Mea culpa.)

Down the street, Mrs. Pinckney, a former nurse, spent a lot of time sweeping her front porch, or sitting on it, or peeping out the front door to see what was going on. Like many women on the street, she wore an apron all day. When she really wanted to see what was going on, she would come outside with a broom and sweep the porch, the steps, and the sidewalk. Mrs. Pinckney walked with a decided limp and she hobbled across the street several times a week to climb the steps of my grandmother's front porch, where much gossiping would be going on.

Sometimes the ladies would call me over (and a friend if I had another child over for company) and press a couple of dimes into our hands and offer a plea in the typical Geechee accent: "Baa-uh-be, I have a headache. Go to the sto' an' bring me back a BC an'a ice-cold Co-Cola. And git yo' se'f somethin' with the change."

Sometimes they asked for a BC powder, sometimes for a Goody. The "Co-Cola" was a Southern-ism for Coca-Cola. The headache powders were interchangeable, packaged in a chewing-gum-sized, rectangular white paper folded to keep the powder inside. The powders sold for a nickel, and the drinks for another nickel when we brought an empty to trade (today we call that recycling).

My friend and I would stroll down dusty Stephens Street, the dirt road that intersected with West 41st Street near our house. We would walk the two blocks to the little store we called the confectionery, on the corner of Stephens and West Victory Drive, and ask for the powders. The people who worked there knew us. Children all over the neighborhood regularly came in with coins to buy a BC and a Co-Cola.

After we paid, we would slide open the top of the waist-high floor-model cabinet that kept the drinks "ice-cold." We knew to reach *deeeeep* into the cooler, plunging our little arms as far as possible into the icy water—the deeper the colder—and grab a single bottle, and then accept the powder from the storekeeper. Then we would get our own treat, usually a few penny candies or a cookie straight out of the jar—no plastic wrapping, just a single cookie that we pulled out with our bare and often dirty hands. There were no concerns in those days about germs in the communal cookie jar. Not to mention the communal pickle jar or the penny candy jar. If there was enough money left, we would get a Nehi soda—orange or grape. My friend and I would share sips from the Nehi bottle on the trip back to the front porch to deliver the requested goods.

At the time, I never questioned why these ladies would get a headache about the same time almost every day. Now I know that BC and Goody powders are aspirin and caffeine, plus with the Coca-Cola chaser there was more caffeine. These women were getting *high!* Right there in the middle of the day. On my grandmother's front porch.

Other families on our block were the McMillans, the Blalocks, and the Quartermans. Behind us were the Johnsons (coincidentally, son Clarence "Duck" Johnson, a couple of years older than me, served on a ship in the U.S. Navy with the man I would later marry).

The families in my village were awfully proud when children brought home good grades on report cards. Sometimes neighbors would reward our good work with a few coins. When I graduated from high school neighbors showered me with small gifts—money or trinkets that might be useful in college, like a dictionary or a box of pencils, and when I came home on visits from college, my grandmother insisted that I go door to door to check in with the ladies up and down the block. Almost to a one, the women would reach into their apron pockets and pull out a dollar or two and press the money into my hand, hugging me and telling me how proud they were of me. My grandmother watched my procession from her front porch. I was embarrassed to take their money and I complained to her about it.

"Do I have to go to each house? I don't need their dollars," I once told my grandmother.

"Yes, you do," she said. "It's not about what you need. Giving you money means a lot to them. The neighbors helped raise you. They corrected you when you were bad and they praised you when you did good. They are proud of you. Giving you a dollar or two makes them feel like they are helping to get you through college."

West 41st Street was more than a community; it was my village. I had to process that the people who lived around me felt like I was their investment for a better life, a better society. They had protected me, encouraged me, taught me right from wrong. And in many ways, when they told tales on my grandmother's front porch, they were some of my first teachers in journalism because they told wonderful stories, which is what we do in the news business. We tell stories.

OUR NEIGHBORS, EVEN THOSE on the next streets over, were the kind who would scold a child if they saw him or her doing something wrong in front of their house and then they would call the family to tell them about the scolding. Sometimes I would get home after school and my grandmother, a leather strap in hand to punish me, would say something like "Why were you lagging behind the group on your way home?" or "Why did you use a bad word in front of Mrs. So and So's house?" If she didn't have a leather strap at the ready, she would order me to go out to the yard and bring back a switch from one of the tall bushes. I had to snap my own piece of pain infliction from a bush and strip it of it's tiny leaves before handing it to my grandmother. And she used it—many times.

Children these days don't get the kind of discipline that was meted out by my grandmother's generation. If they did, I'm sure there would be fewer gang members, fewer teenage pregnancies, fewer youth drug problems, and greater emphasis on schoolwork, prayer (Lord knows I prayed that my grandmother wouldn't find out about some of the things we did), and obedience.

Of course, laws have also changed. In my school years, nothing prevented teachers from giving us a whack. I'm not talking about a beatdown, but a rap across the legs or knuckles—enough to prove that they wouldn't tolerate mess. We *never* talked back to our teachers like some kids do today. We *never* got caught using profane language; if we used it, we were savvy enough to be *waaaayy* across the playground out of earshot of adults.

The women in my village taught me how to tend gardens, decorate rooms, and dress with grace when we would leave home, not dress down to go out. My grandmother taught me how to clean house, host parties, wash, starch, and stretch curtains (maybe that's why I have no curtains in my house today) using a wooden stretcher contraption that would then be placed in the backyard to let the sun do the drying and pressing. The women in my village taught me Southern manners like always saying "yes, ma'am" and "no, sir," and how to be respectful when you are a guest in someone else's house. You always wipe your feet at the door, never put your feet on furniture, say "thank you" when offered a gift or something to drink, and never overstay your welcome.

One of their life lessons I've always adhered to is writing bread-and-butter letters—thank-you notes to show appreciation for hospitality. A proper bread-and-butter letter is always handwritten and sent through the mail. Now, with email, some may send thank-yous via the Internet. But a proper Southern lady knows that a letter of thanks for dinner, a party, or an overnight stay requires an envelope and a postage stamp.

By example, my village taught me humility, that no matter what one's station in life may be, everyone has something to contribute. Whether rich or poor, a product of higher education or educated on the streets of hard knocks, able-bodied or disabled, the village can build character if we embrace the good lessons taught.

THERE WAS ONE EXCEPTION in my village.

Way down on the other end of our block was a place we called the bolita house. I never knew who owned the house or who paid the rent. Unlike with our other neighbors, we never knew the names of the residents in the bolita house. Every now and then a man who lived there or frequented the house would stride down 41st Street with an attitude—a wide-brim hat cocked sideways on his head shading his mischievous eyes. I can almost hear him now, pimp-walking with a step and a half-step, one hand in his pocket jingling coins as if to say to the neighbors "I've got money. Want some? Come and get it."

"Don't go in there," my grandmother and the other women on our street would warn the children. "That's the bolita house."

Bolita—a Spanish word for little ball—was the term used to describe an illegal lottery or numbers game. I wondered how the women on our street knew so much about the bolita house until one day I learned that some of the genteel ladies were playing the numbers themselves. The runners who came out of that house were not polite visitors who dropped by for coffee or tea. They were knocking on doors in the middle of the day, collecting numbers written on tiny pieces of paper and small amounts of money held for safekeeping in the apron pockets of some of the nice ladies, including those who were a part of my village.

Lore had it that players would conjure numbers in their dreams, wake up, and scribble the numbers on a piece of paper to be ready for the bolita man to come by and collect. These were chances of wealth paid for out of eyesight of working husbands who probably would not have approved of their hard-earned coins being spent on a game of chance. I never heard that anybody we knew got rich because of bolita, but I always wondered what else was going on in that house at the other end of the block.

5. Growing Up . . . Under Jim Crow

My growing-up years—the 1950s and 1960s—were greatly affected by laws and social customs that permeated every aspect of life in the American South. The most important mandated that public entities have separate facilities for whites and blacks. This racially based system was collectively recognized as Jim Crow segregation. It defined the neighborhoods where African Americans could live, the libraries we could use, the schools we could attend, the social organizations we could join, the jobs we could get, the cultural events we could enjoy, the medical care we could receive, and even where we could get a drink of water or use the bathroom in public spaces. In short, it guaranteed black people a substandard and unequal quality of life.

This was confusing to small children, who didn't understand why there were double accommodations, and why "Colored" was one of the first words we had to learn to read lest we sip out of the wrong fountain or pee in the wrong toilet. Facilities for African Americans were always far inferior to those intended for use by whites, and Jim Crow laws generated a decades-long struggle for equal rights. This dual system was part of what drove my mother out of the South in search of a more equitable quality of life up North.

The term "Jim Crow" itself has an interesting background. Most historians attribute it to minstrel show performances by Thomas Rice, a white actor who wore blackface and affected a stereotyped black dialect while he sang a song he had written, "Jump Jim Crow," whose lyrics included:

"Come listen all you gals and boys / I'm going to sing a little song / My name's Jim Crow / Weel about and turn about and do jis so / Ebry time I weel about I jump Jim Crow."*

Such minstrel shows were only one aspect of a widespread white popular culture that depicted blacks as lazy, foolish, unreliable, unintelligent, and undeserving of political rights, including the right to vote, to attend public schools, and to equal treatment under the law. No wonder then that stereotyped images in movies, television, books, magazines, and newspapers throughout the twentieth and into the twenty-first century affected how people of all races regarded African Americans. In fact, these stereotypes were often the foundation for lifting up or tamping down our own self-esteem, based on what kind of media we consumed.

Stereotyping meant seeing blacks portrayed as drug sellers, pimps, and prostitutes instead of doctors, lawyers, teachers, or business owners in movie and television roles; and as criminal suspects on newspapers' front pages instead of professional sources in business and government stories. It meant seeing feature stories about white high society in magazines instead of stories and images of black families doing everyday things like decorating their homes for birthdays, cotillions, or weddings. In books, it wasn't until the late 1970s that we began to see a proliferation of novels and best sellers written by African Americans and addressing the audiences of black children, teenagers, young adults, and black women. We are still waiting for a critical mass of books portraying African American men in positive ways as heads of households, supportive sons and brothers, or successful in business. In other words, we still need more books that herald black men as people of strong faith, family, and fortune.

As a journalist I spent a great deal of my professional capital working to improve opportunities for content and human diversity in media. As a newspaper editor and as a member of various professional boards and committees, I studied the history of newsroom diversity and developed training modules to help newsrooms and readers understand the dynamics of staff and content diversity. All of this work was informed by my experiences with Jim Crow while I was growing up in Savannah.

---

* For "Jump Jim Crow," see the *International Encyclopedia of the Social Sciences.*

The intent of Jim Crow segregation was simple enough—to preserve and perpetuate white supremacy. Its history was not so simple. Before emancipation, Jim Crow was not needed in the South because slavery itself kept blacks in subjugation. Further, the practice of slavery required whites and blacks to live in close proximity; actual segregation would have been a hindrance to the machinery of slavery. In the North, however, slavery was basically extinct by 1830, yet white supremacy remained entrenched. Well before the Civil War in many Northern states, so-called black codes (statutes or ordinances) denied black or mixed-race persons access to schools, residential areas, the vote, and other political rights. Prisons, hospitals, and cemeteries were segregated; even in "integrated" churches, blacks receiving the sacrament waited until whites had been served. By 1860, such segregation was pervasive across the "free" North. Blacks could vote only in Rhode Island, Massachusetts, New Hampshire, Maine, and Vermont.

With the defeat of the Confederacy, the emancipation of the enslaved, and the passage of the Thirteenth and Fourteenth amendments, white supremacy and racist social customs did not disappear in the North, but the official black codes there were mostly repealed. In the South, the opposite happened. Immediately upon the end of the war, the white-controlled Southern legislatures began passing new black codes meant to control the newly freed African Americans. Strict vagrancy laws and the beginnings of the convict leasing system virtually re-enslaved many freedmen. New restrictions were placed on interracial marriage, rights to inherit, freedom of movement, and more.*

Some but not all of these measures were undone by the interracial Reconstruction legislatures that were elected in 1866 and by subsequent new amendments and federal civil rights laws. With the Thirteenth Amendment having abolished slavery, the Fourteenth guaranteeing citizenship and civil rights, the Fifteenth granting ex-slaves the right to vote, and the federal government having suppressed white vigilantism (the KKK and similar groups), Southern blacks enjoyed almost a decade of participation in democracy.

---

* For more on the distinctions between the operations of slavery in the South and segregation in the North, see Leon Litwack, *North of Slavery,* and C. Vann Woodward, *The Strange Career of Jim Crow.*

Blacks voted, served in public offices (more than a dozen ex-slaves were elected to Congress), built schools, churches, civic organizations, businesses, and neighborhoods, and raised families.

But actual or threatened violence was ever-present, and bit by bit Southern whites regained political power and control. By 1877, even whites in the North had tired of federal involvement in the South, and Reconstruction came to an end. Over the next few decades, statute after statute was passed to remove African Americans from civic life, to restrict their rights, and even to limit their social and domestic lives. These segregationist measures were called Jim Crow laws. In famous cases like *Plessy v. Ferguson*, the courts upheld these discriminatory measures. Not until the post-World War II era did these restrictions begin to be gradually undone by the combination of litigation, demonstrations, and legislation that made up the twentieth-century civil rights movement.

In the interim, Jim Crow was a crippling presence in our lives. I use Savannah here as an example, but when I came into the world in 1949, more than eighty years after emancipation, this system of legally sanctioned discrimination smothered the entire South.

WE'VE HAD A RECENT refresher on part of this history thanks to rediscovery of *The Negro Motorist Green-Book*, a 1930s booklet that helped black travelers locate hotels, night clubs, restaurants, tourist homes, barber shops, and beauty salons that were race-friendly under Jim Crow laws. The book was re-popularized in the 2018 movie *Green Book*, about a road trip taken through the South by African American classical and jazz pianist Don Shirley. According to the history page in a more recent edition, the book was "a product of the rising African American middle class having the finances and vehicles for travel but facing a world where social and legal restrictions barred them from many accommodations. At the time, there were thousands of 'sundown towns,' places where African Americans were legally barred from spending the night there at all."

The book—its green cover color signaling a "green light" to frequent the sites listed by state—was designed to give black travelers peace of mind that they would only patronize safe establishments.

In Savannah, there was no green book for navigating everyday life, but everyone knew how the system worked. In my family we always had cars, or access to cars, so I didn't ride on segregated buses until my teen years when I started to venture out with friends to the library or the movies. Even then, someone in my family or a friend's parent would usually take us and pick us up for Saturday movies. As children we went to see movies at the all-black Star and Dunbar theaters located in black neighborhoods, but we didn't go the huge Savannah or Lucas theaters downtown. I didn't ask questions about places we never went. It would be a few years later before I noticed that the big theaters downtown were for white people only.

Even the public Savannah Beach—partly maintained by our black parents' tax dollars—was segregated. Similarly, until the late 1960s, parks were segregated and absolutely not equal. Daffin Park was a lush green-grassed area that we would see when driving along the beautiful Victory Drive, once known as the longest avenue of palms in the nation, with thousands of palm and palmetto trees planted in the median, accented by azaleas and other flowers that made spring one of my favorite seasons in the city. On either side of some parts of the four-lane Victory Drive are mansions that exude Southern charm with their white columns and their ancient oak trees draped with Spanish moss.

Daffin Park—still beautiful today—was off limits to black people, but I couldn't wait to look out the window, sometimes asking whichever family member was driving to slow down so I could take in the man-made lake with the tall water spout, the tennis courts, and the paved sidewalks.

On the west side of town, my friends and I sometimes walked a few blocks to Cann Park, a dirt-surfaced space devoid of green grass or athletic luxuries. Cann Park was our hangout area, and sometimes a place to rendezvous with boys. Our modest park had some playground equipment for smaller kids, and the teenage boys cut their athletic teeth on basketball courts. Larry "Gator" Rivers was among them.

"Cann Park had two full courts for basketball, a baseball diamond, and a football field," Gator told me many years later. "They even put a net up in between the two basketball courts for tennis." This area likely served Gator and others well because in 1967 our Beach High School Bulldogs became the first all-black high school to win the state championship in the Georgia High School Association, thus integrating the league.

Gator Rivers, the self-described "best ball handler in the world," was drafted to play with the Harlem Globetrotters. Today he gives back by sponsoring tournaments and working with African American boys in the same neighborhood on the Cann Park courts.

After parks were desegregated in the late 1960s, on my first visit to Daffin Park, I was strolling along the sidewalk with some girlfriends and we encountered a few white boys coming our way. One called out "nigger" just as we were passing them.

I'm sure our bodies stiffened in fear of what would come next. And then it came. One of the white boys spat in our direction. I did not return to Daffin Park for fifty years before I was there one Saturday representing an organization at a community event. Even then—even today—I am uncomfortable in Daffin Park and I'll never go there alone.

Tourists in Savannah today know that one of the most visited and beautiful sites in the city is Forsyth Park, which has as its centerpiece an elegant two-tiered fountain that is the popular site of family and wedding photos and marriage proposals. The fountain has been there since 1858. After desegregation, every time I would drive my grandmother past Forsyth Park she would say, "They let Colored in there now, you know." She never graduated her terminology of us beyond "colored" and "Negroes" to black or African American. Maybe my grandmother had a sense of satisfaction that we had moved forward, that the "Southern way of life" was changing. Yet she never asked me to park the car so she could walk into Forsyth Park. I doubt that in her entire eighty-two years she ever put her feet on the ground in the grand Forsyth Park.

Similar experience extends to my memories of downtown. Saturday afternoon shopping with my grandmother on Broughton Street, Savannah's main downtown thoroughfare, was always a treat. Oper Lee Walker would always be a study in sartorial excellence. "When we go downtown you have to look your best," she would tell me. "We don't want the white folks to think the Walkers don't know how to carry ourselves."

Her "carry ourselves" was a broad comment for how to dress, act, smell, speak, and any other behavior that she thought white people might find offensive. I sometimes challenged her, asking how she knew how white people think. I came to understand that she was a student of human behavior on both sides—white and black. She was protecting me from potential hurt, and all I had to do was look, listen, and learn from her.

She reminded me that, as a colored woman, I would have to always "be better"—that is, make better grades in school, look better, think better, jump higher, wear better-looking clothes, and sit up or walk straighter than white people.

"Bring attention to yourself for good reasons," she said. "We are colored and to get respect, we must dress up when we go downtown," she told me, treating shopping like a birthday party or a night at the theater. We didn't have a theater to go to, but I'm sure my grandmother would have been elegant there, given the opportunity.

It took me a lifetime to know exactly what "better" meant as compared to white people, but the expectation to be "better" never left me when I went away to college and then into the work world. I always knew I was expected to meet a higher standard. Later, as a young mother, I never dressed myself or my daughter, Shelby, in jeans or sweats when we went shopping. I found my grandmother's style influence to be a useful tool to get respect as a shopper.

Of course, when I was growing up in Savannah there were no malls and the hub of economic activity was downtown. The stores along Broughton Street included the typical five-and-dimes S. H. Kress, Woolworth's and McCrory's. These stores sold products to both races but had segregated lunch counters, serving white diners on the ground floor and blacks at a basement counter. The cooks were black; the servers were always white. As in many Southern cities, it took sit-ins in the early 1960s by courageous young people to force lunch counter integration.

Other stores along Broughton Street were primarily owned locally, many by Jewish merchants. Levy's Department Store, Asher's, Fine's, Levy Jewelers, Friedman's Jewelers, B. Karpf, Hogan's Department Store, children's clothier Punch and Judy, and Globe Shoes served the needs of anyone who had the money to shop in them.

At Levy's, perhaps the largest store on Broughton Street, the elevator operators were black, a good job for African Americans at the time. To my mind, Levy's was a grand place. Entering the store we would walk past a wide doorway leading into the Azalea Room, a white-tablecloth restaurant. Every time we entered Levy's, I would ask my grandmother, "Can we go in there and eat?" She would grab my hand and say something like, "Come on child," or "Didn't I tell you not to ask me about that anymore," almost dragging me along. I was too young to fully understand segregation. I could smell the food and see the elegance. I wasn't hungry. I just wanted to eat there, even though we always ate just before we left home for downtown, probably for the very reason of segregation.

Our visits to Asher's included the millinery department, where the extravagant hats my grandmother liked to wear to church were displayed on mannequin heads. There were plenty of mirrors in the hat department's showroom, an open part of the store where customers were coming and going. As a child I thought we were special because the saleswoman took us into a private room with a large wall mirror and she brought in pretty hats embellished with feathers, flowers, and netting. Every season my grandmother would show the saleswoman fabric swatches of her hand-made outfits, and she wanted hats that complemented her upcoming wardrobe. I didn't know at the time that we were being hidden from white patrons who wouldn't want to try on hats if they knew a Negro woman had tried them on first. Often under Jim Crow, blacks were simply not allowed to try on clothing in "white" stores; they had to buy first and hope the items fit when they got home. There was no returning them.

WHEN I WAS IN the fourth grade I got an inkling of why my mother, Gloria, had to leave Savannah. She had moved with a job transfer, but she was clearly not comfortable with how things were in the South she left behind. I had worn glasses since I was seven, and one of my mother's trips back to Savannah coincided with an appointment to pick up a new pair.

"I'll take her," Gloria said when Aunt Catherine told her we had the appointment.

"No, let Cat take her," my grandmother said. I would soon find out why. I wanted my mother to take me. We didn't spend a lot of time together and I wanted to have her all to myself. After all we were just picking up glasses. No big deal, I thought.

When we arrived at the doctor's office and got out of the car, we walked toward the perfectly symmetrical building that had two front doors. I held my mother's hand and led her to the door on the left. We entered a crowded, tiny waiting room with every seat taken. The room was hot and stuffy, full of drab furniture and less-than-pleasant décor. All of the patients and people waiting with them were black. My mother walked up to the reception desk and looked through and across the office area, where she saw another, more spacious waiting room with more pleasing décor. Without a word to the receptionist or to me, she grabbed my hand, marched me out of the door we had just entered, and briskly led me to the other door.

"We are here to pick up glasses for my daughter," she told the woman at the reception desk in the nicely appointed white waiting room. I recall the audible gasps at the audacity of this Negro woman and her child standing in the room reserved for Whites Only.

"Girl, you have to go to the 'colored' side," a woman behind the desk told my mother, who was standing there in her sophisticated Northern-bought clothes and high-heeled shoes, with her perfectly coiffed dark red hair, bright red lipstick, and an attitude.

"No, Mommy, don't do this. Not here," I mumbled softly. Gloria looked down at the fear in my eyes and told me to "Sit! Down!"—each emphasized word was its own sentence.

She politely asked the woman who had just called her "girl" to explain why we could not sit in the nice spacious room where the air was better and the décor was up to date. "Is the price different?" she asked, loud enough for everyone to hear. By now I wanted to hide *under* the chair in which she had just ordered me to sit.

After a couple of minutes of making a scene, which included my mother telling the woman behind the desk that she lived in the North, and a retort something like, "We do things different down here," we were ushered through a door into the area with examination rooms to wait for our appointment, pushed ahead of black *and* white patients. When we were done, my mother firmly grabbed my hand again and walked me back through the "white" waiting room and out the door to the street, new glasses on my face.

In the car, she admonished, "Don't you say a word about this to your grandmother. Just between us, okay?"

We never spoke of it again. But to this day when I pass that building, which is no longer a medical facility, I remember when my mother ordered me to "Sit! Down!" in the Whites Only waiting room.

I HAVE ANOTHER INDELIBLE memory from that Jim Crow era.

My grandmother always looked forward to visiting her sister and brother-in-law, Marie and James Allen "J. A." Burge, in Canton, in Cherokee County in north Georgia. Both were teachers. Like my grandmother, "Auntie" had been a student at Spelman Seminary, a precursor to Spelman College.

I often accompanied my grandmother on these trips, a six-hour ride between Savannah and Atlanta on the Central of Georgia Railway's *Nancy Hanks*. The storied line was named after a race horse that was named after Abraham Lincoln's mother. Like all passenger trains then in the South, the *Nancy Hanks* had segregated cars reserved for whites and others reserved for "coloreds." The latter cars had no amenities beyond a dingy restroom and a water fountain with permanent yellow stains. Some sarcastically called the train the "Nasty Hanks" because of the sorry condition of its cars. There was no dining car for black passengers. I always considered as an adventure the shoebox lunch my grandmother packed for our trip—usually fried chicken, slices of white bread, fresh fruit, and cookies or homemade pound cake wrapped neatly in sheets of waxed paper.

When we got off the train in Atlanta, Auntie and Uncle J. A. would meet us and drive us the couple of hours north through the hilly red clay terrain to their house in Canton.

Wikipedia notes that "the Central of Georgia was the last major Southern railroad to desegregate, as it ran only in Georgia and did not engage in interstate commerce and thus evaded the Interstate Commerce

Commission's 1961 order to desegregate." On our first *Nancy Hanks* trip after desegregation, my grandmother and I were seated in a car with white passengers. The black engineer knew us because of our frequent trips on the route, and he was particularly watchful to be sure we were safe in the new integrated train world.

Sure enough, a white man was having a few too many drinks along the way. The further along we got, the more boisterous the man became. Beyond the increasing decibel level of his voice, I don't remember what he was saying, but we could just feel that there would be trouble. Finally, the man got up from his seat and headed toward us. My grandmother was in the aisle seat; I was seated between her and the window.

"Niggerrr," he blurted out when he got close to us.

Then, WHACK! His hand smacked my grandmother's face. My eyes grew big like saucers and then filled with fear. The white man was removed from the train car for the rest of the trip. It was the last time my grandmother and I would travel together on the train, although I took the *Nancy Hanks* alone a few times while I was a college student in Atlanta. Air travel was then relatively inexpensive and at some point my family began to send me plane tickets, fearing the train was too dangerous for a young black woman to travel alone.

The Central of Georgia's Savannah-to-Atlanta passenger route ended April 30, 1971, the day before Amtrak took over U.S. passenger train service. The nasty *Nancy Hanks* never ran again.

6. Jim Crow as a Matter of Life or Death

The circumstance of my own birth in Columbus, Ohio, was due to segregated medical care in Georgia. Because my mother's younger brother, Watson, was a doctor in Columbus, she was able to stay with his family during the latter stage of her pregnancy and thus avoid the services and facilities set aside for blacks in Savannah at that time.

One such facility was Charity Hospital. According to the historical marker erected in 2003, it was on the site "of the first hospital in Savannah to train African American doctors and nurses. Named for Doctors Cornelius and Alice McKane, it began on June 1, 1896, when a small group of African Americans received a charter to operate the McKane Hospital for Women and Children and Training School for Nurses." Similarly, the Georgia Infirmary was the first hospital for African Americans built in the United States. Chartered December 24, 1832, "for the relief and protection of aged and afflicted Africans," it was established by the Georgia General Assembly and funded by a $10,000 grant from the estate of Thomas F. Williams, a local merchant and minister.

Charity Hospital and the Georgia Infirmary both played an important part in health care for slaves and in the immediate post-slavery era. By the time my generation came along, medical practices were more advanced, yet we still did not have access to the hospitals with white doctors who trained at some of the best medical schools.

In 1964, my family had an unfortunate medical outcome as a direct result of Jim Crow when the man I called "Daddy" (the uncle I had adopted) suffered a stroke and was unable to get immediate medical attention.

Osie Williams, the man who raised me from age eight, went to work in his funeral home seven days a week. He got up every day at 5 a.m. and reached into a casket that had been converted to a chifforobe, a cedar-lined vertical wooden box with a high shelf to hold his collection of Stetson hats and a low shelf for his black leather dress shoes and a wooden box of shoeshine supplies. Under the top shelf, a horizontal pole held the suits and white dress shirts he took to the dry cleaners every week.

Daddy wore a black suit every day, never varying from the standard undertaker attire, always ready to greet grieving families who relied on him to handle their loved ones' final affairs. Like the other black-owned funeral homes in our community, Williams and Williams served only black clientele.

Daddy worked from before daylight until 10 or 11 every night, taking a break in the evening to come home for a proper family dinner and to get Aunt Catherine to handwrite in her perfect schoolteacher printing the obituaries of the day. After dishes were cleared from the kitchen table, he would spread out his disheveled collection of papers, handed to him by family members of the deceased, with hand-written biographical informa-tion and lists of next of kin, which Aunt Catherine would put into a well-composed obit format.

Just before 9 p.m., he would load me onto the passenger seat of his black Fleetwood Cadillac—always a Fleetwood for the undertaker. We would head downtown to the offices of the *Savannah Morning News* with the hand-printed obituaries and a check, which he had carefully written out based on the newspaper's per-word cost for each obit. The check would be the total amount, to be charged back to the accounts of the families of the deceased.

When we got to the newspaper's offices on busy Bay Street, he would remain in the car at the curb while I ran inside with the obituary copy and the check. I would wait patiently for the receipt and then head back to the car. On days when there were dead bodies to tend to at the funeral home, he would drop me off at our pink house on West 41st Street and head back across town to work. One thing about funeral homes—like hospitals, nurs-ing homes, and newspapers, they are always open.

On Saturday mornings, my hard-working Daddy would go in to work as usual, but unless there was an early funeral, he would come back home after a while to freshen up and to have breakfast with us.

Saturday was always a day of work for me, too—no fun allowed until the house was properly dusted and cleaned and clothes and linens were laundered, ironed, and folded. No TV watching, no playing outside, no telephone conversations with friends, no visiting. My friends had the same rules in their houses, so it wasn't so bad.

One Saturday morning in September 1964, I was cleaning my room when Daddy arrived back home and called out "Hey, baby," as he entered the house from the carport through the rec room that had been converted from the back porch.

"Hey, Daddy, ready for breakfast?" I replied.

"Sure thing. Hey, Cat," I heard him call out to Aunt Catherine as he walked down the hall.

Aunt Catherine was in the kitchen, and the scents wafting down the hall were inviting. On weekdays I was fine with a bowl of cereal before school. But weekend family breakfasts were special, especially when it was one of my favorite meals—salmon croquettes and cheesy grits.

The exhaust fan over the stove was on high and I doubt Aunt Catherine heard him call out to her, or even knew he was in the house since the carport was in the back, away from the kitchen up front.

What happened next changed our lives forever.

CRASH!!!!! The sharp quick sound came from the bathroom down the hall between my bedroom and the kitchen. "Daddy, you okay?" I called out, continuing to dust or make up my bed or whatever I was doing at that moment. No answer. "DAAAA-AADDY?" I called out in a sing-song voice.

Then I heard something hitting the tile floor. We figured later that he was taking his shaving implements out of the medicine cabinet when they slipped out of his hands and hit the porcelain sink below. Then his body hit the floor.

The bathroom had two doors. One opened to the hall and the other to the master bedroom. I ran the short distance out of my bedroom and down the hall, and I banged on the door from the hall side. No answer, but I could hear moaning and gurgling sounds coming from the other side of the door. I tried to turn the doorknob; it was locked.

"Aunt Catherine!" I yelled toward the kitchen, not stopping for a second to tell her something was wrong. We raced through the master bedroom, where we found Daddy on the floor—his ample 6'3" body sprawled across the threshold between the bathroom and the bedroom. His white dress shirt and tie were hanging neatly on his wooden valet; his shoes neatly placed next to the bed. He lay on the floor wearing a white undershirt and black suit pants.

We tried to get him to tell us what was wrong. His hazel eyes were unfocused and glassy and he tried to speak but was unable to get out more than a mumble. His body was heavy and limp.

"He's trying to tell us something," I said. "Daddy, what's wrong?" I was fifteen. I had never seen anything like this. I had no clue that he was having a stroke.

Apparently, Aunt Catherine didn't know, either. "Go get a glass of water," she ordered after we dragged his body up onto the bed, his stockinged feet still touching the floor. He lay there, eyes facing the ceiling, tears dripping toward his ears, like he knew what we were saying but couldn't respond.

When I returned with the water we tried to get him to take a swallow. A foamy substance came from one side of his mouth. We knew it was bad.

"Call the funeral home to send the ambulance," Aunt Catherine blurted.

IN SAVANNAH IN 1964, if there was an ambulance service with medically trained personnel, it was not available to black people. The "ambulance" service available to us at that time was run by the black-owned funeral homes on a monthly rotation. If a black person needed immediate medical attention, the funeral home responsible for the service that month would dispatch a vehicle and take the patient to Charity Hospital or the Georgia Infirmary.

I remember my parents telling me about bodies being DOA—dead on arrival. Frankly, I think quite a bit of black funeral homes' business came from DOAs. It may have been the same with white funeral homes at the time; I don't know. Those patients who didn't make it to the hospital in time were immediately transported to the funeral home that had the ambulance duty that day. A family could then transfer the body to another funeral home. But many times, once the body was in our building, it stayed there. Fortunately, we weren't facing a DOA situation, but it was devastating, nevertheless.

On that Saturday morning, I picked up the handset to the wall-mounted rotary phone in the kitchen and nervously dialed the number to Williams and Williams. I knew it then and remember it today by heart. 2-3-4-1-6-3-4, I carefully dialed. The rotary dial wouldn't roll around fast enough.

"Williams and Will—"

"Come quickly," I interrupted. "This is Wanda. Daddy is sick."

The ambulance made it from across town in short order. A couple of funeral home workers rushed in with a gurney and quickly scooped Daddy up from the bed. No diagnostic tools were present, no vital signs were taken. They were just there for transportation.

"Take us to Memorial," Aunt Catherine directed as she climbed into the ambulance with her husband, who was still slurring some unintelligible words.

Memorial was the county hospital. She knew it didn't take black patients, but she also knew it had doctors on duty. The driver—who technically worked for Aunt Catherine since her husband owned half the funeral home and she handled most of the paperwork—obediently followed her direction.

"I'll come over there in the car," I said, rushing back into the house to retrieve the car keys. I was fifteen years old with only a learner's permit. I didn't care. This was an emergency. I knew how to drive and I had to go. My grandmother, who lived next door, had come over by then. She never drove. I don't recall that she ever had a driver's license.

She shooed me out of the house. "Hurry, Cat's going to need you there," she said.

By the time I got to Memorial Hospital on the east side of town, they were bringing Daddy out on the gurney and heading back to the ambulance. Someone at the hospital had made it clear that they "didn't take coloreds."

With teary eyes, Aunt Catherine said, "We're taking him to Georgia Infirmary." Ironically, today's use of that building is as a daycare facility for survivors of stroke.

At Georgia Infirmary, we sat for hours in a hallway, watching Daddy slip deeper and deeper into a silent state of what I would later learn was a coma.

Georgia Infirmary did not have a doctor on duty that Saturday morning. There was no emergency room. No nurses came by to check on him.

They. Just. Let. Him. Lie. There.

EMOTIONS AND ANGER WERE building up inside me. The first man I ever loved, the man who played practical jokes on me, who taught me at the kitchen table how to compose obituaries (which may have been the foundation of my newspaper career), the man who winked at me as he ushered caskets down the aisle when I sat in the back of churches watching him work, the man who took me in when I was eight years old and loved me as if I were his flesh and blood, who taught me how to drive in his Fleetwood Cadillac, who amused us with his spastic version of dancing that he called the "Georgia Hop," the man who resembled my future husband in stature, features, and temperament, the man who served his country in the U.S. Navy during World War II by processing and embalming the bodies of mutilated fallen heroes, the gentle giant at home who cursed like the sailor he was but who showed nothing but compassion to grieving families—this man was slipping away from us and there was nothing we could do about it. We were living in a segregated world that turned him away from a working hospital with doctors and nurses who could have given him immediate and quality medical care.

I sat with Daddy and Aunt Catherine for hours, quiet and contemplative.

"I need to go home," I eventually said. Aunt Catherine didn't speak. She just sat staring at her husband, who was still breathing but lying motionless on the gurney. The two funeral home employees were still there with their boss. They weren't budging.

I could only imagine what Aunt Catherine was thinking. Perhaps remembering their more than twenty-five years of marriage, with no children until they took me in. Perhaps remembering how they founded the funeral home together and how she would go to the office every day after she left her job as a teacher at West Savannah School and do the paperwork and billing until the business was able to bring in more licensed workers so he could spend time in the office. Or maybe she was thinking about how they had built their house on the vacant lot next door to her parents' house, a lot her mother deeded to them after my grandfather died so they could afford to build the home of their dreams. I left her in the Georgia Infirmary hallway, staring at her husband on the gurney, no words, no more tears—just sadness in her eyes.

I drove the two miles home, walked into the house, looked at the empty, disheveled master bedroom where we had tried to revive my stricken daddy. And then I lost it. I doubled over in pain. I wailed. I cried out to God.

DADDY LINGERED COMATOSE FOR weeks in the hospital. Eventually, he was released in a permanent speechless, semi-paralyzed state. Fortunately, because we owned a business and Aunt Catherine was still teaching, from what I could see his illness didn't cause our family undue financial strain. Every two weeks one of the funeral home workers showed up with a check—Daddy's draft as a partner—which Aunt Catherine signed and gave me to deposit in the bank.

Daddy's illness kicked me from a carefree teenage life into one of adult responsibilities. I took on household duties like grocery shopping, writing checks to pay bills, and driving my grandmother wherever she needed to go. I had to grow up fast, attaining skills that would serve me well throughout my life.

I learned how to budget for weekly expenses, how to pay someone to cut the grass, and how to do routine household maintenance. Fortunately, I had followed Daddy around the house when he had pulled out his toolbox. I knew where everything was kept, and I did my best to do some of the things he always had. I knew how to change fuses in the electrical box on the back porch, how to put small items together, and how to tighten furniture when things got loose. I knew the difference between a flat-head and a Phillips screwdriver, and I knew how to use the electric hedge trimmer (except for that time when the cord got in my way and I cut it). My daddy had taught me those things.

Aunt Catherine became a caretaker for her invalid husband. She hired someone to be there during the day while she was teaching. The "fellas," as we called the funeral home workers, came by daily to get him out of bed and help with bathing and shaving. He had to have daily enemas, and sometimes he would wail during the process, which must have been painful. At these times I would sit on the side of my bed down the hall, my face in my hands, just praying that the agony would be over for him soon.

After he was cleaned up, the fellas would put him in a wheelchair and push him "up front" to sit by the big picture window that faced 41st Street. They would gently place him in a recliner and leave a portable metal urinal next to the chair. And there he sat all day. By late afternoon, someone would come from the funeral home and take him to the bedroom, dress him in pajamas, and leave him seated on the side of the bed.

At night and on weekends, his care was all on Aunt Catherine.

Every now and then the funeral home workers would take him across town so he could experience the familiar surroundings of the business. We hoped that being in a place where he had spent so much of his life might spark some recovery. All he could do was watch others work, but going there did put a smile on his face. Those visits were therapeutic for him and gave us a short respite at home.

Though the stroke left Daddy's speech impaired, he understood conversations and everything going on around him. If you asked if he wanted toast for breakfast, he was able to nod yes or no. And we developed a kind of sign language for important things, like needing someone to empty the portable urinal or wanting to sit in the dining room in front of the sunny picture window so he could see what was going on outside. Many times neighbors walking from the corner bus stop would see him sitting there and tip a hat or parasol, and he would motion with his good arm for them to come in and sit for a while and talk to him. He loved having company, even the company of strangers. His face lit up when visitors came inside. He would grin broadly with the side of his face that still had working muscles.

Small pleasures.

The stroke and his death a few years later caused Daddy to miss the seminal moments of my life. He missed my high school and college graduations. He missed presenting and dancing with me at my debutante cotillion. He wasn't able to understand or celebrate my success as a student journalist in high school and college, and he passed away before he could offer my hand in marriage.

7. With 'All Deliberate Speed'

The other big Jim Crow impact on my growing up years in Savannah was in education—segregated, underfunded schools for African Americans in the South were the norm, not the exception.

When the U.S. Supreme Court declared in 1954 in *Brown v. Board of Education* that separate schools for blacks and whites were unconstitutional, the decision overturned the 1896 ruling in *Plessy v. Ferguson*. The earlier case had held that as long as separate facilities for races were equal, segregation did not violate the Fourteenth Amendment guarantee of equal protection under the law.

"Separate but equal" was thus the legal standard that allowed Jim Crow laws to persist for another six decades after Homer Plessy was booted off a train car in New Orleans. In *Brown*, however, the Court arrived at a different conclusion: that "separate educational facilities are inherently unequal."

I was only four years old on May 17, 1954, when the *Brown* decision was handed down, so I can't say what the reaction was at that time in the nation's black communities. What I do know is that nothing changed right away, likely because the decision did not address implementation. A year later, the Court's follow-up *"Brown II"* decision ordered schools to desegregate "with all deliberate speed." That was in 1955, the year I entered first grade.

"Deliberate speed" turned out to be a crawl. Public schools in Savannah didn't begin even token steps to integrate until I was in the ninth grade, and

I personally was never affected beyond knowing about the pioneering black students who first entered the local all-white schools in 1963.

An August 18, 2013, article in the *Savannah Morning News* commemorated the fiftieth anniversary of local school desegregation, describing 1963 as "a watershed time for civil rights in America":

> A group of nineteen black high school seniors, most of them handpicked by Savannah Branch NAACP President W. W. Law, left the safety of their segregated high schools to desegregate all-white Savannah and Groves high schools. In doing so, they changed forever their lives and the face of public education in Savannah.
>
> Twenty-one students were selected and nineteen actually went. Not all would graduate. Two of the group elected to drop out and return to their segregated schools.

I well remember that period in the mid 1960s when school systems across the South began moving toward integration. The local NAACP branch, led by Law, had brokered a deal with Savannah school officials to have an orderly transition.

A biology graduate of Savannah State College, Mr. Law had been unable to get a job in his chosen field of science; such was the dilemma of educated black men who were shunned by firms and agencies that maintained discriminatory hiring. Instead, Mr. Law became a postman, which was a good job, and because it was a federal civil service job, it insulated him somewhat against white retribution for his civil rights activities. Black ministers, undertakers, agents for black insurance companies, etc., had similar advantage over blacks who worked for local white businesses or local governments—schoolteachers, for example—who could be easily fired for activism. Mr. Law, by the way, walked several miles every day to deliver the mail; he never drove a car.

Mr. Law led the black community through many stages of the local civil rights movement, including desegregation of downtown lunch counters and restaurants and for fair employment practices for blacks who were allowed to sweep floors in downtown stores but not to sell from behind counters.

Integration of the public schools was one of the local NAACP's biggest accomplishments. To prepare, Mr. Law reached out to the parents of high-achieving black students and meetings were set up to hear details about how the transition would take place—sending a few black students into some of the all-white schools one or two grades at a time until full integration was achieved. There was no reverse integration at first. That would come later.

Based on my grades, I was one of the students likely to be recruited to transfer to Savannah High School, over on the east side of town, away from my west side neighborhood and friends. Some of my friends at Beach High School were going to those meetings with the NAACP, and I wanted to go, too, just to see what it was all about. But Aunt Catherine and my grandmother didn't think that was a good idea. I stayed and graduated from my all-black high school. Thus my entire secondary education was on Savannah's west side, at Hodge Elementary, Beach Junior High, and Beach High—schools with 100 percent black students, teachers, and staff.

ONE OF THE SAVANNAH High desegregation pioneers was my classmate and friend "Patricia," whom I've known since elementary school. While I was writing this book, I revisited with her that period back in the 1960s when she endured the transition. Significantly, more than fifty years later, "Patricia" still fears retribution from former white schoolmates, and she asked me not to use her real name.

At the time, the transfer students would see us in the neighborhood on weekends and at social events, so the story Patricia retold was a painful refresher, but not a surprise. I already knew about the transfer students being constantly tripped on the stairs while changing classes and being the targets of spitballs in the classrooms. I held my objective journalist composure the day Patricia and I met over breakfast in 2018, but when I sat reading my notes and writing these paragraphs, tears filled my eyes and anger rose in my chest.

One way the NAACP had found the most likely black students to begin the integration process was through churches and their pastors. Patricia reminded me that her father was a minister and that she grew up on Victory Drive, near where Mr. Law lived. So she was a natural recruit, and she said she and the others were eager to go to Savannah High. But what they experienced there was traumatic.

"The students were mean to us, and so were some of the teachers. You had to get used to walking down the hall and being called 'Nigger.' At pep rallies students would shout, 'Beat the Niggers, Beat the Niggers!' Another pep rally chant went like this: 'Go back, go back / Go back into the woods.'

"Being called 'Nigger' was very hurtful. We were called that name every day. At lunch, [black students] always ate together in a group for support and also for protection. Every day something was thrown, something was said. The young men in our group protected us."

Patricia had been a straight-A student in junior high school. But at Savannah High, studies were more rigorous, books were newer, and there were unfamiliar materials like taped lessons for French and new classes like public speaking. I don't recall using electronic French lessons or getting formal lessons on how to deliver speeches in my all-black high school. I got that in college. At Beach High we didn't have classes in public speaking but I got training as a member of The Masquers, the drama club, and in my church where we memorized and performed all manner of orations.

"I quickly learned the meaning of something I had heard—that a 'white person's C was better than a black person's A'," she said. "At Savannah High I got C's and D's when I first got there. . . . We were taught at a higher level. It was the first time I had seen C's and D's in my life. I was determined that if *they* can get an A, *I* can get an A." she recounted bitterly.

And she did just that. Patricia and our friend, Beverly, who also transferred, became two of the first black students inducted into the National Honor Society at Savannah High School. I was inducted into the same Honor Society at my black school. I wonder if the value of my honor is the same as that of my friends who went to Savannah High.

When Patricia entered Savannah State College (an HBCU), she learned that the freshman math she was taking in college was taught from the same level of books and was the same curriculum she had as a senior in the formerly white high school. Because she was qualified, Patricia said, "I tutored math in college." After college, teaching high school math became her career.

OUR SCHOOLS THUS REFLECTED the separate yet unequal status of segregation. Savannah was very much like the "two societies" described in the 1968 Kerner Commission Report on U.S. race relations. Black public schools received on average far less money than white schools. Because of that, school conditions were vastly different. Schools for white students were maintained better than black school buildings, and white classrooms were less crowded.

In Savannah, as in just about every school district in states with Jim Crow laws, our classes were crowded with little regard for the number of students versus the size of the room, not to mention the work done by our teachers. We sat at battered desks with rutted surfaces that made writing difficult. Our books were hand-me-downs from white schools. They were not only written in and on, underlined, stamped, and dog-eared, but they often had torn covers and missing pages.

To do homework, those of us who shared classes would often have to study together or get on the phone. If I needed to know, say, what was on page twenty-nine and a friend had that page, and the friend needed to know what was on page thirty-three that I had, we would tediously read to each other over the phone and take notes. We weren't allowed to use the excuse that we couldn't read the entire chapter or do assigned math problems because of missing pages. We did what we needed to do to learn and get good grades. Years later as a professor, I encountered students who refused to read assigned work. I sometimes erupted with dismay about how hard it was "back in the day" for us to get a full educational experience and how we persevered despite the limitations of separate and unequal access to books and other materials.

Not only were our books used and abused, but they were often sadly out of date. You can imagine the limitations of obsolete history, math, or science textbooks.

Ironically, our black teachers taught us to respect books. We made book covers out of newspapers or brown grocery bags to protect the books and personalize the covers with our names and creative drawings. Our teachers taught us never to write in books, a lesson that served me well through college. Even today I find it difficult to put marks or highlights in books that I own.

BLACK TEACHERS WERE PAID less than teachers in white schools, but they pushed us to stretch ourselves to the best of our ability. So did our families. I could see that in my own home. Aunt Catherine was a teacher for thirty-six years. She was a 1936 graduate of Spelman College (an HBCU) and earned a master's degree in education at Atlanta University (another HBCU) in 1956. Let no one denigrate the value of education at HBCUs. Looking back through the 1967 *Golden Bulldog*, the yearbook for my senior year at Beach High School, I notice how many of our teachers got their post-secondary education at HBCUs in the South. Many attended Savannah State College (now University) and others were graduates of HBCUs in Georgia, South Carolina, Alabama, and Florida.

But when it came to getting graduate degrees, Aunt Catherine was an exception, because most of our teachers had to leave the South. In the introduction to his autobiography, *Bus Ride to Justice*, the celebrated attorney Fred Gray—who represented Rosa Parks and Martin Luther King Jr. during the Montgomery Bus Boycott—described Alabama's "separate but equal" system that tried to compensate for not admitting their black citizens to the state's segregated professional schools:

> The State of Alabama, as did all of the Southern states at that time, had out-of-state aid arrangements for African American students who on their merits should have been admitted to white colleges, universities, and professional schools. Many Southern states inaugurated these schemes to circumvent the 1938 United States Supreme Court decision, *Gaines V. Canada, ex rel.* The *Gaines* case held that states that had a segregated higher education system must provide African Americans with equal educational facilities.

Such was the law that compelled the State of Georgia to send black scholars out of state rather than admit them to graduate programs at in-state white schools. To comply with the law of equal opportunity, the state paid the tuition and other expenses for teachers to go "up North" for their graduate education. My *Golden Bulldog* yearbook documents our teachers' graduate degrees from the University of Pittsburgh, Columbia University, New York University, and similar schools.

WE MAY HAVE BEEN recipients of a second-hand education, but we were taught by first-rate teachers. Because black teachers earned less than teachers at white schools, they had to be more creative in getting needed school supplies. But they did something that black students missed when schools were ultimately integrated in the late 1960s and through the 1970s and beyond. Our teachers cared about us—*really cared*. Our communities were cohesive. Black teachers lived in our neighborhoods, went to church with us, and stopped and talked to our parents in the post office, at the beauty parlor, in the grocery store. If students missed class for more than a couple of days, black teachers would often get on the phone or stop by the house and knock on the door to reach out to parents. No matter the economic or social status, it was difficult for black students to fall through the cracks, like we see happening so much these days.

Our black teachers gave us life lessons with no apologies. Their instruction went beyond the basics of social studies, math, reading, and writing. They grounded us in culture and moral values, and in an era when blacks were considered second-class citizens, they steeled us for challenges we might face outside the safety and protection of our own communities.

In high school, female teachers would pull girls aside as they observed our changing bodies and let us know that "respectable" young ladies must wear the right kind of undergarments to reduce the jiggles that might entice certain reactions from boys. Yes, we're talking girdles. I'm certain boys got their own life lessons from male teachers.

We were taught that those who sat closest to the front of the classroom had the best opportunity to learn. Today when I attend meetings or professional workshops, I still make it a habit to find a seat near the front or close to the leader of the meeting so I can see and hear well and be recognized first when I have questions or suggestions.

We were taught to be patient, to sit still, and to take in the entire lesson instead of fidgeting or packing up forty-five minutes into a fifty-minute class. Social studies teacher Stella Reeves was one of the strictest at Beach High—I unsuccessfully tried to avoid her classes. She had a sign posted beneath the clock: "Time passes, but will you?" It was a reminder that watching the clock was not the best habit for those who expected good grades. Being a good learner means being an engaged learner. In my older years, I find myself quoting Mrs. Reeves's clock message when I counsel young people.

IN MY VILLAGE, OUR education did not start or end at the schoolhouse door.

Aunt Catherine's master's thesis had been entitled "A Study of Relationships Between Language Achievement and Listening Abilities." It was based on research she did at West Savannah School where she taught. Little wonder, then, that when I was eight and we moved into our newly built house on Savannah's West 41st Street, there was a walk-in closet upstairs lined with cedar shelves and filled with books and teacher files. We didn't call it a library, but many years later I realized that Aunt Catherine had created a library, a place where I would often go to pluck a book off a shelf and sit on the carpeted floor and read. That space became my world of adventure.

My family subscribed to Savannah's two daily newspapers, the *Morning News* and the *Evening Press*. On Sundays on the way to church, we purchased the *Atlanta Journal-Constitution* from a street vendor. I learned to love that newspaper and had hopes of eventually working there. I had no desire to work for the Savannah newspapers, which exhibited racist coverage of our community with segregated obituaries, sensationally negative front-page portrayals of African Americans, and the omission of positive news from our community except for the weekly "News For and About Colored People" page.

But we also subscribed to two local black weekly newspapers—the *Herald* and the *Tribune*. By mail we received *Ebony, Jet, Look, Life*, and starting in the 1970s, *Black Enterprise*, focused on African Americans who were emerging business leaders of that time. The *Atlanta Daily World* was available in black-owned shops on West Broad Street, and vendors went door-to-door selling the *Pittsburgh Courier* or the *Afro-American*. Both newspapers were notable for covering and supporting the civil rights movement.

Through subscriptions to black publications at home and school assignments, there was never any doubt that I would grow up reading about people who were the same as my family, people who had the same hair texture, who enjoyed the same kinds of music and books, and who danced to the same rhythms as we did in our community.

When I enrolled at Spelman College, I met students who had not endured the same segregated life I had led. Some of my new college friends had gone to private or Catholic schools in the South, where their resources were not nearly as limited. And while their student bodies may have been African American, some of their teachers—nuns and others—were white. Some of my college friends came to Atlanta from places like New York, Detroit, Pennsylvania or California.

Having grown up in a family where education was a significant value, in my adult years I recognize that our schools, unequal as they were, gave us an education that served us well enough in college and in life. Yet most of us didn't know what we missed under Jim Crow education until we graduated and found ourselves in the company of people who had significantly different experiences. Not to mention, we were denied the right to fraternize with people who were of a different race, which in my case limited my familiarity and comfort with people who did not look like me.

Savannah's public libraries were also segregated. The main (white) library was an elegant columned white building situated in the center of the city. Carnegie, the black library, was on the east side, miles away from my west side neighborhood. Carnegie was a lifeline for many of Savannah's black children when it was our only library. A room downstairs housed the collection for children and was a respite for many of us before we "graduated" upstairs when were in high school.

Linda Robinson Green and I met as high school students in a summer journalism program on the campus of Savannah State College, and we remain lifelong friends. Linda lived on the east side, close enough to walk to Carnegie Library. "My mother didn't like for us to play in the streets," she recalled recently, "so we spent a lot of time in Carnegie. [Future U.S. Supreme Court Justice] Clarence Thomas was our neighbor, and we sometimes walked to the library together."

For those of us who lived on the west side, an assignment that required research materials or a book from the public library necessitated a two-bus trip across town. Most of the time the books we needed were not in circulation at the Carnegie library, which had limited resources. The card catalog designated where the book was housed. We would take the card from the catalog to a librarian and she would "order" the book to be delivered to Carnegie.

"It will be here next week," the librarian would tell us. Then we would get back on the bus and transfer to a second bus. The following week we would reverse the bus trip to the library to pick up our books on order. What a burden it must have been for black teachers to build in two weeks of lesson planning, knowing how long it would take just to secure a book, much less the time we needed to read it.

Years later as a university professor when I encountered students who waited until the last minute to work on an assignment, I would share the Southern equivalent of the "we had to walk ten miles to school in the snow" story by telling students how much planning went into preparing to get a book just so we could do our assignments.

"What if we had waited until the last minute?" I asked students at Savannah State University. I'm not sure my story had an impact on getting students to begin working on assignments sooner. It just infuriates me that in the twenty-first century, young people take so much for granted, even something as simple as how to manage time when they can get any book they need by walking across campus to the library, with a couple of clicks on Amazon, or by "Googling."

ANOTHER ASPECT OF MY all-black high school was tracking—we were put into homerooms and other classes based on who was college-bound and who was not, based on our test scores and grades. I was tracked in the "1" homerooms—known as 10-1 in tenth grade, then 11-1, and 12-1 in our senior year. Most of the close relationships I developed were with students who were in the "1" homerooms with me, because we saw each other almost all day for five days a week.

My passions were the *Beach Beacon*, our school newspaper, and The Masquers, the drama club I led as president. At the end of tenth grade as we were registering for eleventh-grade classes, my friend Virginia Law and I were looking for a course that would be less stressful than our required college-prep math, science, and English courses. Virginia also came from a family of educators. In fact, her mother taught home economics at Beach High. (When we signed up for "Home Ec," we avoided taking it from Virginia's mother and enrolled in a class taught by another teacher.)

Looking for that eleventh-grade stress diversion, Virginia and I settled on Journalism I, taught by Ella P. Law (Virginia's aunt-in-law and no relation to NAACP President W. W. Law). We didn't know what to expect, but Virginia and I were good readers and good writers, having acquired this foundation in school and at home with our educator parents. When I mentioned this to my mother, who had once been an English student in Mrs. Law's class, she said "Ooooh, you're taking a class from Mrs. Law? She was the toughest teacher I had at Beach High."

So much for the stress diversion.

Mrs. Law challenged us, and she recognized something in me—the skill for being creative with ideas, for writing and telling stories, and helping other students with their projects. The class was a laboratory for producing the school paper. I found writing news stories exhilarating. I loved seeing my name in print and hearing "I read your story" or "Good job on that story" from teachers and fellow students. I had what I would later hear described as "a nose for news."

Near the end of eleventh grade, Mrs. Law pulled me aside and asked me to consider something that may have been the trajectory conversation for my career.

"Wanda, you are a good writer," she said. "You understand how to write news and features and you have good story ideas."

That part of the conversation alone would have levitated my spirit for a good long while, sending me floating out of her classroom, down the hall, and all the way home with a great big grin. But she went on.

"I've noticed that you are also a good leader. I see how you work with the other students helping them with their stories, and you speak up in class when we are discussing story ideas. I want you to become editor-in-chief of the *Beach Beacon* next year."

And that's how newspaper leadership started for me, skills that would ultimately lead to management roles at one of the nation's largest newspapers and to become executive editor of my last newspaper before retiring from daily journalism.

Thanks to Mrs. Law, I was about to become editor-in-chief. Along with the title came another perk. She recommended Virginia and me for a summer workshop for black high school newspaper advisors, held on Savannah State's campus.

The 2009 book *Copy: The First 50 Years of the Dow Jones Newspaper Fund* by Rick Kenney documents the founding of this summer program at Savannah State. Paul Swensson, a self-described "newsman," visited the Savannah campus in 1963 to speak to a group of students, faculty, and some high school teachers, undoubtedly including Mrs. Law. Massachusetts-born Swenson had worked at newspapers in South Dakota, Minnesota, and California, and he became executive director of the Newspaper Fund in 1961.

In Savannah, Swensson gave his "Face of the Newsman" address, in which, according to *Copy*, he described a typical "newsman" as having "the nose for news, the discerning eye and the chin for courage. . . . He recalled the repugnance of segregation. He could neither sit in the front seat of a car driven by a black journalism teacher nor in the back seat with the teacher's wife. Because he was lodged at the city's top hotel, his hosts could not visit him in his suite or be served in the coffee shop."

Among the nineteen workshops Swensson proposed and carried out in the summer of 1964 was a trial program at Savannah State for African American teachers and some of their students in the southeastern states.

Kenney wrote in *Copy*, "One of the participants was a high school student, Wanda Smalls, who later attended Spelman College, became a Newspaper Fund editing intern in 1970 and—40 years after that first Savannah workshop—was appointed (executive) editor of the *Montgomery* (Ala.) *Advertiser* after a distinguished career at *USA Today*."

Over three weeks that summer we learned how to write news stories, conduct interviews, lay out (design) pages, and how to shoot and crop photographs. We gained skills for news judgment, how to motivate staff to recognize a good story when they hear about it, how to raise money to support our journalism, and how to avoid getting into trouble with school administrators who universally had more appreciation for censoring the news than for First Amendment freedom of the press.

The Newspaper Fund later gave me the three-week fellowship at Temple University in Philadelphia and the internship in Providence. This was in 1970, the first year African Americans were included in the internship program. Proudly, many years later I was asked to become a member of the Newspaper Fund's Board of Directors, where I served 1992–1999. As an editor at *USA Today*, the *Greenville News* in South Carolina, and the *Montgomery Advertiser*, I made sure we had Dow Jones Newspaper Fund interns working with us in the summer. It was important for me to give back, to help students launch their careers as the Newspaper Fund did for me.

In high school, Mrs. Law positioned me for another opportunity. The *Savannah Evening Press* was starting a monthly tabloid section called *Teen Times*, which would include stories and photographs by high school students about what was going on in the local high schools. Because I would be the student newspaper's editor in my senior year, Mrs. Law recommended me as a reporter for *Teen Times*.

The *Press* and the *Morning News* were not known to have diversity on their newsroom staffs; the papers were not considered balanced in coverage by African American readers. To be fair, the same could be said for the local TV stations' news coverage at the time.

In that summer program, I met Harold Jackson, who attended Johnson High School on the east side. Harold later became the first African American to work full-time in the newsroom at the *Morning News*. Fifty years after he worked at the Savannah paper, I reached out to Harold, who lives in Atlanta, about his time in that newsroom. After graduating from high school and then Savannah State, his career took him on an amazing professional journey to earn two graduate degrees at the University of Michigan in the areas of journalism, radio/TV, and film, teaching and media relations positions at several universities, corporate communications roles at Monsanto and Coca-Cola, and then as founder and president of the JacksonHeath Group, a strategic communications firm.

In July 2007, on the fortieth anniversary of becoming the first African American news staffer at the Savannah newspaper, Harold wrote a commentary recalling his groundbreaking accomplishment:

> Some 40 years ago a quiet revolution took place in the newsroom of the *Savannah Morning News.*
>
> People I had known from only reading their columns and bylines were now my peers. As I walked into the newspaper to assume my duties as a copy boy in the spring of 1967, little did I imagine that I, too, would get a byline and people would come to know me as a reporter the following year . . .
>
> For the next year and beyond, I wrote stories about black capitalism in the city, covered the election of the first black state representative from Chatham County, Bobby Hill, and generally covered the ordinary life of people living in the shadow of this community.
>
> I was also given the job of writing a weekly column for the Sunday edition covering events and activities of Savannah State College, called "College by the Sea." My mother took special pride in seeing my picture on the column each Sunday.

Harold went on to describe the "pioneering social experiment" that allowed him to "build a career as a journalist, magazine editor, television talk show host," etc.

I asked Harold how he was received by newsroom coworkers in Savannah.

"There were people uncomfortable with me being in the newsroom," he said. "They gave me an office in the library, with the primary job of writing and editing obituaries of black people."

While we give much credit to Harold, and to Bobby Adams, a correspondent who covered local black high school sports but never worked in the newsroom full time, I was reminded to look back at my own stories submitted as the first black reporter for *Teen Times*. Years later, I spent a day in the main Savannah public library—the building I could not enter as a young girl. I searched through microfilm for some of my first published stories. When I found the first story under my byline as a "correspondent" for the local newspaper in 1966, I sat back and took an emotional and overwhelming deep breath. The story read:

> Students Sound Off on Styles
> By Wanda Smalls
> School Correspondent
> Like teen-agers everywhere, the students at Beach High School are well aware of today's fashions for youth. Having been asked what they "think about current styles for the opposite sex," they made the following comments:
> Charles Moore—11th grade—"I think they're pretty nice . . . They should do something better about their hairstyles."
> Linda Riddle—11th grade—"Some of them are cute, but some are too 'way out.'"
> LaVerne Oliver—12th grade—"I especially like the Carnaby look on boys."
> Lula Allen—12th grade—"I think Banlon shirts look better on slim boys than on stout ones."
> Angelyn Stewart—12th grade—"I like the silk socks and suits on boys. I like for boys to wear close haircuts."
> Omie Bradley—10th grade—"I don't like tight pants on boys."
> Joseph Snowden—12th grade—"I like long go-go earrings on girls. I don't like dresses with long waists. I like for everything to fit girls."
> Angela Williams—10th grade—"I think most of the boys' styles are too gaudy."

And thus began my professional journalism career, a fashion story that documented Banlon fabric, go-go earrings, the Carnaby look, silk socks, and tight pants on boys. It was my first and last fashion story.

Another story, "Girls Break a Precedent and Get B's," was about seniors

Clara Thompkins and Kay Alston, the first two girls allowed to enroll in the woodworking class.

> Before beginning their first project jointly, a towel rack, Kay and Clara were taught the techniques of assembly, handling of tools and varnishing.
>
> The girls say that the boys in the class do not feel they deserve high grades. They [boys] like to feel that they are still superior in every way. Despite the boys' feelings, Kay and Clara both received a grade of B for the first six-week period."

Way to recognize a good story, Wanda.

A FINAL RECOLLECTION TO share from my Savannah school days sort of bookends segregation.

Tybee Island, formerly known as Savannah Beach, is a barrier island and small city about fifteen miles from downtown Savannah. The island is known for its wide, sandy beaches, with a pier and pavilion on the south end. On the island's north side, Fort Screven has nineteenth-century concrete gun batteries and the Tybee Island Light Station and Museum. The museum focuses on local history. Many historians believe the name "Tybee" derives from the Native American (Euchee) word for "salt," which was one of many natural resources found on the island. It is said that pirates visited the island in search of a safe haven and hiding place for treasure.

In the 1960s, Savannah Beach was off-limits to us. Our parents warned us away from the island as if it were a forbidden fruit. "Just don't go there," they would say, and implicit in the order were Jim Crow laws.

To this day, decades after the "wade-ins" of the 1960s by African American students determined to break down barriers, I still don't know if there was some law on the books that said "Negroes" could not ride onto the island, or if our elders just knew that going there might mean peril to our physical being.

I left home for college and pursued my journalism career elsewhere, so the first time I saw Tybee Island in daylight was in March 1997, the day after we buried my mother in Laurel Grove South Cemetery, the city's traditional black eternal resting place. Her demise had come soon after the doctor told us she would not survive lung cancer, caused, we suspected, by her many years of smoking. Her funeral was even quicker—my mother's wishes. She planned the brief service herself.

The day after the funeral I told my husband, Lloyd, that I wanted to go see the ocean. I wasn't sure why; I just had a feeling that walking along the sea would put me just a few miles closer to God, and I had so many questions about why I was left motherless before my fiftieth birthday. I felt angry, depressed, lonely, sad, yet somewhat relieved that her physical misery was over.

I was also curious about the place my family had once tried so hard to keep me from visiting. And maybe I was feeling just a little guilty.

True, I'd never actually seen Tybee Island, but I hadn't exactly obeyed my parents, either. On the night of my high school prom in 1967, the first and last thing Aunt Catherine said to me before I walked out the door with my date was "don't go to the beach." Later that night, my date told me his parents said the same thing. And so had the parents of the couple we were double-dating with that night.

All four sets of parents had warned us. So what did we do? Like any group of obstinate teenagers, we set out on the lonely, dark U.S. Highway 80 to drive the fifteen miles to Tybee Island after the prom, just to see what the mystery of the island was all about.

We didn't anticipate that the island would be pitch black, devoid of streetlights and traffic in those days. It was a sleepy little island in the middle of a spring night. We saw nothing. We could hear the ocean, but we were not even sure which way to look for it, and we were scared as heck so we got out of there. My fears were buttressed by the race stories we were hearing from across the South in the late 1960s—stories of beatings, lynchings, and arbitrary jailings had us so afraid that all we did on Tybee that night was change drivers and head back home.

Since my date had driven us out to the island while the other couple "made out" in the back seat, we traded places—and activities—for the return trip. To put it delicately, my eyes were closed, so I missed the flashing lights from the police when they pulled us over.

White officers made our driver get out of the car and walk the white line on Highway 80. None of us had been drinking, as far as I knew, but I was surprised to learn that our friend didn't have a license to drive. He was arrested, so my date drove the other girl and me home. I never told my family about our detour to Savannah Beach.

For African Americans in Savannah, beach paradise was elsewhere. My social centers as a child were the segregated Girl Scout troop hosted at St. Matthews Episcopal Church, the West Broad Street YMCA where we learned social graces in "charm school," and Sunday School at Second African Baptist Church, the historic congregation founded by slaves and free blacks in 1802. Before I was born, my grandfather was a deacon and Sunday school superintendent at Second Baptist; Aunt Catherine played the piano, and my grandmother was active as a deaconess and in service groups.

In the summers when our church planned Vacation Bible School or Sunday School excursions to the beach, we made the four-hour bus trip to American Beach, on the southern end of Amelia Island in Florida. Settled and built by Abraham Lincoln Lewis, CEO of the Afro-American Insurance Company as a retreat for his company's employees, American Beach was known as one of the South's "black beaches." Going there allowed us to enjoy the water free of racial intimidation. It was a long bus ride—a sacrifice of time, considering the Atlantic Ocean was just fifteen miles from our church's front door on Savannah's downtown Houston Street.

Hilton Head Island was another nearby oasis for black families, especially the few elite families from Savannah who built houses along a couple of streets at the entrance to the island many years before the big resort corporations "discovered" the island. On Hilton Head, just across the bridge in South Carolina and forty-five minutes away from Savannah, we took pleasure in spending time on Collier Beach and Singleton Beach, black beaches with open-air pavilions not far from the shorelines for running into the surf, where we attended Saturday night parties, dancing to the 1960s Motown sounds.

My friend Virginia's family had a house on Hilton Head, and they invited me to join her there many weekends during our high school years. We would pack the car with weekend food supplies and return to Savannah Sunday night. Those were joyous weekends of freedom from Savannah's oppressively hot, humid summer days. We would sleep in the twin beds in Virginia's room with the windows open at night, enjoying the sounds and breezes from the surf.

So, on the day in 1997 when I ventured to Tybee Island to reflect on the loss of my mother and think about how I would move forward without her, as we entered the island, Lloyd drove slowly along Butler Avenue, the island's main drag. We took in the quaintness and serenity and admired the eclectic beachy architecture, the tropical landscapes, and the laid-back lifestyle.

We parked on the south end of the island and walked along Tybrisa Street past the shops and restaurants. We strolled the length of the big pier that jutted into the Atlantic Ocean to look at the water—which, even in early March, gave me a feeling of warmth and peace. Here we were, just a few miles from where I grew up on Savannah's west side, and yet a world away.

That day we decided to book a vacation on Tybee Island and we returned a few weeks later, and the year after that and the year after that. Lloyd quickly learned how to find the locals-only fishing spots. We gravitated to vacation rentals along Chatham Avenue and the Bull River, where most of the houses have their own docks, and where the views and fishing are unbeatable. I came to love solitary walks along the shoreline of the South Beach, or sitting with a mug of coffee at dawn in one of the beachside swings, watching the sun come up.

Tybee became a place of celebration for us. We chose the island as the site of our anniversary getaways each May. Over the next twelve years, we rented small condos and, later, beach houses, inviting friends from other cities where we had lived to join us. When Lloyd and I relocated permanently to Savannah in 2013, our daughter, Shelby, asked we would spend our vacations.

"Vacation?" I exclaimed. "We don't need to go anywhere! We're living near Tybee Island and we can go there every day if we want."

Times change. Tides change. And, thankfully, so do people.

8. Continuing the Legacy

I come from generations of college-trained women, so I don't remember conversations about *if* I would go to college. It was always known that I *would* go to college. In addition to my grandmother, my grandmother's sister, and Aunt Catherine, Ernestein Walker Baylor, a second cousin who became a history professor at Morgan State University, graduated from Spelman College in 1949.

As for me, once I realized that journalism was my passion, I wanted to go to the University of Georgia, which at the time was the only school in the state offering a degree in journalism, a program that began there in 1915. Charlayne Hunter-Gault, a native of Due West, South Carolina, had been one of the first black students to enroll at the University of Georgia in 1961, and she graduated there in journalism in 1963 and went on to a distinguished career in both broadcast and print. I had the pleasure of working with her at Columbia University in the summer of 1972. In 1961, I had seen the turmoil on the network news when state patrol officers were escorting Charlayne and her fellow pioneer, Hamilton Holmes, onto the Georgia campus amid the taunts and rioting of segregationist white students. The two black students enrolled, then sat out some time and finally re-entered the university after court intervention. It was a tumultuous time and my family, rightly so I now acknowledge, didn't want that for me.

So I was Spelman-bound, though not without resistance from Daddy.

Before his stroke, we had family conversations about where I would be going to college. "Stay at home," he told me, "and we'll get you a car so you can drive to Savannah State," the HBCU that was about five miles from our house. It was a matter of convenience and also probably loving protection for parents to keep their children close by for college. Maybe it was a Southern thing. It certainly was, culturally, a pattern in many African American families.

But Aunt Catherine and my grandmother had other plans for me. They were determined that I continue the family legacy at Spelman College in Atlanta, which I was happy to oblige. I couldn't wait to leave Savannah, not just because of what I experienced as a racially oppressive environment, but because home after Daddy's stroke had become such a sad place.

"If you go to Spelman you won't need a car," the women in my family would remind me, because I would be living on the campus in Atlanta.

When the time came, I applied only to Spelman, which was not nearly as competitive to get into as it is today. In 1967, the year I enrolled, the student body at the African American college for women was fewer than one thousand. In 2018, more than nine thousand women applied for one of Spelman's six hundred freshman-year spots, in a student body of about twenty-two hundred. I am grateful that I didn't have to compete by today's competitive standards.

We didn't tell Daddy right away, but a few weeks before it was time for me to leave for Atlanta, we went into the bedroom where he was sitting on the side of the bed as he waited for whatever care was to come next.

"Daddy, I was accepted at Spelman and I'm going to go to college there."

His eyes became damp and then came the tears. There was anger and frustration in his face, and he fisted his left hand, the one that was not affected by the stroke. He repeatedly pounded the mattress.

"No. No. No. No. No," he slurred. He obviously remembered the conversations about my staying home and going to college in Savannah. It was heartbreaking, but I knew I had to do what was best for me. I grew up knowing that I was someday going to be a Spelman woman, and Aunt Catherine assured me that I was doing the right thing.

After I left for Atlanta in 1967, I lost track of some of the details of Daddy's care, but I know it was tough on Aunt Catherine without me around to help. My grandmother's health also declined while I was in college and she eventually moved next door into our house so Aunt Catherine could more easily look after both of them. Every time I came home from college I could see the weight of the caretaking burdens on her. She tried to put on a good act, but I knew she was bone-tired.

On May 31, 1971, my grandmother was proudly wheeled into Sisters Chapel for my Spelman graduation. She passed away two months later. At her funeral, the Reverend Edgar Quarterman, our pastor at Second Baptist Church, said in his eulogy that he had visited her at home in her final months: "She told me she was praying that God would keep her around long enough to see Wanda graduate from Spelman College. She saw her graduate and I know she is at rest now."

It was the first time I had heard that story.

By then Daddy was in a nursing home in Savannah. He died the next year. Aunt Catherine lived on as a widow in the pink house on West 41st Street until 1991.

MEANWHILE, I HAD BECOME a Spelman woman, fulfilling the family legacy.

> *Spelman, thy name we praise,*
> *Standards and honor raise.*
> *We'll ever faithful be*
> *Throughout eternity*
> —From *The Spelman Hym*n, by Eddye Money Shivery, '34

"You went to Spelman, didn't you?"

"Yes," I always nod.

"Uh, huh. I can tell."

Thus begin many conversations about what we typically know as "The Spelman Woman"—quiet, gracious, smart, leadership-focused, elegantly put together, African American women educated at Spelman College in Atlanta.

The school was founded in 1881 as the Atlanta Baptist Female Seminary by Sophia B. Packard and Harriet E. Giles, two Christian white women who moved south from New England with a mission to educate black girls.

Spelman began in the basement of Friendship Baptist Church, and the campus was created at a nearby location on nine acres of land with five original frame buildings as what was described as a "model school" to train young women to become teachers and nurses. The two founders ultimately encouraged other friends in New England to move to Atlanta to teach. Some of their well-to-do friends, especially the Rockefellers, provided funding.

In 1884, the name changed to Spelman Seminary, in honor of Laura Spelman Rockefeller and her parents, longtime activists in the movement to abolish slavery. The first high school class graduated in 1887. As the campus and academic programs grew in the early twentieth century, the school became Spelman College in 1924. Today there are twenty-five buildings at Spelman; when I arrived as a freshman in 1967, five were named for members of the Rockefeller family.

Women in my family were building a tradition of becoming Spelman women in the early decades of the 1900s. My maternal grandmother, Oper Lee Watson, and her sister, Eliza Marie, attended Spelman. Aunt Catherine attended Spelman beginning in the second grade, and she graduated from Spelman College in 1936.

Spelman was thus a part of my village long before I was a student there. As a child in Savannah I tagged along to monthly meetings of what was then called the Spelman Club, a network of women in cities across the nation whose passion for Spelman led them to raise scholarship funds and to recruit promising local high school students to attend their alma mater. Even in grade school, legacy family members would become clones of the Spelman women we were getting to know.

My Savannah Spelman village influence drove some of the rules for me at home. Wearing a dress or skirt, never pants, was de rigueur because at the time, Spelman women *never* wore pants or super casual clothes outside the house. Spelman women were good writers, appreciative of the arts and culture, and those from the South spoke in a gentle Southern voice but learned to communicate effectively and firmly to show how well-prepared they were to become leaders. These traits governed my childhood and prepared me to become a Spelman woman.

"We had to dress up with hats and gloves, stockings and leather shoes every time we left the campus," Aunt Catherine would tell me, even for a shopping trip to Rich's downtown on Atlanta's Broad Street. It was as if

Spelman women were in uniform, wearing modestly fitting dresses and perfectly prepped for suitable off-campus presentation. Even when I enrolled at Spelman in 1967, we could not wear pants until after 7 p.m., and then only on campus, never at the all-male Morehouse or co-ed Clark colleges across the street. In my freshman year, even at night when we could "take company" with a young man in the dormitory lounge, we could not wear pants.

9. Privileged Black Girl

"Wanda Smalls, you have a phone call," a schoolmate shouted after she answered the ringing wall-hung pay phone on the second floor of Abby Hall, a dormitory at Spelman College. "She said to tell you hurry up. She's calling from Russia."

The year was 1969, my sophomore year. My mother, Gloria Marie Walker, was on the phone.

Gloria—I called her that—began her career working in retail sales at Camp Stewart (later Fort Stewart), a Georgia military base about an hour from Savannah established in 1940 as an anti-aircraft artillery-training center. As Camp Stewart's troop level increased during World War II, a Post Exchange was needed. When the war ended, the site was used by a small Georgia National Guard contingent but otherwise abandoned.

Somehow, Gloria survived what must have been a mass layoff of employees after the war. She transferred to the Army PX at Fort Dix, New Jersey. I was left behind with my grandmother in Savannah.

Gloria's professional story is one of her rise through the ranks of retail sales and merchandising, especially considering her own growth years as an African American under Jim Crow laws. After Fort Dix, her next step was to New York City to work in the headquarters of the Army and Air Force Exchange Service (AAFES). With the ultimate title of senior executive buyer, she was one of very few African American or women executives in AAFES.

Gloria's categories ranged from automobile parts and accessories to women's apparel, from luggage to watches. But the area she most enjoyed was as a toy buyer. It was a big job during the Vietnam War era of the

1960s and early 1970s. The military ranks soared and AAFES became one of the world's largest retail organizations. Gloria told me she had the second largest buying budget for toys worldwide—behind then-powerhouse Sears, Roebuck and Company.

She regaled us with stories of traveling the country on buying trips to toy company headquarters and factories, where she learned about trends and materials used to make the merchandise and placed orders for vast numbers of toy trucks, train sets, board games, Play-Doh, and dolls. G. I. Joe, the line of military action figures produced by Hasbro, was popular with her military family customers, as were dolls for little girls. Every February she spent a week at the annual Toy Fair, a trade show in New York City where toy manufacturers show off their upcoming lines of merchandise.

Once she flew me to New York and slipped me onto the Toy Fair floor with her credentials. She wanted me to see how she worked such a large and important event, going from booth to booth introducing herself, shaking hands, asking questions and making appointments for future discussions with those companies whose items she would ultimately consider for her PX buys.

She was thorough, making sure working parts were safe for tiny hands, couldn't be swallowed by children still young enough that they put things in their mouths, and that stuffed animals had eyes that were sewn on instead of glued so they wouldn't come off. The Toy Fair visit showed me how someone who cares about her job must be committed to details on behalf of the end user—not just filling orders, but fulfilling the mandate for quality, consistency and safety. I would carry these lessons with me throughout my work life as I nurtured professional and personal relationships. Firm handshakes, looking people in the eye, doing enough homework in advance to ask the right questions, getting to know professional people on a personal level by asking about their children who were completing high school or getting married, and following up with hand-written notes. My mother never had to *tell* me how to do these things. She *showed* me how she did them.

On one of my trips to New York she convinced me to get up early and accompany her to work one day. I did so with reluctance because I knew she would find a way to put me to work. She did. She placed a stack of file folders and documents before me and told me she needed my help with filing. She showed me how to make files and categorize information. Years later, when her office was moving, and the staff was cleaning up files and putting documents in boxes, they found a letter I wrote to President Lyndon Johnson. The cynical letter, written in my teen years, was stashed away in a random file folder.

> Dear President Johnson,
> I wanted to report to you that my mother, Gloria Walker, and the staff members in her office at the Army and Air Force Exchange Service are breaking the law. They have me here working and I am not getting paid. I am sure you are aware of child labor laws. Please tell them that they should either pay me or stop forcing me to work.
> Sincerely,
> Wanda Smalls

I remember tapping out the prank letter on a manual typewriter at my mother's desk while she was in a meeting. She said she had to laugh when she finally read it.

As A BUSINESSWOMAN GLORIA had one important thing going for her—clout. She had a vast budget and she represented an organization that was a perpetual retail customer. Being the renaissance woman she was, Gloria recognized quickly that all of the dolls and action figures were made in the image of white people. None looked like the vast number of African American families who were her customers, those serving in the U.S. armed forces. Thus began her quest to change the toy industry's habit of producing only white dolls and expecting little black girls to identify with them, or producing G. I. Joe only in the image of white soldiers.

We didn't have the name for it then, but what eventually became a business imperative for "diversity"—addressing the needs of a business audience based on statistical analysis of her own customer base—was what Gloria established, with a bit of cajoling, in the toy industry. She approached one company after another about designing dolls with African American features, breaking through norms of ignoring a segment of the buying population. Gloria personally worked with the CEOs of Hasbro and Mattel and they agreed to alter some of their toy designs.

Elliot Handler, who founded Mattel with his wife, Ruth, produced a line of toy Peanuts characters from the popular comic strips created by artist Charles Schulz. Apparently, sales through AAFES boosted Mattel's bottom line, and when Handler's company celebrated their quarter-century anniversary, they commissioned Schulz to draw a cartoon in honor of my mother, the toy buyer. The single-frame cartoon is a conversation between characters Charlie Brown and the blanket-dragging Linus, with Snoopy, the intrepid Beagle relaxing atop his doghouse.

The first line of black dolls came with the coloring of little black girls, but not with the Afro-centric features that made the dolls look like me and other black girls I knew growing up. Eventually, the doll features evolved to having broader noses, thicker lips, and more realistic color tones. I remember the day when I was still in elementary or middle school a doll came in the mail to me in Savannah. It was the era of mechanical toys. The box introduced me to "Wanda Walker," a doll my mother, working with designers, helped create, giving her my first name and the double meaning of my mother's last name and the fact that this doll walked.

I took Wanda Walker out of the box and found the wind-up stem in her back. She was about a foot tall and she wore a pink dress trimmed in white lace. Her hair was black with a shiny coarseness. She wore what looked like black patent leather shoes and white socks also trimmed in lace. When I placed Wanda Walker on the hardwood floor in my grandmother's living room, the doll put one foot in front of the other in a stiff mechanical move, her arms swinging as she walked to the whirring sound of the wind-up motor inside her body. It wasn't a perfect walk. She would bump furniture or trip over any nick in the hardwood floor, but she walked, and she looked somewhat like me in terms of her color.

Gloria went on to work with toy companies and designers to encourage them to transform their lines of Barbie-like and G.I. Joe-type products.

After a time, companies recognized the importance of expanding toys and action-figure lines into the images of segments of their customers. Today dolls—including Barbie, who began life as a fashion model—are inspired by the cultures of people who are African American, Asian, Hispanic, Caribbean, Middle Eastern, physically disabled, curvaceous and full-figured, and of course portraying a wide variety of careers. Undoubtedly, this has been a lucrative transition for the toy industry. Who knows? Maybe dolls created after my mother's retirement have Gloria Walker to thank for their success with the popular Barbie, Cabbage Patch, and others with diverse features that followed.

IN THE PRE-DAWN HOURS of August 28, 1963, a bus pulled out of New York City with my mother as the organizer. In addition to her professional acumen, Gloria was a bad-ass feminist and an adventurer. During the civil rights movement in the 1960s she was energized to protest and take a stand for justice. Having been born in 1929 into some of the worst years of Jim Crow laws and racism, and the lack of rights for women, she was motivated to support the March on Washington.

Gloria had gone around to her co-workers at the AAFES headquarters in New York and encouraged them to join her by paying for a seat on the bus and standing out in the hot August sun on the Washington Mall to rally with the estimated quarter-million people who heard Dr. King deliver his famous "I Have a Dream" speech:

> Now is the time to make justice a reality for all of God's children. It would be fatal for the nation to overlook the urgency of the moment. This sweltering summer of the Negro's legitimate discontent will not pass until there is an invigorating autumn of freedom and equality —1963 is not an end but a beginning.

That day was a highlight of my mother's life. She told me that story over and over throughout her retirement years, how they marched, sang songs, cheered and hugged strangers of different races, people they didn't even know, but with whom they found kinship in that epic moment of the civil rights movement. She told me they went home motivated to make a difference in their own spaces of life.

In 1969, my mother called me a couple of times during her three-week tour of communist Russia, then the Union of Soviet Socialist Republics—the USSR. She was traveling with Valerie, an AAFES colleague who had immigrated from Russia to the United States. When Valerie told my mother that she and her sister were planning to visit family in the USSR, somehow the conversation led to Gloria going along. My mother was always curious about the world, but until then she had never traveled abroad. Some of her interest in international cultures was fueled by the 1964 New York World's Fair, when she sent for me to come to the city so we could take in the exposition together. I was fifteen.

The World's Fair was an amazing amalgam of cultures—a potpourri of international music, dance, food, architecture, languages, clothing, souvenirs, toys, and, most of all, a hope that through visiting the various pavilions and restaurants the world would become a smaller place with a better understanding of how we might blend our mutual visions for a better world free of conflicts and misunderstandings.

With her curiosity piqued for world travel and the opportunity to travel with someone who spoke the language, my mother jumped at the chance to join Valerie on the adventure to the Communist nation. The women took rooms at a resort along the Black Sea, an area steeped in history where tourists were welcome. While the American travelers could not go to where the Russians lived, Valerie's Russian family members were able to visit her at the resort.

On one of her calls to me while she was on the trip, Gloria told me about their encounter with a woman she met while taking in the sights of Moscow's Red Square.

"I was standing in a sea of people," she yelled quickly over the phone's distant-sounding line. "Then I saw a woman across Red Square. She was black like me."

As if in a slow-motion film the two black women moved toward each other until they stood face to face. They talked. Lily Golden was the daughter of Oliver Golden, an African American expatriate of the early 1900s with roots in Mississippi, and Bertha Bialek, a daughter of Polish Americans of Jewish descent. After initial pleasantries, Lily touched my mother's face and asked how she was able to find makeup for her medium-brown complexion. Then she noticed the hosiery my mother was wearing and she expressed envy that Gloria was able to find stockings the color of her skin. They talked about American culture—fashion, books, music—things not available to Golden at the time.

When my mother returned home, she put together a care package for her new friend, Lily. Inside the box was a collection of properly colored makeup for Lily's brown skin, brown hosiery, and books written by contemporary African Americans. My mother was a fan of authors like James Baldwin, Richard Wright, Ralph Ellison, and Langston Hughes, and of jazz artists like Duke Ellington, Billie Holiday, Sarah Vaughan, and Count Basie, so I assume she sent Lily parts of her own book and music collections. My mother and Lily Golden exchanged letters and postcards for a few years after their encounter in Red Square, and about once a year for a while my mother would mail a box of items she thought her friend might appreciate.

They had one more thing in common. They were mothers of daughters who grew up to become journalists. In the mid-1990s, I was seated in a

Kansas City, Missouri, hotel ballroom that was filling up with hundreds of people at a luncheon for the annual convention of the National Association of Black Journalists, an organization I joined in 1981. I looked down at the printed program and my eyes got big when I saw the name of the speaker—Yelena Khanga, Lily Golden's daughter. Khanga was on a book tour in the States to promote her memoir—*Soul to Soul: A Black Russian Jewish Woman's Search for Her Roots.*

I quickly pulled out one of my business cards and wrote on the back, "Daughter of Gloria Walker in the USA," and my mother's current mailing address. The program had not started. I nervously made my way through the huge hotel ballroom to the dais and introduced myself to the speaker. I was nervous because this woman didn't know me. Would she be pleasant to a stranger with the bizarre story of their mothers' friendship? Might she be warm in her greeting and tell me she remembered the care packages from long ago that helped her mother identify with her own African American heritage?

I have to say her reaction was somewhere in between. I think I rambled, a sign of my glee as I recanted the story of how our mothers met and about their pen-pal friendship, and I asked Khanga to pass along my card to her mother. I don't know if she did. My mother, by then retired and again living in Savannah, did not hear from her friend Lily again.

When Vice President Lyndon Johnson became president after the assassination of President John F. Kennedy in 1963, he moved some federal agencies to Texas, no doubt to boost jobs and the economy in his home state. AAFES was one of those agencies. My mother and her colleagues who were eligible and willing to move eventually occupied a newly built facility in Dallas, also thanks to LBJ's Texas boosterism.

WHEN SHE TRAVELED ON business and passed through Atlanta, Gloria would sometimes arrange a long flight layover. She would taxi over to Spelman's campus to take me to dinner or just visit in my dormitory and meet my friends. During my college years she was buying toys for AAFES and she once arranged to ship a large box of stuffed animals so I could share them with women on my floor. Stuffed animals were popular in those days, perhaps as an expression of our personalities. Some of us gave names to our stuffed animals and my friends took her into their rooms to show how their animals were displayed.

Gloria always arrived on campus dressed like the professional business-woman she was. Years later Tina McElroy, my freshman-year roommate who became a journalist and novelist, would share her impression and memory of my mother: "Wanda, your mother was the first black woman I ever saw who carried a briefcase."

When my daughter Shelby's birth made Gloria a grandmother, we had a frank conversation about her smoking. I asked her to find a way to stop—not just for her own health, but for the health of her only grandchild.

"I won't bring her to visit if you keep smoking," I told her, mindful of scientific reports about the dangers of secondhand smoke. She adored Shelby and of course, could not tolerate not having her visit. My mother, then in her mid-fifties, went to her doctor for a prescribed nicotine patch that helped her kick the habit she had maintained for at least three decades. The results were quick and successful. But her past smoking habit would eventually catch up to her.

Gloria's last assignment with AAFES was in San Francisco, where she returned to an urban life more similar to the time she spent in New York. She rented an apartment in a round building (the rooms were pie-shaped) on Gough Street on Cathedral Hill. Her apartment faced the tourist-popular St. Mary's Cathedral.

In 1978, when the military and AAFES realized after the end of the war in Vietnam that they did not need a full contingent of resources, she retired with full benefits at age forty-nine. AAFES gave my mother one more fully paid move across the country and she returned to Savannah to live out her retirement years. As it would turn out, they were far too few.

10. The Spelman Years

By the time I entered Spelman College as a freshman in 1967, the transition from Jim Crow to the civil rights movement was far along. Spelman students already had a history of being active in local civil rights activities: sitting in at lunch counters, marching, protesting, picketing with signs, and organizing in SNCC and other groups. Some went to jail for their bold stand for equality.

In my time, activism was felt on campus, too, against school rules and policy. Our 10:30 p.m. weekday/11:30 p.m. weekend curfews were strict. Violation of curfew resulted in punishment of social probation, a verdict meted out by women we called dorm mothers. In Morehouse North, my freshman-year residence, our judge and jury was Sheila, a Nigerian woman who was a graduate student at Atlanta University. She sternly presented the rules in her native accent during freshman orientation, in a conversation intended to scare us enough not to break the rules. In private, my close friends and I mocked Sheila's accented admonitions. She would say, "I d'on lak that sheeet, no!" I didn't come from a cursing environment, so just her use of the s-word was enough to keep me in line, well, except for one time.

As freshmen we were not allowed to ride in cars except with close family members unless our parents placed a letter on file giving a family friend permission to fetch us for dinner or some social event. Our normal mode of transportation was walking or public buses.

One night some high school friends from Savannah drove to Atlanta because our high school basketball team was playing in the state championship. I had the audacity to walk off campus and meet friends who were in a car. No permission from home; I just got in and went to the arena. Our team won the game. But on the way back to campus we had some kind of car breakdown and I missed curfew. I was placed on social probation for two weeks. Social probation meant returning to the dorm after every class to sign a sheet in the office to verify that I was still on campus, no activities off campus, and no taking "company" in the dormitory's lounge. A few days were cut from my social probation due to my good behavior.

WE MOSTLY RESPECTED THE rules, but we saw fit to challenge them. Our families considered our actions radical compared to what they experienced a generation before us.

In the fall of 1968 in my sophomore year, Spelman women, led by the Student Government Association, began a confrontation that led to a peaceful and successful revolution. There was give and take on both sides.

Memory tells me we created a lock-in in Sisters Chapel, the stately building where we attended Thursday vesper services, Sunday worship, glee club concerts, and graduations when the college was still small enough that we could fit the entire Spelman family inside.

During a raucous night of speeches and student leadership, we came up with a list of demands. Our demands changed the college in ways that would affect future generations of Spelman women, yet probably caused postmortem consternation of the spirits of Spelman's founders Miss Packard and Miss Giles, the Christian white ladies from New England who founded the college. Spelman's ancient, staid, largely euro-centric culture was about to change. Our demands included student representation on key campus committees—including on the Board of Trustees—African and afro-centric relevance in courses and exchange programs, internships in the black community, expansion of library resources, and more respect from campus security forces. Some of the demands that were more relevant to underclassmen like me were relaxation of curfews, compulsory dress (we wanted to be able to wear pants to classes), and the strict rules for mandatory Thursday morning vesper services in Sisters Chapel.

At some point a student took to the stage and said something like "It will be a cold day in Hell before the administration will agree to our changes."

When we finally opened the doors to Sisters Chapel, we went outside and saw snow flurries, a rare weather event in Atlanta. Our prayers worked. The administration accepted most of our demands and it was time to get back to classes.

IN TAKING THESE STANDS, no doubt we were inspired by and influenced by the strong women who preceded us.

One was Bernice Johnson Reagon, now popularly known as founder of the soulful music group Sweet Honey in the Rock. As described by Professor Harry G. Lefever in *Undaunted by the Fight: Spelman College and the Civil Rights Movement, 1957–1967,* young Bernice Johnson, then a student at Georgia's Albany State College, was active with other students in the civil rights movement. One evening in 1961 they attended a mass meeting where Dr. King, Ralph David Abernathy, and Wyatt T. Walker were in attendance. Lefever wrote:

> That night, at a mass meeting held at Shiloh Baptist Church, King addressed a packed crowd of nearly one thousand. "Don't stop now," he told them. "Keep moving. Don't get weary."
>
> Three young activists led the singing—Bernice Johnson, Rutha Harris and Cordell Reagon. As the three blended their voices into a harmonious trio they invited the audience to sing along. . . . Bernice began with the traditional song, "Over My Head I see Trouble in the Air."
>
> But as she sang she changed the words, changing "trouble" to "freedom."
> *Over my head I see freedom in the air.*
> *Over my head, oh Lord, I see freedom in the air,*
> *Over my head I see freedom in the air,*
> *There must be a God somewhere.*
>
> Shortly after the mass meeting at Shiloh Baptist Church, Bernice's musical leadership was disrupted. She, along with others, was arrested and imprisoned for participating in a demonstration at the Albany bus station.

She spent two weeks in jail, and then, because of her participation in the demonstrations, Albany State (a public HBCU) expelled her in December 1961. A month later she enrolled at Spelman. Bernice dropped out of Spelman in November 1962 to travel with the Freedom Singers, a group formed during the demonstrations while she was a student at Albany State. She returned to Spelman in 1968 (by then Bernice Johnson Reagon) and graduated in 1970, a year before I graduated.

I have a vivid memory of her talent when, on some Sunday mornings I would leave Spelman's campus and walk up Chestnut Street to Rush Memorial Congregational Church, where Bernice and sometimes the Freedom Singers could be heard before I got to the door. Many years later I reunited with Bernice when we were both living in the Washington, D.C., area and she was leading Sweet Honey in the Rock.

Another well-known activist student was Marian Wright Edelman, president and founder of the Children's Defense Fund and the first woman chair of Spelman's trustee board. Marian joined a sit-in in the "white" section of the Georgia State Legislature. On March 15, 1960, she was with some two hundred students from colleges across the Atlanta University Center (Spelman, Morehouse, Clark, Atlanta, and Morris Brown) who were ready to protest for their rights to "equal protection of the laws." The students sat-in at Atlanta lunch counters in the State Capitol, City Hall, the county courthouse, bus stations and train terminals, cafeterias, and five-and-dime stores, thus helping to break down segregation.

Also in the movement was future novelist Alice Walker, who attended Spelman 1961–1963 and in 1965 graduated from Sarah Lawrence College in New York. Walker demonstrated and was arrested for her protests while she was a student at Spelman.

Years later when I was at *USA Today*, I encountered Walker, by then the author of *The Color Purple*, the 1983 Pulitzer Prize-winning book later adapted into a film and musical. I was in the conference room running a news meeting when I looked up and through the glass wall saw Walker standing at the reception desk having a conversation with Dixie Vereen, who then was the photo director for *USA Weekend*, a sister magazine publication in our company. Dixie had taken a *Weekend* cover photo of Walker some years before that, and when Walker came to visit our building, Dixie brought her to see the huge framed copy of that picture—in which Walker has her legs stretched out on a beautifully painted bench in front of a well-lit bay window—hanging in our suite of offices.

I excused myself from the meeting to meet our guest, to let her know I was a Spelman graduate, and to make sure she knew that Stacy Brown, the young receptionist, was also a Spelman woman, someone I had hired right out of school to give her a start in the business world.

Some time after that, Vereen came to my house for a party and brought with her a smaller framed copy of the same photo of Walker; it still hangs in my home.

Reagon-Johnson, Edelman, Walker—they are just a few of our Spelman notables. Who doesn't know the names of many others, including Keshia Knight Pulliam, who played little "Rudie" on the Cosby Show; Rosalind Brewer, former CEO of Sam's Club and now COO of Starbucks; poet and author Pearl Cleage; actress Esther Rolle, who starred as Florida Evans on *Maude* and *Good Times;* Bernice King, daughter of Dr. Martin Luther King Jr.; Christine Farris King, Dr. King's sister who retired as a longtime professor at Spelman; Dr. Audrey Forbes Manley, U.S. surgeon general and later president of Spelman; LaTanya Richardson Jackson, Hollywood actress and partner in the arts with her husband, Morehouse College graduate Samuel L. Jackson; Aurelia Erskine Brazeal, United States ambassador to the Federated States of Micronesia, Kenya, and Ethiopia; opera singer Mattiwilda Dobbs; Stacey Abrams, who set the political world on fire in 2018 as the first black woman to run for governor in Georgia; Tayari Jones, author of the best-selling novel, *An America Marriage*; J. Veronica Biggins, one of the highest ranking females in the banking industry and who served with distinction on Bill Clinton's transition team in 1992.

Tens of thousands of Spelman alumnae are not as well known as those named above, yet contribute daily as some of the nation's and the world's distinguished doctors, scientists, lawyers, artists, scholars, writers, lawyers, elected officials, teachers, professors, non-profit and corporate executives, public speakers, administrators, ambassadors, and entrepreneurs.

It is humbling to know that many of us came from similar circumstances —little girls who grew up in neighborhoods just like mine, some deep in the South and steeped in traditions of family and faith, and abiding by Spelman's motto, "Our Whole School for Christ."

MY FRESHMAN YEAR MAY have been my best year at Spelman. I quickly connected with a group of young women who lived on the second floor in Morehouse Hall North. One was my assigned roommate, Tina McElroy, an English major like me. Tina grew up in Macon in middle Georgia. Tina describes her parents as business owners who ran juke joints and bars.

Tina and I pretty much took the same classes and got the same assignments for reading, writing research papers and book reports. I was always the planner, getting my reading and research done quickly and writing papers well before deadline. Tina was the socializer, hanging out in dorm rooms with some of the other students. Down the hall there was a big room, a space large enough to house three or four girls. That's where the late-night card games took place, and where on many nights I could find Tina if I was looking for her.

We had wonderful teachers in the English Department. Richard Carroll, the department chair, was a small, quiet, mild-mannered man who taught us the history of the English language. Gloria Gade Wales was a fiery professor who introduced us to feminist and African American voices in literature. June Aldridge put the fear of God in us with her teaching style. She was a serious instructor, teaching us the fundamentals of English and reading, assigning numerous papers to write without ever cracking a smile. We nicknamed her "Stone Face." Later I learned that in her retirement years she admitted that she knew about the nickname, and she laughed about it—finally, we put a smile on the face of our Professor Stone Face.

Tina and I were part of a group we called "The Nine," a less-than-creative term for nine students who formed a close friendship as soon as we arrived on campus. The Nine supported each other, teased and laughed together, and cried over things like fickle boyfriends, tough class assignments, and acne breakouts. There was Deborah Durant, my sophomore year roommate, who came from the Bronx, New York, determined to major in physical education. Caroll Myers from Barnwell, South Carolina, smiled all the time. Dorothy Bailey, also from South Carolina, spoke in her native Gullah accent and had an infectious laugh. Lois Williams, the daughter of a Detroit doctor, was an English major like Tina and me. Marilyn Baugh was from Amityville, New York, and came to Spelman to become more fluent in languages; after freshman year she lived in the "The French House," a small residence hall where she and other students were encouraged to speak only French. Caryl Carter, from the Houston, Texas, area, was also a language student, majoring in Spanish—we called her Chili Red because of the color of her hair, but the moniker also fit her cussin', fiery personality. Petite Brenda Coleman came from Pine Bluff, Arkansas, and I have to say she took much ribbing from our group about—well, let's say the small nature of her legs. When Tina published her first novels she gave minor characters the first names of our friends in "The Nine."

As a nineteen-year-old sophomore in the fall of 1968, I met John Henry Smalls, my biological father for the first time.

"Wanda, you have a visitor in the lounge," someone told me on a Sunday morning when I was relaxing or studying in my dorm room. "He said his name is John Smalls."

I knew the name, of course, but nothing and no one had prepared me for this visit. I would learn that he lived in Philadelphia, and that he was recently in Savannah visiting his mother and inquired about me. Someone passed along word that I was in school in Atlanta.

"Tell him to wait for me," I told the person who announced his presence. I hurriedly got dressed and rushed downstairs. When I descended the open staircase into the lobby I saw a man with a little boy seated next to him. The man stood to greet me.

"Hi, Wanda, I'm your father," he said in a deep voice.

Where the hell have you been, were the words that came into my mind, but I couldn't get those words out. Instead I accepted a weak hug and said something like, "Nice to meet you."

We sat down and he introduced the boy. "This is your brother, Shawn. He lives here in Atlanta with his mother. He's nine years old."

My father explained that he was divorced from his second wife, Shawn's mother. He told me a little about his own family—his sister, Susie, who lived in Philadelphia, and his brother, Tommy Smalls, who ran the club Smalls Paradise in New York City and was a popular DJ known as Dr. Jive. Beyond that I don't remember much about the conversation. I kept looking at Shawn, mostly to see if he had features similar to mine.

I have a brother! was all I could think about. Why did I not know this? Why am I just finding out that I've had a brother for nine years? Nine years!

Shawn appeared to be quiet and shy. He never spoke. Maybe he just found out he had a sister. Maybe he thought I was going to move in with him and his mother and he might lose his room. Maybe he wished he had a brother instead of a sister. Who knows what a nine-year-old thinks when he meets a sister he never knew?

I lost track of time and the conversation rambled—something about my father contacted Aunt Catherine and she gave him permission to stop in and see me, permission that was needed at Spelman with the college's then-strict rules about visitors. I just sat there trying to take it all in.

When it was time for them to leave, my father gave me the name and phone number for Shawn's mother, Catherine Smalls, who, like my grandmother, was a beautician. Like mine, Shawn's parents were divorced. Then our father made out a check for $20 and handed it to me.

"I want you to have this and I promise to send you more money from time to time," he said.

And with that and a quick goodbye, they were gone.

The next day I took the check to the campus cashier's office in Rockefeller Hall. The office had a bank-like system where students and parents could make deposits and withdraw funds when needed. Aunt Catherine mailed $20 to the cashier's office for me every month. In those days that was more than enough for spending money. I endorsed and handed over the $20 check from John Smalls. A few days later I was in Rockefeller Hall and as I walked past the cashier's office, she called out to me.

"Wanda, come here. I need to tell you something." I walked closer to the teller's window where she was sitting. "That check for $20 you brought in the other day," she said quietly, "it bounced. We have to take $5 from your account to cover the fee."

I went from doubling my monthly allowance to losing $5 from my account. I never mentioned this to any member of my family. I never reached out to John Smalls to let him know the check didn't clear. He never sent me more money. I was done with it, and with him.

I never saw him alive again. Ten years later in 1980 when he passed away, Catherine Smalls, Shawn, and I traveled to the funeral in Philadelphia. I went mostly to take one more look at the face I hardly knew, a memory I wanted to keep, and also to meet a few relatives I knew would be there. I met my father's sister, Susie, and her children and grandchildren, and the widow of my father's brother. My father's family was not very welcoming, and I never saw any of them again, either.

SPELMAN HAS A HISTORY of partnerships and exchanges with students from other colleges. Since the late 1950s, Spelman students have been recipients of study-abroad scholarships made possible through the philanthropy of Charles Merrill Jr., son of the co-founder of the Merrill Lynch investment firm. He established the program for scholars at HBCUs, starting with Spelman and Morehouse colleges. Many students in my own generation received these scholarships and were able to study at some of the finest universities in the world.

During my sophomore year, in the fall semester in 1968, seventeen white students came from the College of St. Teresa in the almost all-white community in Winona, Wisconsin. They arrived to study on our campus; likewise, Spelman sent some of our African American students to St. Teresa.

In the February 1969 monthly edition of the *Spelman Spotlight*, at a time when I was a reporter on the student publication, a story titled "Is it Fair?" by Linda Patterson set the scene for the benefits and disappointments of the experimental partnership with St. Teresa.

> What may appear to outsiders as a harmonious situation between the seventeen exchange students . . . and the Spelman women should be looked at more closely.
>
> The little town (Winona) is all white except for one black family, the Rouses, for there was once an unwritten rule that no Negroes could live there. The tension over the exchange program is due to the combination of

the white students' ignorance of blacks and the blacks' new self-awareness [referring to the Black Power and Civil Rights movements of the 1960s across the nation, but especially on HBCU campuses like those in the Atlanta University Center].

Most of these (white) students have had no direct contact with blacks before, and some had never seen them except in books, magazines and on television.

Eventually I learned from a fellow student that the administration didn't prepare the campus community for the arrival of the white students, most of whom were not well accepted by their black roommates. There were no conversations with Spelman's black students before assigning roommates. I can only imagine that the white students felt isolated and rejected, an isolation much like African Americans suffer when we are put in minority situations. When troubles flared, Spelman brought in a mediator, but hostilities still ran high.

There was at least one exception to the hostile integration of Spelman College. That same year we welcomed a white woman into The Nine (but we never renamed the group The Ten). Deborah "Debbi" Leavenworth was a junior transfer student from Keuka College, a Baptist school in Keuka Park, New York. Her minister father had a friendship with Dr. Martin Luther King Jr. and Dr. King's minister father, who was known as Daddy King. James Lynn Leavenworth, director of theological education for the American Baptist Church (ABC), was a Spelman trustee representing ABC at all Baptist or Christian higher education institutions. The Kings—father and son—had been guests in the Leavenworth home in Collegeville, Pennsylvania, and Debbi learned about Spelman through that friendship.

"At the time, Spelman was looking for white students to apply," Debbi told me in an interview while I was writing this book. "My acceptance, I found out later, made Spelman eligible to receive federal funding because I integrated the student population. I wanted to go to Spelman because I was majoring in social studies and I wanted to be in an urban setting. I applied to transfer to several places, but Spelman gave me the best scholarship."

Debbi immediately became friendly with The Nine. She was the first white girl with whom I ever had a serious conversation. I had never gone to a school where there were white students, and the few white professors we had at Spelman were just professors, not friends.

Together with our "Nine" friend Deborah Durant, Debbi rehearsed and performed in the Glee Club. In the dorm, Debbi was comfortable hanging out with us as we told stories about boyfriends, difficult professors and school assignments, and our dreams for the future. Debbi quickly stopped being the "white girl" to us and became just another friend, I suppose just as it should be.

"My life at Spelman was not easy, but I had trusted friends who made me proud to be there," Debbi (now the Reverend Deborah Leavenworth Carter) told me. "And I learned so much about myself and other people. I loved the glee club and I enjoyed playing my flute at Spelman."

As planned, the white exchange students from the College of St. Teresa left Spelman's campus and presumably completed their educations in Wisconsin. As far as we know, in 1970, Deborah Leavenworth became the first white woman to graduate from Spelman College.

IN 1970 I WAS awarded a fellowship to a three-week crash course in copy editing before being assigned to a newsroom internship in Providence. I was assigned by the Dow Jones Newspaper Fund to study in the journalism program at Temple University in Philadelphia, not far from where the Leavenworth family lived in Collegeville. There was about a week between classes ending at Spelman and the Temple program beginning. Debbi and her family invited me spend that gap week with them.

This was my first time staying in the home or even sharing a meal with a white family. I don't remember much about my stay, but this experience broadened my knowledge about people who are of a different race and helped me understand one thing—people are people, no matter their race or where they live. Another benefit to those few days with the Leavenworths is that it prepared me to live on campus at Temple and to coexist in a program with white students.

I returned to Spelman after that summer in Philadelphia and Providence as a professional journalist, ready to assume my student body-elected position as editor of the *Spelman Spotlight*. I led a team of reporters and others, some of whom I stayed in touch with for many years after we graduated, especially those who went into journalism. I had been a reporter for the *Spotlight* before becoming editor, and I was proud of the work we were able to do, the professionalism we brought to the newspaper, in large part because of our professor and mentor, Alan Bussell. I remember the day in my sophomore year that I met Mr. Bussell. I was standing in line in Reid Hall, Spelman's gymnasium, to register for classes. In the era before computers we did everything on paper. The non-air-conditioned gym was hot and sticky, and the lines were long.

As I waited my turn, I overheard comments from nearby that probably changed my life. Two things stood out: the words "journalism" and "Clark College." At that moment I got out of line in Reid Hall and walked across Spelman's campus and through the main gates, onto Chestnut Street, which led to Clark College. All of the colleges in the Atlanta University Center consortium allowed us to take classes but get credit at our own schools.

I walked into the building where Clark's registration was taking place and found Mr. Bussell, the journalism professor. I told him I wanted to be a journalist, and he assured me that I would benefit from his classes, which at the time amounted to only a couple of courses. I signed up for both, and I was thus in the first group of journalism students at Clark College (which later became Clark Atlanta University when it merged with Atlanta University). Slowly, the Clark program expanded from two sections each of news writing and news reporting, to copy editing, then broadcast journalism courses, and more.

I walked back to Spelman and into Reid Hall, where I took my place at the back of the line and resumed waiting to register for my remaining classes.

MY COMMITMENT TO SPELMAN College has never wavered. When Johnnetta Cole was president of Spelman she established the Corporate Women's Roundtable, a group of powerful women who were leaders and executives in some of the nation's most important corporations. The group's mission was to advise Dr. Cole on opening doors for Spelman students through internships, mentoring, campus speakers, and the experience of travel.

Ideally, we were to help make it possible for students to shadow corporate executives and be mentored by them. As senior editor at *USA Today*, I was in a position to help students in these areas.

While a member of the Roundtable, which met a couple of times a year, I was elected by the National Alumnae Association of Spelman College (NAASC) to the alumnae seat on Spelman's Board of Trustees. This was a high honor and I looked forward to serving. I called Dr. Cole and told her that, based on my time considerations, I would be resigning from the Corporate Women's Roundtable. As a *USA Today* editor and mother of a young child, I could not put in the time to serve in both groups. I served two terms as an alumna trustee. When my second and final trustee term was about to end, Dr. Cole called me at home the evening before I was to fly to Atlanta to attend my final board meeting.

"Sister Wanda, we cannot allow you to leave this board. We need you to stay." At the time I was chairing one of the board's key committees, a role I quite enjoyed. Dr. Cole informed me that there was a category called honorary trustee that would allow me to attend all board meetings and continue to lead and serve on committees, but not be elected to a board officer position, which was fine with me.

"At some point there will be an election and it is my hope that you will be elected back to the board as a full trustee," Dr. Cole said. She and the board, then under the leadership of Dr. June Gary Hopps (Spelman class of 1960), were true to their word. I was elected again to the Spelman board and in total I served nineteen years as a trustee. I chaired board committees of student affairs, community service, and board affairs. I served with some incredible board members, many of whom I mentioned earlier in the chapter as well-known Spelman alumnae, and also with people like venture capitalist Terry Jones; the late Donald Hollowell, Atlanta civil rights attorney; Donna Shalala, chancellor of the University of Wisconsin-Madison before she became Secretary of Health and Human Services in the Clinton Administration; former Atlanta Mayor Shirley Franklin; Dr. Hopps, former dean of the Graduate School of Social Work at Boston College, and Ronda Stryker, a director of the Stryker Corporation, a Fortune 500 medical technologies firm.

And then there were the graduation speakers and community service honorees I was able to meet and spend time with. I met Ruby Dee, who asked Shelby to take her young grandson outside to play on campus because he was bored being cooped up in the president's campus house with grownups, and Hank Aaron, who took a picture with Shelby. "Stand here and take a picture," I told her, and after the picture was taken, she asked me, "Who was that old man I took a picture with?"

"That was Hank Aaron, a baseball great," I told her. "Ask your father about him when we get home."

I met Bill Cosby, whose son Ennis, a graduate of Morehouse College, was killed in Los Angeles in a robbery attempt. Many of our Board of Trustees meetings were held in a room named for Ennis Cosby. I spent time with Bill Cosby when he was graduation speaker at Spelman, and then one day when I was working at *USA Today* in Washington, President Cole called me to ask if I could join her with Cosby for lunch at a restaurant in the Watergate Hotel. Cosby and his wife, Camille, donated $20 million to Spelman (returned years later after Cosby was convicted in a sexual abuse scandal).

In 1992 I took my mother to Spelman's graduation because writer Maya Angelou was the speaker. Gloria and I had read all five of Angelou's memoirs up to that point—from *I Know Why the Caged Bird Sings* to *All God's Children Need Traveling Shoes*. After the graduation ceremony, the two women, who were about the same age, sat on a sofa in the Spelman president's house slapping thighs and telling stories like they were friends who had not seen each other in a long time.

"Baby, go get me a glass of water," Angelou told me, turning to my mother in laughter. "Young legs," indicating, I guess, that she needed help from someone at least twenty years her junior. The two women sat there for hours like school-girl friends, calling each other Gloria and Maya, sharing stories about things that mattered to them as generational black woman peers—places they had traveled, books they had read, jazz music from the 1940s, living in New York City, slang phrases from their Southern upbringing, and things like that. Their meeting predated cell phones with cameras, otherwise I would have been taking candid shots and posting them on social media.

Spelman was known for bringing notable artists to campus as speakers and performers. One of my favorite memories as a student at Spelman was the week I spent with poet Nikki Giovanni, who hung out and led discussions with small groups of students, sometimes sitting around in residence hall lounges in the evening, reading poetry and talking about writing. This was in my last semester before graduation, and I was one of few residential students who had a car. I was asked to escort Giovanni back and forth from the historic black-owned Pascal's Motor Hotel.

Giovanni was a young poet, five years older than my senior-year classmates and me. In English classes we had studied the art of free verse, poetry that does not have the limitation of regular meter or rhythm. I had written some of this free verse and one of my poems was published in an anthology of poetry while I was a student at Spelman.

I hung on to every word as Giovanni read her poems and asked us to interpret her writing. After graduation, I began to collect Giovanni's books. She recorded poems with the New York Community Choir and released the album *Truth Is on Its Way* in 1971. On the album, her poems were arranged with the choir's gospel vocals and organ and piano accompaniment. I purchased the vinyl album, which I still own, then the cassette tape, and then the CD. I have rolled along with Giovanni and that album through all of the technology changes, listening to *Truth Is on Its Way* on long neighborhood walks and on the treadmill, and in times when I needed inspiration—in the car, at home, and at work.

I was a professor at Savannah State in 2016 when the university invited Giovanni to speak on campus. The ballroom in the student center was standing room only as we listened intently to Giovanni, then about seventy years old, talk to an audience that included students of the millennial generation who probably had never even heard of Nikki Giovanni until their professors told them to attend the event. Giovanni shared her story in her normal raw language, with humor, passion, and profanity. Lots of profanity. She read some of her poems—even some from *Truth Is on Its Way*. I know most of those poems by heart, and I was mouthing the words as she spoke.

After almost ninety minutes of speaking, when Giovanni was wrapping up her talk, I slipped out of my seat and quietly, slowly walked along the back of the ballroom to position myself near a table that was set for her to sign copies of her books. I hadn't brought any books from my collection. Instead, in a tote bag I carried the album cover for *Truth Is on Its Way*. I was first in line, and when she was comfortably seated and ready to sign I pulled out the well-worn album cover and handed it to her.

She looked up at me and said "Oh, my goodness, you've had this one a *long* time."

"Yes, I have," I replied, aware of the line forming behind me, and not taking the time to remind her of our Spelman College experience more than forty-five years earlier.

WHEN MY MOTHER PASSED away in 1997 she left three houses for me to sell, two with no encumbrance of mortgage. As I handled her affairs I knew I wanted to help Spelman with part of the estate. I inquired about establishing a scholarship to honor the women in my family who were Spelman alumnae before me. Even though Spelman does not have a journalism studies program, I wanted to ease the way for interested students to pursue careers in communications.

The endowed scholarship, with matching funds from Gannett, the newspaper company I worked for, was set up to support students who have a demonstrated interest in journalism. I have no say in which students get the scholarship, but once a year, along with the financial accounting from Spelman's Office of Institutional Advancement, I receive a letter from a student thanking me for the support she received from my donations.

One letter came in 2014 from Dawnn Anderson, an English major from New York. When she wrote the letter, Dawnn had already completed an internship at the *New York Times*, was associate news editor for a campus publication, and had interviewed President Ellen Johnson Sirleaf of Liberia.

Dawnn wrote: "Through the guidance and mentorship of faculty, professionals, even friends at Spelman College I am encouraged to soar to new heights. As a recipient of the . . . scholarship, I am humbled that you believe in me enough to invest in my future. Following graduation from Spelman, I hope to attend Columbia University's School of Journalism and begin my career as a journalist. Thank you for allowing me to make my dreams a reality."

English major Laura Eley from Richmond, Virginia, wrote in 2017: "Every year my mother and I scramble to find funds to help me continue my Spelman matriculation and thanks to . . . you, a small burden has been lifted. I dream of becoming a media professional fighting to redirect the black narrative."

A few times as I have walked the convention center floors at the annual conference of the National Association of Black Journalists, young women looked at my name badge and realized I was the benefactor of one of their scholarships.

"You are Wanda Lloyd?" one asked excitedly. Before I knew what was happening arms enfolded me and I heard sweetly whispering in my ear: "Thank you, I got your scholarship at Spelman. I didn't think I'd ever get to meet you."

JUST WHEN I THOUGHT I had given all I could to Spelman, and Spelman had given me everything and more than I deserved, in 2016 I was called to Spelman again.

Lloyd and I were relaxing on the mezzanine level of the Mayo Clinic in Rochester, Minnesota, a magical facility to which we were referred to treat his medical condition that doctors in Georgia and South Carolina were unable to handle to our satisfaction. While we were waiting between appointments, I pulled out my silenced cell phone and noticed several calls from Area Code 404. Someone from Atlanta was trying to reach me. I listened to the messages and returned the calls.

"Wanda, I wanted to let you know that the Board of Trustees has voted to give you an honorary degree."

I almost dropped the phone, surprised, humbled, proud as heck.

"President Campbell will present the award at Founders Day in April. Please call me back and confirm that you can attend."

Spelman awards honorary degrees twice a year, in April during the Founders Day convocation and at graduation in May. I had voted in so many Board of Trustees meetings to award honorary degrees to people in government, the arts, science, philanthropy, sports, and humanitarian endeavors to such recipients as Cicely Tyson, Maxine Waters, Jacob Lawrence,

Camille Hanks Cosby, Nelson Mandela, Oprah Winfrey, Danny Glover, and Andrew Young.

Honorary degrees to alumnae of the college are a special honor because of the recognition that we have not only excelled in our chosen fields, but because we have kept our linkages to Spelman and given back to the college. Only two other members of my own class of 1971 had been so honored: author and playwright Pearl Cleage and author Tina McElroy Ansa, my friend and freshman year roommate. With my honorary degree, we would have the largest number of Spelman honorary degrees of any Spelman class. In 2016, Spelman's honorary degrees would go to Stevland Morris (Stevie Wonder), U.S. Attorney General Loretta Lynch, and Wanda Lloyd. This time, the trustees had voted to honor me.

On April 5, 2016, Tina (who was awarded her honorary degree in 2011) and I set out on a road trip to Atlanta. In four hours in the car we reminisced about our time at Spelman and all that has been blessed in our lives in the years since we graduated.

My heart smiles when I think about the three generations of women in my family whose lives were impacted by Spelman College, and how Spelman gave me the opportunity to meet people from whom I have drawn knowledge, perspective and wisdom. How friendships were born, some of which are still growing today. How I gained leadership skills by editing a college newspaper, working on the yearbook, and being a resident assistant in a freshman residence hall; becoming fluent in language arts, appreciating the ability to sing in the glee club with classically trained musicians, speaking publicly, growing in spirit and faith through services in Sisters Chapel, helping to set policy as a member the Board of Trustees and most importantly, the opportunity to expand the gifts God gave me—the gifts of reading, editing and writing.

From the Spelman Hymn: "Spelman, thy name we praise!"

11. Pathway to Providence

"Wanda, Wanda, wake up. You have a telegram."

Aunt Catherine interrupted a nap I was taking one afternoon in December 1969 while I was at home during Christmas break. A Western Union messenger had rung the doorbell and delivered something that needed my attention.

"A telegram?" I said questioningly, lifting my head from the pillow. I had never received a telegram and I had no idea why someone would send one to me. What I did know was that telegrams delivered only two kinds of information: Very important *good* news or very important *bad* news—job offers, pleas to send money, births, deaths, international distress signals, wars. In our family, birthday greetings were often sent in telegrams, but I was born in July and this was December.

My telegram read:

> Congratulations. You have been selected winner of a $700 Newspaper Fund editing intern scholarship. This award will be made on the completion of the 1970 summer work-study program described to you previously. You have been assigned to the editing course at Temple University in Philadelphia. Letter to follow. Merry Christmas. Sincerely, Thomas Engleman, Executive Director, The Newspaper Fund

I soon learned that my internship assignment would be the *Providence Evening Bulletin* in Rhode Island, a place I had heard about but never imagined I would live in. We studied state capitals in grade school when we researched and wrote reports on natural resources for every state. I knew Providence was far away, but it might have been in another world as far as I was concerned.

I had applied for this internship under the tutelage of Alan Bussell, our dedicated journalism instructor at Clark College. Clark (now Clark Atlanta University) is across the street from Spelman; both schools were and are a part of the Atlanta University System (AUC). An AUC agreement allowed students at the member colleges to take classes on any of the other campuses and get academic credit at their school. Bussell started the journalism program and initially was the only instructor. He suggested that students seek internships, and he told us about the Dow Jones Newspaper Fund. As a college student I had not put it together that this was the same Dow Jones organization that had sponsored the summer program for minority high school teachers and a few high school students at Savannah State three years earlier.

"There are two kinds of Dow Jones internships," Bussell told us. "One is for reporters and one is for copy editors.

"Copy editors, what's a copy editor?" someone in the class asked. It turned out that Bussell had been a copy editor himself, at a newspaper in Memphis before he moved to Atlanta to teach. He was a young, white single guy with a passion for journalism and for working with students who demonstrated interest in the subject. I was one of those interested students. I had been a student reporter in high school and was one now in college, so I knew what a reporter's job entailed—developing story ideas, asking questions in interviews, doing research, and writing stories. But copy editing would be a challenge. I chose the challenge and applied for the copy editing internship.

To qualify for the reporting internship, students submitted their resumes and clips (copies of stories they had already published). But to apply for the copy editing internship we had to prepare for an intense copy editing test. Bussell coached me through the test prep and, based on the good news in the telegram, I apparently did well.

THE THREE WEEKS AT Temple were arduous but I learned a lot about how to "work" copy by making sure the writing was easy to read; grammar, spelling, and punctuation were correct; and all facts, dates, and statistics were correct. In the book *Copy!: The First 50 Years of the Dow Jones Newspaper Fund*, author Rick Kenney reminded me that the program included rigorous instruction in editing basics, headline writing, libel, newspaper organization, typography, and page design:

> There was a daily critique of the *New York Times* and the *Philadelphia Inquirer*, each of which was delivered to the class. Interns were challenged to "play editor," to consider news play and ethics, the pressures on the press, and trends in the newspapers. The group considered what newspapers might be like in ten or twenty years, when, if journalism took hold in their lives, they might be among the managers in newsrooms.

Professor Edward Trayes led the program at Temple, and he was tough on us. He was one of those teachers who felt a personal responsibility to send into newsrooms students who could be competitive with veteran copy editors. We had weekly tests at Temple. We mastered the *Associated Press Stylebook*, which we were told would be the Bible of news reporting, writing, and editing. We studied geography, math, and grammar. We spent a lot of time learning to write headlines that "sing," as Professor Bussell used to urge us. Good headlines tell a story in a few words; headlines that sing also often use a twist of words that make the reader want to jump right into the story.

As the program at Temple was ending, Professor Trayes met one-on-one with participants. In my meeting he said he felt I was prepared to do the work in Providence, but he wanted me to know that I might be the only black person in the newsroom.

"I hope you are prepared for that," he said.

I don't recall how I responded. I know I was scared to death but determined to be brave and to do what needed to be done to succeed in the internship. After the weeks of training at Temple, my passion for copy editing had grown exponentially, and I could not wait to get to work on a real copy desk in a real newsroom alongside experienced editors.

The Newspaper Fund has remained in my life. When I was later in a position to hire interns, I reached out to the Newspaper Fund's executive directors to let them know I wanted interns in our newsroom. When the Fund expanded their board of directors to include alumni of their programs, I was put into service as a director from 1992 to 1999. And when I later chaired the Department of Journalism and Mass Communications at Savannah State University, one of my first acts was to establish a summer program for high school students. We successfully wrote a grant for the Newspaper Fund to support the program in 2014, forty-nine years after I participated in a similar program at Savannah State. My efforts were coming full circle, paying it forward for the next generation.

THE PROVIDENCE NEWSPAPERS—THE MORNING *Journal* and the afternoon *Bulletin*—had several interns in 1970, and by letter they introduced me to two other young women, both white, so we might consider living together to share expenses. I had never lived with white people before. The burden of my childhood-ingrained fear of white people was by then tolerable and fading, and I was beginning to appreciate the opportunity to learn about people who were different. The other two interns were from New England. One, I recall, was a student at Bates College in Maine. They were reporters, working day shifts at the morning paper. I was assigned to the afternoon paper. Our schedules were different and as roommates we hardly saw each other.

Internships didn't pay much, but together we were able to afford living in a five-bedroom, five bathroom house in an upscale neighborhood not far from the newspaper office downtown. The house was owned by a stockbroker and his family who spent summers on nearby Martha's Vineyard. The house was big enough for each of us to have a private bedroom and bathroom. We left the massive master bedroom vacant except when we had visitors that summer; my mother stayed in it when she visited me one weekend.

We split expenses, including for utilities, which we were responsible for in addition to sending a monthly rent check to the family, and we were expected to keep the grass cut and watered. But since we didn't see each other most days, things were pretty lonely in that big house where we were mostly home alone.

So one day we went to an animal shelter and adopted an adorable puppy, whom we named Pax for the Roman goddess of peace. It was 1970, after all, the year John Lennon's "Give Peace a Chance" was popular.

One afternoon I was walking Pax and came upon a woman who said her name was Gloria, same as my mother. Gloria was walking her little Shih Tzu, a long-haired Chinese breed with a bow on its head to keep hair out of the eyes. Like the dogs in my family when I was growing up, our Pax was a lovable mutt of questionable heritage. Gloria's Shih Tzu was obviously an expensive pampered pet with the pedigree papers to show for her cuteness and purity of bloodline.

Gloria and I stood a moment talking about our dogs.

Then she said, "It's too bad you have to walk the dog *and* take care of the children."

That's when I realized that Gloria assumed I was the nanny or maid for the family that lived in the house in her neighborhood. When I explained that I was a college student holding down a professional internship at the daily newspaper downtown, I could see she was embarrassed. She apologized and we became friends over the summer as we met on afternoon walks with the dogs. I never told my roommates about my first encounter with our neighbor and her fancy dog. But I couldn't wait to recount my story in my next letter home to the family: "I met a Shih Tzu and I was mistaken as the nanny—at the same time."

Here I had come all this way from not only the waning era of Jim Crow, but far away from the South where discrimination was a part of everyday life. A woman I had just met immediately jumped to the conclusion that because I was black I must have been the servant for a white family. I was in New England which, to me, might have been a foreign country. It was a place where I rarely saw people who looked like me, mostly because I didn't have a car that summer and didn't venture far from the presumably all-white neighborhood where we were living or where I worked downtown.

I remember writing my grandmother that summer, telling her about my experiences in Rhode Island.

"I saw a black person today," I wrote in one letter. "I looked in the mirror."

Another incident that summer was an unfortunate reminder of how far we had not come. Because I was working for the afternoon *Bulletin*, usually getting to work by 6 a.m., I left the house by about 5:15 a.m. and walked down the street to the corner bus stop. At the end of the block I would cross the street and wait for the city bus going in the direction of downtown Providence. The first day, a white police officer drove by on the other side of the street. He went to the next block, and I watched him slowly double back in my direction. He pulled up to the curb, leaned over the passenger seat, and rolled down the window.

"Good morning. May I help you?" he asked.

"No, I'm fine, just waiting for the bus to go to work," I said.

"You're on the wrong side of the street."

The neighborhood was on a hill and I could see that, in the direction on the side of the street where I was standing, downtown was a few miles down the hill.

"Isn't this the side to go downtown?" I asked. "That's where I work."

"Downtown? Where do you work?"

I explained to him that I was a summer intern at the Providence newspaper and I would be waiting for the bus there every day for the summer.

"Oh," he said. "I thought you work in the neighborhood," he replied.

I realized the officer also thought I was a household servant working for one of the families nearby. He thought I was waiting to go *into* that upscale neighborhood, not *out* of the neighborhood.

We said a few pleasantries, and he continued on his morning patrol. For the rest of the summer, that officer waved or said good morning every day when I was waiting on the corner.

AT THE END OF the summer internship, Joe Ungaro, the managing editor of the *Evening Bulletin*, called me into his office for a chat. He thanked me for working there.

"You've learned a lot this summer," he said. "The editors on the copy desk tell me you are a good fit for our newsroom. You've contributed a lot here."

"Thank you, Joe," I said, "I enjoyed it."

"Would you like to come back when you graduate? We'd like to have you work here full time."

Wow, that caught me by surprise. I had spent the better part of the summer soaking up everything I could from my co-workers on the copy desk, but I was hesitant about making lasting personal connections because I was sure I would never see this group of people again. I also considered the fact that Providence was a long way from my family in Savannah and that the winters in Providence would not be nearly as comfortable as being somewhere in the South, like Atlanta.

"Thank you," I replied. "I appreciate the offer but I think I will stay in the South after I graduate, closer to home. I really like Atlanta and I'm hoping I can work at the newspaper there."

"Okay, but keep in touch with us," Joe said. "We would be happy to have you back in our newsroom."

I returned to Atlanta for my senior year, confident in my new skills, but certain, too, that I would never return to Rhode Island.

AT SPELMAN THAT FALL of 1970, I had great stories to tell about what I had learned in Providence. I excelled in the rest of the classes I took with Professor Bussell, in a program that had expanded to include a few courses in broadcasting. I took every journalism course offered. Even though I was majoring in English, I crowded in a few extra electives so I could get a full academic experience in journalism. I was editor of the *Spelman Spotlight*, and working in Providence over the summer made me a professional journalist in my senior year in college. Because my parents had forbidden it, I had not gone to the University of Georgia, where journalism was offered as a major. But I was determined to take advantage of every opportunity available to me in the Atlanta University Center.

In our senior year many of my friends in Bussell's classes were trying to figure out what they would be doing after graduation, and I needed to figure that out, too. The Newspaper Fund internship had given me some great skills, not to mention a summer salary and scholarship funding.

Another scholarship came from Cox, the Atlanta-based company that owned the *Atlanta Journal* and the *Atlanta Constitution*. I was a recipient of the Ralph McGill Fellowship, a stipend for college students who are from the South and who, the fellowship program believed, would stay in the South and work in journalism. The fellowship was in honor of Ralph Emerson McGill, the long-time anti-segregationist editor and publisher of the *Atlanta Constitution*. McGill, who won a Pulitzer Prize for editiorial writing in 1959, grew up in eastern Tennessee. After high school he attended Vanderbilt University in Nashville, but he did not graduate because he was suspended his senior year for criticizing the school's administration in an article in the student newspaper. He served in the Marine Corps during World War I. Martin Luther King Jr. mentioned McGill in his 1963 "Letter from Birmingham Jail" as one of the "few enlightened white persons" to sympathize with the civil rights movement.

Like with the Dow Jones Newspaper Fund, I was the first black student to be named a McGill fellow. And while I didn't get to meet the namesake, who died in 1969 while I was a student at Spelman, I had grown up reading the Sunday *Atlanta Journal-Constitution*. My goal was to work for McGill's newspaper as a copy editor.

I made an appointment with William "Bill" Fields, an editor who served in various roles at the Atlanta newspapers. It was Fields who reached out to let me know I was a recipient of the McGill Fellowship in my junior year at Spelman. Like many young people, I was not focused on who he was at the time, but I remembered he was a nice gentleman who seemed to want me to do well. I think I met him on campus when he came to speak to one of our journalism classes.

By the time I was ready to meet Fields in his office on Marietta Street in downtown Atlanta, he was vice president and executive editor of the morning and evening Atlanta newspapers. I was ready to show him my updated resume and have a conversation about my successful internship experience at Temple University and at the *Providence Evening Bulletin*.

"Come in, sit down," Fields said, graciously motioning me to a chair. "What's on your mind?"

I handed over my resume and I told him as quickly as I could about all the good opportunities I had in journalism. I told him I was editor of the *Spelman Spotlight*, and I shared my summer accomplishments. I told him I was from Savannah, but I had no desire to return home to work for the local newspapers there.

"I want to stay in Atlanta," I said, "and work for the *Constitution* or the *Journal.*"

Mr. Fields listened intently as he studied my resume.

"Well, we invested in your education with the fellowship and we would be happy to have you working here as a reporter."

Did he just say "reporter?"

"Thank you," I said, "but I am a copy editor. I want to work as a copy editor, not as a reporter."

During my internship in Providence I had come to love copy editing. I had been a reporter for student publications, but what really gave me pleasure was to get my hands on stories and make them better, to work with reporters, photographers, and other editors, and to lay out pages that would be appealing to readers. Besides, I was shy at that time in my life and not comfortable going out and talking to strangers, which a reporter has to do. No, I was a copy editor and no one was going to talk me out of being one. Also, during my internship I was told by one of my colleagues that copy editors make slightly more money than reporters, and copy editors get to management faster. I was a copy editor.

Fields went on to tell me how important it was for the Atlanta newspapers to hire "Negroes" as reporters. We were still living in the period of the civil rights movement and black people in Atlanta were demanding that the newspapers hire journalists who could help improve the accuracy of reporting and writing about what was going on in the community. The reality was that newspapers were struggling to find what they called at the time "qualified Negroes" to work in the nation's daily newspaper newsrooms.

The Kerner Commission had as recently as 1968 pointed the finger at the nation's mainstream media as a reason for much of the violent unrest that had erupted in America's cities in "the long hot summer" of 1967. Atlanta was one of the cities that had seen racial violence. It was a city struggling to safely integrate schools, transportation, and lunch counters, and to offer fair housing and job opportunities to black people.

"Why can't I work on the copy desk?" I asked Fields.

"Look, you can come to work here tomorrow, if you want—as a reporter.

But if we put you on the copy desk, working inside the building, no one (black readers, presumably) will know you are here."

I thanked him for the conversation and the offer. I returned to campus and placed a long-distance call on the pay phone in my dorm to Joe Ungaro, the managing editor in Providence.

"Joe, if the offer is still open, I'd like to come back to work on the copy desk as soon as I graduate."

WHILE I WAS IN Providence for the internship I didn't have a car, but I had purchased a used Dodge Challenger during the Christmas holiday break my senior year. Not many students who lived on campus at Spelman had cars in 1970, and many of us relied on some of our male friends at Morehouse College across the street to get us around Atlanta if we needed to leave the campus.

"I'm editor of the student newspaper and I need a car to take the page layouts downtown to the printer," I had told my family. My grandmother wasn't buying that.

"You have scholarships," she said. "What if they see your car and take away your scholarships?"

Thankfully Aunt Catherine understood the reality of my scholarships. I was about to begin the final semester of my senior year. I had maintained a merit-based academic scholarship all four years. I worked on campus as a resident assistant, and I earned a stipend for being editor of the student newspaper; the combination took care of my room and board. My stipends from the Newspaper Fund and the McGill Fellowship rounded out my financial package to more than cover books and fees. My college education was completely paid by the time I brought up the subject of getting a car; I was entering my final semester, college was about to end, and I had no student loan debt. That was enough to allay my grandmother's fears.

Now I needed to pay for the car. My family had opened a passbook savings account for me when I was a child and they insisted that I put aside small amounts of money from my weekly allowance. When someone in the family was going to Carver State, the black-owned bank where I had the account, I grabbed my passbook and went with them to make deposits.

When I received cash presents for birthdays or Christmas, or for high school graduation, I put the gift money in my savings account. My mother was investing in savings bonds, which we stored in a safety deposit box at the bank. Ostensibly, the money in my savings account was to be used for college, but since I had enough scholarships and stipends to cover tuition and fees, I emptied the savings account and paid cash for a previously owned beige Dodge Challenger, which I named Angel.

The day after my graduation, Gloria and I loaded up my car and began driving to Providence. She would help me find an apartment and then fly back to Dallas, where she was living at the time. After we checked into a hotel in Providence, our first stop was a visit at the newspaper office. I took my mother into the newsroom to meet my coworkers. We mentioned that we were looking for an apartment and some of my colleagues gave us leads on places to look. We grabbed a copy of the newspaper and started going through the classified ads looking for apartments.

My mother called some of the listed numbers, asking if they still had vacancies. A few said yes so we picked up a map and started driving to the locations. That's when reality hit us. We were out of the South but not away from discrimination. When we knocked on doors sometimes we would see a peep out of curtains but got no answer at the door. Sometimes doors were opened slightly ajar and we were told that the apartment we called about less than an hour ago was no longer available. After many years living in New Jersey and New York City before her job transferred her to Dallas, my mother's voice over the phone did not sound like she was black. And if it did, I'm not sure many people in Providence would have known what a typical black voice sounds like. We had doors shut in our faces—literally and figuratively. Welcome to Rhode Island.

In the 1960s, Rhode Island, the smallest state, was known as the watch production capital of the United States, with many jewelry manufacturers located there. Also, Samsonite, the luggage maker, had its manufacturing headquarters in the state. Watches and luggage were two of the categories my mother was responsible for buying for the Army and Air Force Exchange Service (AAFES) , so she had been to Providence a few times before.

She had become close friends with one of her vendors and his wife, a white couple who lived on a rocky beach in Bristol, Rhode Island. They invited us to dinner at their house while my mother and I were looking for a place for me to rent. Before the end of the evening, they did two generous things. They told us about University Heights, a large garden apartment complex known to be racially accepting because of the large student population at nearby Brown University. And they invited me to stay in their house in Bristol until I found a place to live.

University Heights was perfect for me and not far from the newspaper office downtown. The day after our dinner in Bristol, my mother and I were escorted to a model apartment, and before long I was placing a deposit and making arrangements to move in when the next one-bedroom unit was ready to be leased.

My RETURN TO PROVIDENCE was an easy transition. It took me years to realize how fortunate I was to land my first full-time professional job in a place that was familiar, with people who already supported me and wanted to help me grow professionally. In the Providence newsroom in 1971, I recall there was only one other female, a white woman reporter. Her name has faded from my memory, but I remember that she covered religion—one of the soft news topics. When the top editors and those who ran sections of the newspaper would go into the conference room and make decisions about which stories were most important for page one, no women were ever at the table to help make decisions about the content and play.

Besides the religion reporter and me, the only other women worked at the dictation desk, an area of the newsroom where a group of fast typists worked on manual typewriters with telephone receivers with attached shoulder rests to reduce neck strain on long calls while they were transcribing information. Reporters and people from the community called the dictation desk and the women would type the content just as it was called in, and then send it over to an editor, who would read the stories and distribute them to the copy desk based on the topic—local news, features, business, sports, obituaries, etc.

Even the pool of what we then called "copy boys" had no women in the mix. Copy boys were young, mostly under twenty-one. They were there to "rip" copy off the wire machines, run stories from one news desk to another, and, frankly, a couple of times a day they would walk through the newsroom to take orders and our money for coffee and snacks from the nearby mom-and-pop restaurant. Living in Rhode Island was the first time I heard the term "regular coffee," which means coffee with cream and sugar. It was New England-speak.

Having women working in the newsroom in Providence must have been an afterthought because the women's bathroom on our floor was retrofitted from a closet in the morgue (library, or archive). I remembered that on the first day of my internship the year before I had been handed a key to the ladies' room. The room was tiny, and because of where it was situated we kept the door locked for privacy when someone was in there.

One of the transcriptionists used her key and came in one day as I was standing at the sink washing my hands. She struck up a conversation, explaining that the ladies at the dictation desk were discussing the oddity of the young black female copy editor; I was something they had never imagined for the newspaper's staff. Almost every newsroom in the nation was staffed just like Providence, mostly white and male. The women's movement had not yet fully come to newsrooms.

I replied that I was an intern, a college student taking journalism classes, that I had studied journalism since I was in high school, was editor of my high school newspaper, had worked on my college newspaper, and would be the editor of the *Spelman Spotlight* at the end of the summer.

"An organization (the Dow Jones Newspaper Fund) chose me for this internship. They sent me to Temple University in Philadelphia for a crash course for three weeks this summer, and they assigned me here to work for the rest of the summer."

"Oh, you are in college," was her response.

During our quick conversation I learned that neither she nor any of the ladies on the dictation desk had gone to college. They had not fathomed that a person who is black and female would have the opportunity to get a college education, much less work in the newsroom. She actually told me that. That may have been the first time I realized what a unique opportunity I had to enter journalism and newsrooms at the beginning of the 1970s.

I later learned that most of the journalists in the Providence newsroom had not gone to college. In the generations before mine, most reporters started their careers as copy boys and then apprentice reporters. They were smart people, but the business did not require a college degree at the time (don't try that today). In the years before I got there, experience was the key to getting a newsroom job and moving up in the industry. But that opportunity and trajectory didn't work for women and black people. More was expected of us.

My car, Angel, was just fine for the mild winters in Georgia, but I soon learned that I needed snow tires for New England winters. However, even snow tires couldn't help me get to work one morning. I left my apartment in darkness. As soon as I took a few steps I slid down a short hill. There had been an ice storm overnight. I had no experience with ice on sidewalks, grass, or roads. This took me by surprise.

I managed to get back up on my feet and took careful steps down the rest of the hill, walking on the crunchy grass, avoiding the slick sidewalk to the parking lot. Boom. I fell again. I was going to have to get some boots with traction.

When I got to my car Angel was completely covered in a sheet of clear ice. If I could have lifted the ice in one piece, I would have had a perfect mold of my car. I couldn't get the door key into the lock. I had no idea what to do. I somehow made it back up the hill to my apartment and I called the newsroom. I asked for my supervisor, a man we lovingly called Meddie.

Norman Medrech was the chief of copy editors for the newspaper's state editions. Despite his sometimes-gruff manner, Meddie was a man of wisdom and experience.

"Hi, Meddie, this is Wanda. My car is iced over. I can't even open the door. I won't be able to come to work today."

Meddie was silent. I don't even remember if he said "goodbye." I went back to bed.

A few minutes later the phone rang. It was Meddie.

"Wanda, look outside your window. There is a taxi waiting in your parking lot. Get in it!"

That was my first big lesson in the importance of working out solutions to problems. Never use weather as an excuse for not going to work.
Be prepared, learn to cope, have a backup plan. That lesson would follow
me the rest of my career, through snowstorms in Washington, D.C., where
I learned to always have a shovel, some sand or kitty litter, and a suitcase
with a change of clothes in the trunk of my car from October through
March; to Tennessee where I learned that ice would sometimes delay but
hardly ever cancel classes in the program I led at Vanderbilt University,
because the sun usually melts ice quickly enough to move ahead as planned
by about 10 a.m.; to Alabama, where during Hurricane Ivan in 2004 we
set up cots and sleeping bags and slept on the floor and under desks in the
newsroom for days and nights until streets were cleared and power was
restored. Newspapers are like hospitals, law enforcement operations, and
university housing. They never close. My lesson was that the work must go
on. Unless the government declares an emergency evacuation, weather is
no excuse to stay home.

When I walked into the Providence newsroom that icy day, I swear I
heard people sniggering, my coworkers probably thinking "there is that
stupid girl from the South. She can't even handle an ice storm."

PROVIDENCE IS A PLACE with a colorful culture. When I was there in the
early 1970s, the population of Italian and Portuguese immigrants and
their families was large. Several descendants of immigrants worked in the
newsroom, and many immigrant surnames regularly appeared in stories
we edited, so my first challenge was to learn how to pronounce names that
were unfamiliar to me. This was particularly important because copy editors
had to be sure names were spelled correctly. I learned to love Portuguese
sweetbread, which sometimes coworkers would bring into the newsroom
or I would find at a bakery. I would never have had that cultural experience
if I had not lived in Providence.

I also met the mafia.

Shortly after I returned to Providence with only the clothes packed
in my car and a shipped trunk from Spelman, my grandmother passed
away. When I went home to Savannah for the funeral, Aunt Catherine

told me to go into my grandmother's house and pick out any furniture I needed for my new apartment. At the time I was sleeping on a loaned single mattress on the floor, and I had used money left over from buying the car to purchase a sofa. That's all I had. I picked out my grandmother's bedroom set, some small tables and lamps and a few other odd pieces to furnish my new place.

Aunt Catherine sent me a check to pay for the furniture shipment, and the moving company assured me of twenty-four hour advance notice before delivery. One Saturday morning while I was at work I received a call on the copy desk's phone line.

"Ma'am, we're in Providence with your furniture," the truck driver said, telling me the amount of money he needed—in cash.

"I don't have the cash. Today is Saturday. The bank is closed but I can write you a check."

"I can only take cash. I have to keep moving so I'll just go on up the highway with your stuff and call you in a few days when we come back through Providence."

A colleague on the copy desk overheard my dilemma. "I can get you the money. Ask him what time to meet you at home."

Puzzled, I told the driver to meet me at the apartment.

When I hung up the phone, my colleague, a fellow copy editor, led me into the composing room area where Linotype operators were typesetting the stories and compositors were placing rows of lead type into forms for printing the pages for the Sunday editions.

My copy desk colleague said to a man I didn't know: "She needs cash to get her furniture delivered. She'll pay you back Monday when the bank opens." He told him how much I needed; about $600, as I recall.

The printer reached into his pocket, and I swear he pulled out a thick wad of hundred-dollar bills secured with a rubber band. He peeled off the bills one at a time, placing them gently into my hand. He asked me no questions, and after rewrapping the bills with the rubber band, he put the rest of his wad back in his pocket. Then he turned back to his work.

I didn't have time to be stunned by such an amazing gesture. I thanked him and ran out the door to go home. Over the weekend someone who knew better told me I may have just met the mafia, someone positioned to loan money and in some cases charge high interest payments.

Nevertheless, on Monday, I left the newsroom at exactly the time for the bank to open. I withdrew the money I needed to repay my new friend in the composing room. No interest was mentioned, none paid.

I SPENT THE FIRST part of my time in Providence working on the national and international copy desk, editing copy, writing headlines, and identifying photos to go with some stories. It was a continuation of my summer internship and I quickly got really good at what I was doing. One day an editor asked me to fill in on the state desk because of a staff shortage. I loved working on the state desk. There is a difference between editing copy that comes over on the wire services, like all national and international stories did in Providence, and editing copy written by the newspaper's local reporters. On the state desk, the stories were written by reporters assigned to various bureaus throughout the state. I loved digging into raw copy and also following a story from one day to the next. Working on the state desk put me in a position to work closely with the bureau chiefs in places like Bristol, the beach area where I had stayed a few days when I arrived, and Newport, a Navy community, or in places with names like Cranston, Warwick, Scituate, Pawtucket, Central Falls, and Woonsocket. We also edited stories from nearby communities in Massachusetts, places like Nantucket and Worchester. These names were a totally different language for someone who spent most of her life in the South. Working on the state desk was a great orientation for an editor to learn how to adapt, learn about different communities, understand local idiosyncrasies and the range of local cultures. I soon earned a permanent slot on the state desk.

A FEW WEEKS AFTER my return to Providence, I was seated at the copy desk when I had a visit from a woman named Dorothy from the personnel department. Dorothy had processed me into the job, making sure I had signed the requisite papers to get my weekly pay and health insurance. Dorothy wanted to know how I was doing.

"Have you made any friends in Providence?" she asked.

What Dorothy really wanted to know was whether I had met any *black* people. Even though I had worked in Providence the summer before, since I didn't have a car as an intern it was a certainty that I didn't get around to explore the city. I had heard that black people lived in South Providence. But with no friends and no personal transportation, the summer passed without a visit to the black community. That was about to change.

"No, not yet," I told Dorothy.

"There is someone I want you to meet, a woman who works downstairs in the advertising department. Do you have time to go down there with me?"

Dorothy introduced me to Bonnie Culbreth, a black woman a few years older than me. Bonnie had a warm smile and I could tell she totally understood her role in this introduction. She would take me under her wing and help me meet black people in Providence. Bonnie and I exchanged phone numbers, and I went back to the newsroom.

The next Friday afternoon I was in my apartment, resting after my 6 a.m. to 3 p.m. workday when the phone rang.

"Wanda, this is Bonnie. We met at the newspaper this week."

"Oh, hi, Bonnie. What's going on?"

"Listen, there is a free concert tonight in Roger Williams Park over here near my house. Curtis Mayfield is performing. Do you know who he is?"

"Oh, sure, I have one of his albums. I like Curtis Mayfield."

"Great," Bonnie said. "Why don't I give you my address and you can drive over here, leave your car at my house and ride with us. My friend, Ann, is also going."

I quickly got dressed for my first night out in Providence—ever. We would be outside so I wore a pair of slim-fitting, light-blue tie-dyed jeans, a T-shirt of some sort, and sneakers—a popular outfit in the '70s. I had just turned twenty-two. I was young and full of curiosity. And now I had a new friend.

We drove in Bonnie's car to the park. The concert was a loosely organized crowd, all black as I recall, mostly young adults and a few young families. Mayfield had just dropped his album *Super Fly*, with songs like "Pusherman" and "Freddie's Dead" among my favorites.

When the concert ended and we were walking back to Bonnie's car she asked if I was in a hurry. She needed to make a stop before going back to her house. I had nowhere to go—except to be at work at 6 the next morning.

"Ann and I have boyfriends in the Navy, stationed at Davisville (Rhode Island). They come up to Providence on the bus on Friday nights and we just need to pick them up at this place."

"Sure, I'm okay with that," I replied.

In a few minutes we pulled up to a bar, a small wooden building with people standing outside. I wasn't sure what was going on inside but it seemed like the party was outside.

"The Hurry Back" was the name on the sign. I peered at the collection of black people. Bonnie pointed out her boyfriend as we were parking and Ann pointed out hers.

"Oh, who is that tall good-looking guy with your boyfriend?" I asked Bonnie.

"That's Lloyd," Bonnie said, referring to his last name I would later learn, nomenclature very common with military people. I'm not sure she even knew his first name.

"You want to meet him?"

Of course I wanted to meet him.

Bonnie introduced me to Willie Lloyd, who invited me inside to have a drink. We sat at the bar for a long time, making small talk and getting to know each other. Lloyd was six feet, five inches tall, very slender, with medium brown skin color. He had the prettiest brown eyes, which he said he inherited from his mother. He chain-smoked cigarettes, a common habit in the 1970s, and he drank "Seven & Seven," a drink containing Seagram's 7 Crown and 7 Up cola. I wasn't much of a drinker—not because I had anything against drinking, I just had not acquired the habit—and didn't know what to order.

Lloyd offered to order for me—a Brandy Alexander.

The bartender brought me a sweet, milky concoction, a brandy-based cocktail consisting of cognac, crème de cacao, and cream, with nutmeg sprinkled on top. I took a sip. I liked it. I had at least one more that night.

When Lloyd opened his wallet to pay for the drinks, I saw a picture of a baby. He was honest and open about it. He told me he was married—separated—and his estranged wife and baby were living in Chicago with family.

We sat for a while, talking, drinking and listening to music. People were constantly feeding the jukebox and "Me and Mrs. Jones" by Billy Paul played over and over and over.

After a while we moved the party to Bonnie's house, including Ann and her boyfriend. At some point in the early morning hours I said I needed to get some sleep because I had to work at 6 a.m.

Lloyd walked me outside. Before I could see it happening, he was seating himself on the passenger side of my car, where we continued to talk, kissed, and talked some more. I kept saying I had to get some sleep and who knows, I may have nodded off a time or two in the car.

At some point he dropped some news on me. The bus that returned sailors to the base left at midnight. He had nowhere to go. I was too tired to be agitated. I turned the key in the ignition and took him home with me.

12. A Summer in the City

One afternoon in May 1972, a year after I graduated from Spelman, the phone rang in my apartment. The male voice on the phone introduced himself as Jack White, a reporter for *Time*. He went on to explain that he was calling on behalf of Robert C. "Bob" Maynard, who was about to direct the Summer Program for Minority Journalists at Columbia University.

"They need a copy editor on the faculty this summer and, as best as we can determine, there are only two black copy editors working at daily newspapers in the entire country," he said.

I was one of them. The other, a man, was apparently working in Atlanta, had a family, and had no desire to leave Atlanta and spend the summer in New York.

"Are you interested? Do you want to know more about the summer program?" Jack asked.

"Sure, I'm interested but I have no idea if I can go to New York for three months. I'll have to check with my editors."

White said he would have Maynard call and tell me more about the program. We hung up and I began to process that someone had tracked me down and wanted me to work in New York. I didn't even know if that was possible—to take a leave and then come back to a job. I didn't have much time to think about it. The phone was ringing again. Bob Maynard was calling.

The next day in the Providence newsroom I told Managing Editor Joe Ungaro about my conversation with Maynard, who, I had learned, was a national correspondent at the *Washington Post*.

"What do you think I should do," I asked Ungaro. "They want me to fly to California this weekend to meet with Bob Maynard."

"Go," Ungaro said. "It sounds like a wonderful opportunity to train more minorities for journalism. Plus, you will learn a lot." He assured me that my job would be there for me at the end of the summer.

THE SUMMER PROGRAM WAS the brainchild of Fred W. Friendly, the former CBS news executive who along with Edward R. Murrow was credited with perfecting the genre of the television news documentary. Friendly was a member of the Columbia University journalism faculty when he approached Maynard about starting a program that would train minority post-graduate students in a non-degree program to get them ready for professional newsroom positions. The summer program had two components—broadcasting and newspaper journalism—and Friendly was executive director for both. Geraldo Rivera, who went on to become a famous television reporter and talk show host, got his initial TV training in the program.

Our 1972 team of faculty members for the newspaper component was Charlayne Hunter-Gault, one of the two black students who integrated the University of Georgia; *New York Times* reporter Earl Caldwell, who had embedded with and documented the Black Panthers and became embroiled in a key U.S. Supreme Court decision clarifying reporters' rights; Howard Ziff, a gruff city editor-type journalism professor at the University of Massachusetts-Amherst; Maynard, who later received a Nieman Fellowship at Harvard University and then joined the editorial board of the *Washington Post;* and me. Maynard later became the first African American publisher of a metro daily newspaper, the *Oakland Tribune,* and in 1983 he purchased that newspaper from Gannett, making him the first African American to hold a majority share in a mainstream daily newspaper.

At age twenty-two and one year out of college, I was the youngest person in the program, younger even than the students. I may have been too young or too naive to be intimidated. I may also have been too naive to be impressed by the greatness around me at the time. Today I am awestruck by the opportunity I had to work in this program with its star-studded faculty.

My job at Columbia was to edit the weekly laboratory newspaper that we named *Deadline*. Each week we went about building a story budget for the eight-page tabloid newspaper with stories by our student participants who covered live news in New York City and on the Columbia campus. We worked with hot-shot New York newspaper designer Peter Palazzo, who came up with the *Deadline* design concept. And every week it was my job to copy edit the stories, write the headlines and picture captions, lay out the pages, and by Thursday night hop in a taxi and take the copy to a printer in Manhattan where I gave instructions for my page designs. The newspapers were delivered to our newsroom at Columbia before I would arrive Friday morning. This was real-time journalism production for a weekly newspaper.

During the summer I also created lectures of basic editing, mostly to help our students present copy that was better prepared for publication, and to help them understand what happened to their stories in the editing phase. On Fridays the program's faculty, staff, and students gathered in Maynard's apartment to listen to speakers in a seminar setting. The speakers were politicians, journalists from some of New York's biggest media organizations, and community activists.

While living in New York that summer, I took full advantage of the arts. I went to galleries, concerts, and dance performances. I bonded with Sandra Dillard from Denver, one of the students in our program. Sandra and I shared a love for the theater and just about every weekend we attended a show on Broadway. That was the year of shows like *Pippin, Don't Bother Me, I Can't Cope, Purlie,* and *Man of La Mancha.*

Joe Ungaro, my managing editor in Providence, was right. When I returned to Providence at the end of the summer, my body of knowledge about editing and writing had increased exponentially. Having worked in New York City around some amazing journalists, I was a better editor and more aware of my place in journalism. I was also firmly dedicated to improving the lot of minority journalists and helping to make America's newspapers more accurately reflect the communities they served. And I was beginning to come out of my shell of quietness. I had no way of knowing it, but years later I would be called upon to launch and lead a similar program to increase newsroom diversity.

The summer program in New York was just the beginning of my visits to the Columbia campus. Over my career I returned to Columbia four times as a juror for the Pulitzer Prize, and in 2006 I received an award for lifetime achievement in Columbia's "Let's Do it Better" workshops on journalism, race, and ethnicity, led by journalist and professor Arlene Morgan.

Aunt Catherine had not been to New York since 1964, when we attended the New York World's Fair. "Come visit me this summer," I wrote her right after I was settled in New York. At first she said she could not travel that far away from Daddy, who was by then in a nursing home in Savannah. I continued to call and write, entreating her to take a break. Finally she said yes, and we set a date for her to travel in early August.

I bought and sent her a plane ticket. She would sleep in the bedroom of one of my three Columbia suitemates, a graduate student who would be traveling during Aunt Catherine's visit.

I bought tickets for a Patti LaBelle and the Bluebells concert at Lincoln Center. We would go to Queens one day to visit Uncle James and Aunt Lillian, who lived in Woodside, and on the weekend we would drive up to Providence so I could show her my apartment and the newsroom where I worked.

I was giddy with excitement the day Aunt Catherine arrived. She came with the stress of worrying about her husband, but she said she was ready for a short vacation and the plans I had made. Aunt Catherine loved music. She was a trained pianist and had been a member of the Spelman College Glee Club. She had played piano for Sunday School in our church in Savannah, and she directed the chorus at West Savannah School, where she taught for many years.

I had been to Lincoln Center several times, but always for more highbrow entertainment—classical music or performances of the Alvin Ailey Dance Company. The Bluebells concert would be different. LaBelle, along with Sarah Dash and Nona Hendryx, put on a show that left an indelible memory for Aunt Catherine and me. Aunt Catherine went into Lincoln Center awed by the New York venue and the people who were there, yet probably wondering "Patti who?" But she came out raving about the experience (except for the decibel level of some of the music), and we gleefully sang "Somewhere Over the Rainbow" Patti-style on the taxi ride back to Columbia's campus.

It was a happy shared moment, something we talked about for the rest of her life. But when we returned to the residence hall that night, our world sank. One of my suitemates said we had gotten a couple of phone calls from a James Walker. That was Aunt Catherine's brother.

"He said to call him right away."

"Hi, Uncle James. You called us?"

"Yes, I'm afraid I have some bad news. Put Cat on the phone."

"Hey, James," she said and she started to tell her brother what a great time we had at Lincoln Center. She only got a few words out when her voice dropped, her face saddened.

"When? What time."

DADDY HAD PASSED AWAY. Aunt Catherine had left Uncle James's number with the nursing home in case they needed to reach her. Instead of completing our planned vacation week, including the drive to New England, we flew back to Savannah to bury my Daddy, who compassionately waited for his wife to be with family before taking his last breath.

Left: My grandmother, Oper Lee Watson Walker, loved to shop downtown on bustling Broughton Street. Jim Crow laws sometimes denied her full enjoyment of the experience.
Below: My mother, Gloria Walker, as a teenager in Savannah.

Top: dressed in a milkmaid costume on the steps of my grandmother's house, likely on the way to a kindergarten program. Bottom: I wore this red-dotted Swiss dress for my sixth birthday party at my grandmother's in 1955.

Left: Aunt Catherine, right, and I flew to New York to join my mother for the 1964 World's Fair. Below: With my grandmother before church on Mother's Day; she never felt well-dressed without gloves. Bottom: With friends Clintina Hallman, center, and Brenda

Coleman, right, dressed up for a Sunday service at Spelman College; I'm holding white gloves, clearly influenced by my grandmother.

Right: With members of the Eta Kappa chapter of Delta Sigma Theta, the sorority I proudly pledged in 1969; I'm fifth from the right, wearing a sweater with white cuffs.

Above: Having fun with fellow Spelman Glee Club members Deborah Durant, left, and Debbi Leavenworth; Debbi may have been the first white student to graduate from Spelman.

Above: The copy desk in the newsroom of the Providence Evening Bulletin, *my first professional newspaper. I am surrounded by some of my copy editing tools—manual typewriter; gum eraser; copy on glued-together pages; open glue pot; over my left shoulder, the pneumatic tubes that swooshed copy to the composing room; and the wire machines through which national and international stories arrived. Photo by J. David Lamontagne,* Providence Journal. *Below: The* Atlanta Journal *newsroom sent me off with a party, including cake and gifts. The kind gesture was unexpected, because I had only worked at the newspaper for six months.*

Above: With my baby, Shelby, when she was a few months old.
Below: With Shelby on Easter Sunday in Alexandria, Virginia.

Above: Willie and me at a conference in the early 1990s. Below: With Shelby and my mother, relaxing in downtown Savannah in 1991.

Right: A photo that was in the 1993 Gannett annual report with a story about my efforts to diversify the nation's newsrooms. Below: The cover of the report; I was a senior editor at USA Today at the time.

While on the board of directors of the American Society of Newspaper Editors, I met President George H. W. Bush, top, and President Bill Clinton, bottom.

Novelist Tina McElroy Ansa and I have been close since we were freshman roommates. In 1998, we were both on the cover of the Spelman alumnae magazine.

Top: As executive editor of the **Montgomery Advertiser.** *Left and below: With Shelby and Willie at the send-off party when I retired from Gannett and the* **Advertiser** *in 2013; Shelby surprised us by flying to Montgomery for the affair.*

Above: In a now sadly ironic 1988 photo, Spelman College then-President Johnnetta B. Cole and I had a moment of laughter with entertainer Bill Cosby in Washington, D.C., when he donated $20 million to my alma mater; the money has since been returned. Below: My friend Tina McElroy Ansa and my daughter Shelby attended when Spelman awarded my honorary Doctor of Humane Letters degree in 2016. It was fitting that the ceremony was held in Sisters Chapel, the venue of Tina's and my 1971 graduation with bachelor's degrees in English.

13. A Newsroom 'Family' in Miami

One afternoon in the spring of 1973 I answered the phone in my apartment in Providence. The call was from Larry Jinks, who said he was an editor with the Knight company group of newspapers. Knight owned newspapers in Florida, Pennsylvania, North Carolina, Kentucky, Illinois, and Georgia. Jinks said he was recruiting to fill Knight newsroom positions and he was especially looking for experienced copy editors. He didn't say they were specifically looking for black copy editors, but I knew that was part of the reason he found me.

"Your name came to our attention," Jinks said. "Would you be interested in talking about what you are doing and whether you might be interested in making a move?"

One thing I have learned over the years is that you never know where or when the next opportunity is coming. You may meet someone or work with someone who drops your name in a conversation. Sometimes people are just quietly watching you, and they admire your spirit, not to mention the quality of your work. Most importantly, early in a career the best thing to do is to stay in touch with professors from college by checking in on social media, or picking up the phone every now and then and let them know what and how you are doing. A lot of professional recruitment happens through alumni networking.

I don't know how editors at Knight heard about me in Rhode Island. At that time I had few contacts in the business, and I had not put out the word that I was looking for a career move. I was just two years out of college and still learning a lot in Providence.

Jinks and I talked about my specific work experience in Providence, my internship crash course at Temple University, and the work I did on the faculty at Columbia. He told me what the Knight papers were looking for, and before long he invited me to travel to one of their newsrooms for a copy desk tryout. We just needed to settle on which newspaper I would visit.

"Well, I've been in Providence for two years," I said. "I am cold. What newspapers do you have in a warm climate?"

"That would be the *Miami Herald*," Jinks said.

"Okay, that's where I want to try out."

A FEW DAYS AFTER the interview and copy desk tryout, I accepted an offer to move to Miami. I drove Angel to Miami in early June. I purposely chose to move to the South again, but Angel didn't have air conditioning and the Miami heat was unbearable. So after getting settled into an apartment, my first order of business was to trade up to a car with air conditioning. When I drove onto a Dodge car lot, the sales people got a good laugh at my Rhode Island-purchased snow tires. I drove away in a brand new orange and white Dodge Charger. It was an ugly car, but it was new and air-conditioned and I had gotten a decent trade-in.

My first assignment at the *Herald* was to work on the national/international copy desk. Like most copy desks, we were located in the middle of the vast newsroom, surrounded by the city desk, where stories were assigned to reporters, and the state desk, the area that covered south Florida communities outside Miami.

On my first day working, someone on the city desk held up a telephone receiver and asked out loud "Is there a Wanda Smalls working here?"

I looked up from the story I was working on. "I'm Wanda Smalls."

"You have a phone call over here. What's your extension?"

I called out my phone number and the call was quickly transferred.

"This is Elsie Carper at the *Washington Post*. I'm looking for the Wanda Smalls who used to work in Providence. Is that you?"

In 1973, the universe of black journalists working in mainstream media was small. Some of the larger white newspapers were just starting to think about looking for black newsroom staffers. The pool of trained black journalists would mostly come from the black press or the small number of black colleges that were starting journalism departments. In those days, the more informed recruiters knew to reach out to professors at schools like Howard University, Clark College, Florida A&M University, and a handful of others that had the foresight to know that newsrooms needed black journalists who had classroom instruction and experience with internships and campus media.

After the urban unrest during the civil rights movement, which a small number of black media—mostly weekly papers—covered in major cities, some black journalists were persuaded by white newspapers to jump over from the black press, where salaries were small. The lure probably went beyond money. Some were convinced that they could have a greater impact working for the bigger daily newspapers with more resources and more readers. But the pool was small, not nearly large enough to fill the growing needs of mainstream media organizations. As a Spelman English major, I had been lucky to take journalism classes at Clark College, even though I could not declare a journalism major. When I graduated, I had a job offer at a mainstream newspaper. In fact, at Clark, I don't remember any black newspapers coming to recruit us.

In Washington, the legendary Elsie Carper was a long-time administrative editor and newsroom recruiter. She worked the small minority network of newsroom professionals and had called me a few times when I was in Providence, asking if I would consider coming to Washington for a one-week tryout for the *Post's* copy desk. Good recruiters keep track of their top candidates, and they call from time to time to catch up with potential hires and let them know there is still an interest in bringing them in to interview. Carper was a good recruiter.

"I thought you were going to let me know when you were ready to make a change and leave Providence. I just heard you're in Miami now. What happened?"

I explained that things had moved quickly, that I had not been looking for a change, but that Knight called and asked me to come down for a tryout. She was quiet; I got the feeling that Carper was not someone who took rejection well.

The truth is that I had no desire to move to Washington at that time. I was a young, single black woman, and there were commonly known statistics of four single black women to every single black man in Washington. At some point I was hoping to find myself in a relationship that would lead to marriage and a family. Washington, D.C., was not in my plan.

I had briefly dated Willie Lloyd in Providence, and we playfully talked about marriage during our brief relationship. But he was still technically not available. Plus, after a couple of tours in Vietnam, the Navy deployed him overseas again a few weeks after we met, and we were out of touch for years.

IN THE 1970S FEW African Americans pursued copy editing as a career. Most black journalists were passionate about reporting and writing, and they had designs on telling stories that made a difference in black communities. Plus, I would learn that not many black journalists in those early days integrating mainstream newsrooms even knew about the opportunity to start their careers through the editing route. From my Atlanta experience when I was denied the opportunity to start as a copy editor, I knew that white editors preferred blacks for reporting, not as copy editors. Yet because there were few of us in numbers, my editing experience ultimately put me in a place of high demand. In fact, I don't know any African American copy editors who are older than I am. If I wasn't the first, I may have been the second or the third African American daily newspaper copy editor.

Copy editing has never been a glamor spot in newsrooms. The copy desk, an essential part of the news production chain, was usually a place where former reporters were assigned because either they wanted a more consistent schedule, they wanted to get on the track for newsroom management, they had good institutional knowledge of the community, or they had screwed up somewhere along the way and were forced to come in from the reporting ranks.

Through the mid 1970s, I only knew of a handful of people who enjoyed working on copy desks instead of reporting. That's why some copy desks were known to be a place of eccentric frustrated former reporters, yet with a lot of experience. I got used to receiving potential job offers from newspapers. I wasn't arrogant, but I knew I could choose the newspaper and city where

I wanted to work because they needed my black face in their newsroom.

For example, in 1972, when I was working in the Summer Program for Minority Journalists at Columbia University in New York City, *New York Times* recruiter Peter Millones spent a lot of time in our student newsroom, perhaps supporting the participants being sponsored by the *Times*. He tried in several conversations to persuade me to meet with *Times* editors. He even took me to lunch at Sardi's, a restaurant known for the hundreds of celebrity caricatures on its walls. It is common to see movie stars sitting at the next table in Sardi's, and I'm sure Peter took me there hoping to impress me. He did. But New York was one of those places that I've never wanted to live or work. That summer of 1972 was enough New York City for me.

I was not aware when I interviewed in Miami that the Knight company had a big push on hiring black journalists. But in the *Miami Herald* newsroom, I found a family. For the first time in my career I was in a place where I saw a number of people who looked like me. The black reporters were Louisiana native Eleanor Rushing, a sweet, soft-spoken recent graduate of Grambling State University (an HBCU); Dorothy Gaiter, who grew up in Tallahassee and met her husband, reporter John Brecher, working in the *Herald's* newsroom; Gayle Pollard, a Washington, D.C., native who had just completed the master's journalism program at Columbia University; Shelia Payton of Milwaukee, who earned a bachelor's in journalism at Syracuse University; Joe Oglesby, who came to the *Herald* with a degree in English from Florida A&M University (also an HBCU); and St. Louis native Thomas Morgan III, who came to the *Herald* with a degree in journalism from the University of Missouri and a stint in the U.S. Air Force that included being a White House aide in the Nixon and Ford administrations .(Tom later became president of the National Association of Black Journalists.)

The most important benefit of our black *Miami Herald* family was being loved and mentored by faith-driven, big-hearted Beatrice Hines, or "Mama Bea," as we called her. Bea had moved to Miami as a young child with her mother, a domestic worker, when her parents separated. Bea first worked as a file clerk in the newspaper's library, and she enrolled at Miami Dade Community College where she studied journalism. In 1970 she was promoted to general assignment reporter, becoming the *Herald's* first

African American woman reporter. Bea became a long-time columnist for the newspaper until she retired. However, she never truly left the *Herald* because now in her eighties, she is still writing columns on a freelance basis.

Bea came a long way professionally, but what she did for others is what I most cherish about her. She has always been a praying woman, and she kept all of us black journalists in her prayers. She was an outstanding seamstress, a skill that supplemented her income as she raised two young sons, Ricky and Shawn, after her husband died. Bea not only made clothes, but she became a milliner, making extraordinary hats for church ladies. Sewing was my hobby, and I had plenty of time to sew while I was living in Miami. Bea and I shared tips about where to shop for fabrics and how to alter pattern designs to build our unique wardrobes. After my night shift in the newsroom, I would often stay up into the early morning hours working on sewing projects. I would sometimes bring my in-progress garments into the newsroom to complete the handwork during my dinner break. I always enjoyed showing off my creations to Bea.

After leaving Providence, where I was culturally lonely in the newsroom, it was comforting to have African American colleagues in Miami. We quickly became a family, because except for Bea all of us were far away from our own families. In Miami we celebrated each other's birthdays, Thanksgivings, and other holidays. Bea was the only one in our group who lived in a house, so she hosted many of our celebrations.

As journalists we relied on each other. We had to. The newspaper did the right thing in bringing a large group of African Americans into the newsroom around the same time. There is a lot to be said for critical mass in a workplace to help people who have common cultural backgrounds feel comfortable. But another step was probably needed. The black reporters sometimes felt that they were not respected for their professional skills, and there was no support to help white editors understand why black reporters were not always successful—or happy.

Several times some of my fellow black women journalists called me on my copy desk phone line and asked to meet in the newsroom's ladies restroom, which had a lounge area with a sofa. Two or three of us would gather there and let the reporter vent, and often cry, before we gave her some encouragement and suggestions for how to handle a situation, and then we all went back to work, hopefully bolstered by our common support.

To be clear, Miami was the best of times and the worst of times. Best, because we had each other, and worst because the newspaper skipped a step—they didn't give editors the training and support needed to adequately supervise reporters who came from different cultures instead of belittling every little thing black reporters tried to do. I'm sure this is not unique to journalism and newsrooms and probably happens in workplaces everywhere. What good is it to hire people who are different and then hold them to a standard that doesn't fit with them culturally or emotionally?

To be sure, the *Herald* hired a powerhouse group of black journalists, which we proved as we *left* the newspaper. Almost all of us went on to work at bigger newspapers like the *New York Times,* the *Washington Post,* the *Los Angeles Times,* and the *Wall Street Journal.* Among us were future Nieman Fellows at Harvard University, the founder of a nonprofit to provide scholarships for students at HBCUs, authors, editorial page writers, and newsroom executives. Based on the accomplished people *Herald* editors hired, they did a great job sprinkling the staff with people of color who had outstanding potential, even though most of us eventually left with the best part of our journalism careers ahead of us. Oglesby left the *Herald* but ultimately returned as editorial page editor. Across the nation newspapers have struggled for decades to recruit and retain people of color. Many years and numerous training models have gone into trying to overcome this deficiency. The situation has improved somewhat, but mainstream newsrooms have still never fully reflected the readers they serve.

FOR MOST OF MY career I made some good decisions, and I reaped many good rewards. But one day in Miami, I woke up and had the darndest idea. And I acted on it.

I was starting to miss Atlanta, where I had gone to college. I was a long way from Aunt Catherine, who in 1974 was alone in Savannah. My grandmother passed away a few months after I graduated from Spelman, and Daddy the following year. We also lost "Auntie," my grandmother's sister, and her husband in north Georgia, and a couple of elderly cousins.

Aunt Catherine had retired from teaching, and all I remember her doing was settling family estates. I wanted to get back to Georgia, and I had this idea that I should take one more shot at working as a copy editor in Atlanta.

So one Saturday morning in the fall of 1974, a little more than a year after I arrived in Miami, I dressed in professional clothes and gathered a few copies of my resume, which was always updated—just in case. I stuck the resumes in a portfolio and drove to the airport in Miami, where I purchased a one-way ticket to Atlanta. In those days air travel was relatively cheap. I had no luggage, just my handbag and the portfolio that held examples of some of the pages I had designed, clips of stories I edited with headlines I had written, and my resume copies.

In Atlanta I took a taxi downtown to the office of the Cox-owned daily newspapers, the morning *Constitution* and afternoon *Journal*.

"Good morning, my name is Wanda Smalls and I'd like to see the managing editor of the *Atlanta Journal*," I told the man working at the security desk.

Here's where stupid took over. I had no idea if the managing editor was working that day, but I had gotten on a plane and traveled all the way from Miami to see someone whose name I didn't even know. I didn't even think to stop and buy a newspaper at the airport so I could read it and at least *look* for the name of the editor I was going to try to meet. I'd had one conversation about working at the Atlanta newspapers a few years earlier, when then-Executive Editor Bill Fields told me they would not hire me as a copy editor because they needed to put black reporters on the streets so people would know the paper was complying with community demands for newsroom integration. I was a copy editor; I didn't want to be a reporter.

So here I was, trying again. I missed Atlanta, having been away for three years after I graduated from Spelman. I missed being able to drive onto the campus and attend glee club concerts and theatrical productions. I missed the hustle and bustle of downtown Atlanta with large department stores like Rich's and Davison's. I missed walking along West Hunter Street and "Sweet" Auburn Avenue, where I was likely to see any number of civil rights icons walking among the common folks. Some of my Spelman friends had settled in Atlanta, and I wanted the opportunity to hang out with them. I wanted to go "home" to Georgia.

The gentleman at the security desk picked up the phone.

"There is a Miss Wanda Smalls here to see you," he told the person on the other end of the phone. "Yes. She said she is from the *Miami Herald*."

"Okay, I'll send her up."

So far so good.

I asked the gentleman who was sending me up the name of the managing editor.

"Mac—uh, Durwood McAllister, ma'am."

McAllister was walking across the room to meet me when I got off the elevator. I scanned the newsroom and recognized the familiar signs of Saturday duty by a contingent of journalists who were busy, but not harried, all of them white and mostly male. Typical staff, I figured. My ears caught the usual clackety-clack of the teletype machines as wire stories came across, and the occasional yell of "copy" by editors demanding that copy boys rush over and hand-deliver copies of stories from one editor to another. I caught the scent of glue used by copy editors who were pasting stories together in the editing process. This all felt so familiar.

I followed McAllister into his office, pulled out a copy of my resume, and handed it to him as I shared a bit of my background. I was talking fast and in my most professional voice. I didn't know how much time I had with him and I had a lot to say.

The conversation was pleasant enough but it didn't last long, maybe not even thirty minutes. He made it clear that he didn't have any copy desk openings at the time, but at least he didn't say he would *never* hire me as a copy editor.

Then, when he was ready to end our visit, McAllister got up and made motions that we should head toward his office door. As he was shaking my hand and backing me out of his office, he said something like, "I'll call you if we have an opening."

And then it was over.

I went down the elevator and out onto the street. I hailed a taxi and went back to the Atlanta airport and bought another one-way ticket. When I arrived home in Miami that Saturday afternoon I did some laundry.

14. A Bad Fit in Atlanta

Unlike the afternoon newspaper in Providence, working for a morning paper like the *Miami Herald* meant working nights, because the deadlines were about twelve hours different. In Miami, my copy desk shift started about 2 or 2:30 p.m., and I usually worked Tuesday through Saturday nights. Anyone who understands how newspapers operate would know to call a friend who works for a morning newspaper in the morning and call an afternoon newspaper person in the evening, but before 9 p.m. when it was time to get to sleep.

That's what happened late one morning in November 1974, a few weeks after my impulsive Saturday trip to Atlanta to ask for a job at the afternoon *Atlanta Journal*. The phone rang. Durwood McAllister, the managing editor, was calling me.

"Wanda, you came in here a few weeks ago asking for a copy desk job. Do you still want to work here? We have an opening."

And that's how I got to live in Atlanta again, finally working for the *Atlanta Journal*, a newspaper I had read many years in Savannah as the Sunday *Journal-Constitution*. And I didn't have to pretend to want to be a reporter. I was going there as a copy editor—the job I wanted.

McAllister told me the weekly salary and said, "We can give you $400 to help you move. Is that okay? Can you start working in three weeks?"

I took the $400 moving help, a reasonable amount in those days for a single person living in a small apartment, and I turned in my letter of resignation at the *Miami Herald* that afternoon. I called Tina McElroy, my friend and former Spelman roommate, to share the good news. Tina, who grew up in Macon, Georgia, had stayed in Atlanta after we graduated, and she was working at the morning *Constitution*. I told her I would be moving quickly and looking for a place to live. Tina was sharing an apartment with her sister, Faye, also a Spelman graduate, and they let me sleep on their couch for a few nights. I talked to their apartment manager and in a few days I moved into a unit in the building next door to the McElroy sisters.

DESPITE MY HIGH EXPECTATIONS about returning to Atlanta, I was ill-prepared for the disappointment I soon felt, and I learned a great lesson about taking shortcuts when making important decisions, especially decisions about my career. As much effort as I put into getting the job, and as excited as I was to return to Atlanta, the *Journal* was a bad career move. McAllister didn't require me to do a tryout on the copy desk, which should have been a big clue that things might not be what I expected. I had not asked the right questions. Actually, I hadn't asked any questions.

By then I had worked at two daily newspapers where the quality of work was high, alongside reporters and editors who were supportive and instructive. If I edited a story that left out important details, or submitted a headline that didn't say exactly what the story was about, the story came back to me with direction for a do-over. At both newspapers I was expected to grow as an editor, to improve my understanding about how to make a story better for readers. We were not there just to correct spelling and grammar, but to dissect reporters' writing and make sure the language flowed well, to be sure we filled "holes" in stories—missing facts or figures that might make readers scratch their heads because of the incompleteness of the information. We were expected to write headlines and photo captions that were engaging, accurate, and fit the allotted space.

In Providence and in Miami, we were given time to work on stories to the best of our language skills, news judgment, and creative layout abilities. I learned early that every story needed three reads. The first was to see what the story was about, while fixing glaring spelling or grammar problems. The second read was to get deeper into the story and work on its flow and accuracy. The third read was to put myself in the mind of the reader. And think: Is the story perfect yet? Can the language be improved for better understanding? Are there holes—questions—to be filled?

In Providence and Miami I had worked my way onto the state copy desks, assignments where I had the opportunity not just to edit stories but also to lay out pages, to talk to section editors about their vision for photos and graphics, and to reach out to reporters when I had questions about their stories.

In Atlanta I was assigned to what was called the universal copy desk, where we worked with stories from all sections of the newspaper. We had to read stories quickly and slap quickly written headlines atop them. Another group of editors across the newsroom selected photographs, and another group designed the pages.

In my other newsrooms, there was a copy desk for local news, one for sports, one for business, one for wire stories (national and international news) and one for features. The advantage to having specific copy desks is that editors build expertise in their topic areas. For example, a features desk that dealt with fashion or religion stories might have copy editors who were steeped in knowledge about certain fashion designers or who understood the difference between the dogmas of the Lutheran versus Presbyterian churches. A sports copy desk normally had fanatics, especially those who were fans in the local sports areas such as football if the city had a professional team, or hockey if the city was in an area where hockey was played.

Anyone who has ever known me knows I have never cared about or understood sports of any kind. Growing up as an only child in a house where sports were never played or watched on TV left a void in my life. But on the universal copy desk in Atlanta I was given sports stories to edit. I know I didn't do those sports stories justice.

In Providence and in Miami, I had spent time in the composing rooms, seeing my stories through the production process to be sure pages were built to my design. I had autonomy and power to put my professional stamp on headlines and pages. Not so in Atlanta, where I never sized a photo or ordered a graphic or fit stories onto pages.

I was touching and barely improving an enormous amount of stories. In my previous two newsrooms I worked with about a dozen—some days a few more, some days a few less—stories. One day in Atlanta I decided to count the number of stories I touched. With every story I put down a line or slash mark on a piece of paper until the end of my work shift.

Egad! I edited and wrote headlines for more than sixty stories that day.

This was not good. I wasn't learning new skills, I wasn't developing my editing chops, and I was not providing a good service for readers. I frequently thought about my professors Alan Bussell at Clark College and Ed Trayes at Temple University. Both had taught me the meaning of the term "shoveling" copy, which means quickly reading a story and letting it move along because you don't have time to ask questions and make the story better. How disappointed they would be in me if they knew I was in a place that allowed, no, required me to shovel copy. I had made a career mistake because, in my haste to get back to Atlanta, I just didn't ask the right questions.

THE TRANSITION IN THE 1970s from hot type to cold type may have been the biggest change in newspapers since German printer Johannes Gutenberg introduced the printing press and movable type in the fifteenth century. Newspapers had perfected printing using pretty much the same manual and technical process, producing stories one line at a time, and adding every other element on a page as a standalone thing. I have always thought of building a newspaper page as something like putting together a puzzle.

My crash course at Temple taught us the history and the process for producing lines of type and how to edit not just on paper, but in the back shop, the composing room where lead type was figuratively and literally flying. During my internship in Providence I learned how to read pages with lines of lead type upside down and backwards after stories were placed on the pages in chases, heavy metal tables with wheels where the pages were shaped and built.

The people who worked in newspaper composing rooms were organized in unions which were sometimes called chapels, a term taken from British union organizations that apparently grew out of real church groups. Chapels would hold meetings and negotiate with management on behalf of union members. I learned never to touch the metal, a violation of typesetters' union rules that might lead to one of the printers yelling "chapel meeting" and walking off the job, thus slowing production and leading to missed deadlines, missed press runs, and delayed delivery of newspapers, not a popular outcome from the perspectives of readers and advertisers. I am happy to say I never caused a chapel meeting.

In the 1970s, new technology was fast approaching. Generations of copy editors—myself included—had started their shifts by placing a glass glue pot, a metal "pica pole" ruler, a proportional crop wheel, and sharpened thick-leaded copy pencils on the desk. Now they were sitting before a monochrome cathode ray terminal, which we often called a video display terminal or VDT. These were not desktop computers but "dumb" terminals, connected by cabling to a mainframe computer somewhere in the bowels of the building. The mainframes were large enough to fill a room. Most journalists in newsrooms never saw or thought about the mainframes, whose inner workings were irrelevant to our daily duties, until they went down. The newspaper had to have capable technology guys—and yes, they were all guys at first—to keep the mainframes running.

I have always enjoyed being on the cutting edge of technology. As a child I took pride in having the latest models of record players or TV sets, although those things are now in the junkyard of memories for those of us who used them. At Spelman, I may have been the only freshman living in Morehouse North in 1967 to have an electric typewriter, a high school graduation present from my mother. My roommate, Tina, still teases me about her having to endure my late-night tap, tap, tapping out research papers, book reports, and *Spelman Spotlight* stories when she was trying to read or sleep.

At the *Atlanta Journal*, despite my disdain for the lightweight work I was doing on the copy desk, the newspaper moved to the cutting edge of technology when the decision was made to switch from hot to cold type—meaning typesetting not with molten metal but with paper-output photographic film processes. That meant the demise of the traditional composing room for printers and compositors, and the loss of some of those jobs. With the new technology, reporters would essentially typeset their own stories. Copy editors would no longer have to avoid touching metal type because changes to stories and pages would be made on-screen using a keyboard.

In the new production area, the tradesmen who were able to keep jobs were retrained for the new technology. They would take layout direction from editors who were designing pages not on paper mockups but on a screen. After stories and images were input, they would come out of special printers on large slick sheets of white paper and elements would be cut out and glued onto a board the exact size of a newspaper page. Then an image would be made of the entire board. The composing room staff had to learn a whole new way of producing pages.

The experts and consultants who came into newspapers to show us how to make this transition were up-front about certain changes. The new technology would require fewer people. There would be payroll savings. Younger staff members would probably gravitate toward the new technology and be ready to move the organization forward. Some workers currently on staff, including in the newsroom, would reject the new ways and would choose to leave. More importantly, others would reject the new ways but would stay and grumble for years about how much they missed "the good old days." The new mainframe computers would require new skills, probably performed by people who were not currently working in the newspaper industry.

The most striking part of the change, as I recall it, is that the transition would take place overnight. The ancient Linotype machines and vats of molten lead would be disassembled and hauled away after deadline one night. Then a day after the last hot type newspaper was produced, the next day's newspaper would be produced using cold type. There would be no opportunity to turn back.

All of this was unfathomable for some who worked in newsrooms. From the moment we heard about the changes, and especially when we got word of the training schedule to get us ready for the transition, the conversation on the copy desk shifted from topics like "Hey, listen to this story" to expressions of doubts and negative anticipation of the changes coming our way. I was young, twenty-five at the time, and I was not going to be like some of the negative nabobs. After all, I had an electric typewriter at home. What was the big deal? We could do this.

One of the senior editors called me aside one day and said they needed two people from the copy desk to spend half of our working time for a few weeks in a training room in another part of the building, where they would learn to use the new terminals. He wanted me to be what today we might call an early adopter of the new technology, to learn how to use it and then to train others.

I was ready for this assignment and picked it up quickly.

On the day we made the transition to cold type, I remember in particular a copy editor named Pat Patterson, a sluggish-moving, cigarette-smoking older gentleman who had been a reporter for many years before coming inside to work on the copy desk. Patterson had great knowledge about Atlanta from his experience on the streets covering various news beats. As he grew older, put on some weight and, frankly, acquired a negative attitude about a lot of things, he exhibited a wry sense of humor. He was one of what my friend and fellow newspaper editor Rexanna Lester describes as social rejects on copy desks, an apt description. Patterson sometimes made fun of stories he edited, reading parts out loud and making off-color comments that would never be tolerated in today's #MeToo, #blacklivesmatter, #gaypride environment.

I always assumed Patterson suffered from hemorrhoids because every morning, he went into his locker and brought out among his work tools a dirty bed pillow flecked with tiny spots of blood. I worked with Patterson for six months, but I don't recall him ever taking that pillow home to wash it. The only saving grace was that he sat on the pillow all day, hardly moving except to take a bathroom break, so I didn't have to look at it much.

Near the end of the training for the new technology, I returned to the copy desk each afternoon immediately after deadline, and for about an hour, as the new terminals were installed next to the typewriters, I trained my colleagues one by one. I noticed that Patterson kept putting off his lesson, grumbling the whole time. On the morning the changeover took place, when we entered the newsroom, things looked and sounded different. An overnight crew had swapped out the noisy copy desk typewriters for the new VDTs. The monitors were humming softly.

Patterson peered over his glasses across the newsroom at all the new-fangled equipment, then he went to his locker and one final time he retrieved his personal items, including his well-worn, stained pillow. He never sat down to work that morning. The last time I saw him, he was getting on the elevator, grumbling something most of us didn't want to hear. We had a newspaper to put out that day, and Patterson never returned to work at the *Atlanta Journal.*

At 4:30 one morning in February 1975, the phone rang in my Atlanta apartment. I peered at the clock next to my bed, not believing the early hour. I answered through my sleep.

"Hello."

"I *told* you I was going to marry you!"

"Hello?" This time was a question.

"I *told* you I was going to marry you!"

Wait a minute. I recognized that voice.

"Willie Lloyd?" I was waking up quickly.

Lloyd was the man I had met a little more than three years before, when I went with my friend Bonnie to the Hurry Back bar in Providence to pick up her sailor boyfriend. Lloyd was one of the sailors standing outside the club. Bonnie introduced him to me by his last name because that's how his fellow sailors referred to him. The name stuck.

After a long night hanging out with some new friends in Providence, I just couldn't seem to shake this Lloyd guy—not that I wanted to. He had escorted me to my car in the wee hours of the morning when I announced to the group at Bonnie's house that I needed to go home to get some sleep because I had to work very early the next morning. Lloyd didn't have anywhere to go, having missed the midnight bus for the one-hour trip back to the Naval base, so I took him home with me.

When we got to my one-bedroom apartment, he said he needed to sleep. We had both been drinking. Without asking, he stripped down to his underwear and got in on one side of my full-sized bed, the side I normally slept on, next to the nightstand and my alarm clock. As soon as his head hit my pillow he passed out. With just two or three hours before my alarm would go off, I also needed sleep, so I climbed into bed on the other side and fell asleep.

Somehow, I managed to get up when it was time, and I showered, dressed and drove downtown to the newspaper. That afternoon when I returned home Lloyd was still sleeping in my bed. I was in need of a nap, so I crawled into the bed again. Later, the phone woke us both. It was Bonnie.

"We're going down to Newport to listen to some jazz tonight. Do you and Lloyd want to go?"

Dang. How did Bonnie know that Lloyd was still with me?

Lloyd was waking up, reaching for a cigarette.

"Bonnie wants to know if we want to go to Newport with them tonight? Do you want to go?"

Lloyd quickly nodded yes, exhaling smoke through a one-sided grin. When I hung up the phone he said he needed a change of clothes. He asked me to drive him to the Naval base at Davisville south of Providence. When we got there, I waited in the car as he jumped out and sprinted into the barracks. I brought a book and I was prepared to patiently read, assuming he would take a shower, maybe shave, and get into some clean clothes.

In just a few minutes, he came running out of the barracks.

With a suitcase! He was moving in.

"WILLIE LLOYD? HOW DID you find me?" We hadn't spoken for more than three years. We were close for about six weeks during the summer of 1971. He was on the Naval base during the week, but he came to Providence to spend weekends with me, arriving on Friday evenings on the same bus that had brought him the night we met at the Hurry Back. I became one of those Providence women who retrieved her man from in front of the bar on Friday nights. A commuter train to Davisville left Providence before dawn on Mondays, and, conveniently, the train station was across the street from the newspaper. I would drop him off for the train at 5:30 a.m. and then go into the newsroom to begin my workweek.

Later that summer my grandmother became gravely ill and I was summoned to Savannah to say a final goodbye. Before I left Providence, I wrote Aunt Catherine's phone number on a scrap of paper and handed it to Lloyd.

"Call me if you want to," I told Lloyd. He didn't call, which was not alarming because long-distance calling was expensive and not a common thing in those days. Two weeks later, my grandmother died, and I returned to Savannah for her funeral.

My memory fades about the last time I saw Lloyd that summer. The Navy soon sent him to Diego Garcia, a small island just south of the equator in the Indian Ocean. The island was under British rule, and the American military was there between 1968 and 1973 to forcibly remove the native population to nearby islands to allow establishing a critical military base.

"How did you find me?" I asked Lloyd the morning his phone call woke me up in Atlanta.

He said he had completed eight years in the Navy, deciding not to make it a full career, and he was divorced and living in Northern Virginia near his mother and sister. He sounded lonely, like he was having a pity party.

"I was looking through an old suitcase at some papers and I found a little piece of paper with a phone number," he said.

He wasn't sure whose number it was but he was hopeful. He called long distance information to ask where area code 912 was. The operator looked it up and told him it was for the Savannah, Georgia, area.

"I found her!" was his response.

The time was about 4 a.m., and he dialed the number. Aunt Catherine answered.

"Hello, my name is Willie Lloyd. You don't know me but I used to know your niece, Wanda, when she lived in Rhode Island. I was in the Navy up there."

Aunt Catherine was always the person I could call at any hour, and no matter when it was she would be alert and ready to talk. So she willingly talked to this stranger who said he knew her Wanda.

"Oh, my Osie was a sailor. I just love sailors," she responded.

Lloyd had managed to capture Aunt Catherine's heart at 4 o'clock in the morning. He went on to tell her he had returned to Rhode Island to be discharged from the Navy and he went looking for me in Providence. "I want to find Wanda. Can you tell me where she is now?"

"Well, no, I can't tell you that. But I can take your number and have Wanda call you."

He gave her the number to write down, then he said, "Wanda was working for a newspaper in Providence. Does she still work for a newspaper?"

"Oh, yes, she works for the *Atlanta* . . . oops. I can't tell you that."

That's all he needed. After they hung up, Lloyd dialed long distance information and asked for the phone number of a Wanda Smalls in Atlanta. More than three years after we last saw each other, that's how he found me. He would have made a good reporter.

I arrived in the newsroom by 6:30 a.m., apparently looking like I hadn't gotten enough sleep. As I walked toward the copy desk, a coworker named June noticed that I wasn't looking well.

"Wanda, are you okay?"

"I'm just tired. This man I used to know called me before 5 o'clock this morning and asked me to marry him."

"Whaaaat? Are you going to marry him?"

"Girl, please! Do I look like a fool?"

That was on a Tuesday.

Lloyd arranged to fly into Atlanta on Friday that week so we could get reacquainted.

By Sunday night we were engaged.

A FEW DAYS AFTER my engagement to Willie Lloyd, I called Elsie Carper, the editor for newsroom administration and recruitment at the *Washington Post*. The last time I spoke with her was my first day at the *Miami Herald*. I only worked at the *Herald* for eighteen months, and I was determined not to move to Washington as a single woman. But now I was engaged. When Lloyd and I discussed our job situations—I had been in Atlanta just a few months, and he had a good position as film production manager with the United Way of America in Alexandria, Virginia, just across the Potomac River from Washington—it made sense for me to be the one to move.

I told Carper I was getting married and would be moving to the Washington area. In short order, she arranged a fully paid trip to Washington for a one-week tryout on the copy desk. This was the step I had skipped when I took the job in Atlanta. The *Post* put me up at the Jefferson Hotel, a couple of blocks from the newspaper. Carper told me there was no current opening, but "let's get the tryout out of the way so when an opening comes, you'll be ready." I was fine with that.

15. Witness to Greatness in D.C.

Lloyd and I set Sunday, May 25, 1975—Memorial Day weekend—as the date for our small family wedding and reception in the living room of Aunt Catherine's house on West 41st Street, next door to the house where my mother was born.

When I first took Lloyd home to Savannah shortly after we were engaged, Aunt Catherine asked him a very traditional question for parents to ask with respect to their girls.

"Can you take care of Wanda in the style that she is accustomed to living?"

Lloyd didn't even pause in his response.

"No, ma'am. Wanda is smart. She has a good education and a good foundation, so she will help take care of us."

Aunt Catherine, barely 5'4", smiled up at my 6'5" husband-to-be and said, "You're honest. I like that. If you are asking for my blessing, you have it."

ON A SATURDAY MORNING shortly after Lloyd and I were married, we were settling into a rented townhouse in Annandale, a community in northern Virginia, when I received a call from Elsie Carper. We hadn't spoken since I was in Washington for the tryout in her newsroom. Once again she had tracked me down, this time at our new home phone number. She now had a job for me, and she asked if I could come in on Monday.

This was my first move to a new city without having a job lined up first, and I was stepping out on faith that things would work out for my career. The Washington area is full of media organizations, and if the *Post* hadn't called I was prepared to start pounding the pavement to look for an opportunity.

But I had no idea how quickly Lloyd's belief in my career would be tested if the *Post* hadn't come through. At the end of my one-week *Post* copy desk tryout, my last interview had been with Benjamin Bradlee, the venerable editor who oversaw the newspaper's vast news operation. To say I was scared and nervous to meet Bradlee would be an understatement. It was a step that every potential *Post* hire had to endure. Our meeting was swift. Bradlee's questions were short and invited brief answers from me. As frightening as that meeting was, I assume I passed whatever test Bradlee conducted, because now I was about to join his team in the storied *Post* building at 1150 15th Street NW in downtown Washington.

I reported to Jack Lemmon, the newspaper's night managing editor. Lemmon was a mid-westerner who, some said, had the appearance of Lou Grant from the *Mary Tyler Moore Show*. He supervised the Metro copy desk and the news desk, which included the editors who planned and designed Page One. Jack had reviewed my resume and knew I had experience seeing pages through to deadline in composing rooms. He wanted to start me right away as one of the night production editors. My overnight shift—7:30 p.m. to about 3 a.m.—was the most stressful time of a morning paper's production schedule. I worked alongside union compositors in a lead-gray, dungeon-like, noisy room full of white men who were shouting back and forth to be heard over the din of the Linotype machines and the rolling of the heavy, metal chase tables across uneven brick floors. It was like working in a factory.

Production editor was a job we didn't have at my three previous newspapers. Welcome to the big time, I said to myself. I was now working for a newspaper with a huge staff and the luxury of having editors assigned exclusively to the composing room. Production editors were the last line of defense, the last to edit copy on the lead pages, the last to rewrite what we called "busted" headlines that were too long for the allotted space, the last to correct misspelled words, and the last able to add quick and necessary facts to a story or fix errors caught in the proofing process between editions.

Production editors communicated with the newsroom staff above us on the fifth floor via a constantly ringing telephone and with paper instructions delivered by a labyrinth of pneumatic tubes. If you've ever made a deposit at a bank from the drive-up lanes, you likely have put your check and ID into a tube that shoots over to the teller behind a glass wall through a system that sounds like a wind tunnel. The old newsrooms all had a system like this, with pnuematic tubes running to various parts of the building.

At the end of the editing process upstairs, my job was to get the copy or the correction where it needed to go. While I quickly caught on to the routine in the composing room, I found myself in some uncomfortable situations. I don't know if a woman had ever served as a production editor at the *Post* (I doubt it), but I'm pretty sure I was the first African American woman in that role. In an era when women working in professional environments usually wore dresses or skirts, the nature of the composing room required me to wear pants every night. I spent a good part of my shift bending over the chases and looking up at compositors, pointing to the pages and yelling above the din something like "this headline is going to be changed" or "put this new slug of type there." Remember, I could not touch the type because of union rules. But I had to get close to the pages and to the men working on those pages to point out where changes had to be made.

Many of the men who worked in the composing room were supportive and kind as I learned the ropes of being a production editor. I already knew my way around a composing room, but this one was on a bigger scale. A few times I would recognize the intentional close brush of my behind by some man passing by me, or I heard men make disparaging comments not about me specifically but about women's physical assets in general. They might have been describing their own girlfriend or wife, or some woman they saw that day. On some nights I felt like I was on a busy city street walking through the raucous catcalls of construction workers.

In a few weeks I reached the point where my stomach would churn at the thought of getting on the elevator to the composing room floor. I was beginning to wonder if this job was some kind of *Post* rite of passage, or whether I had the stuff to endure this huge newspaper. There were fleeting moments when I wondered if I was good enough for the *Post*. I was too ashamed to mention my self-doubts to anyone, not even to my new husband. Somehow I got the nerve to go back to work day after day.

I WAS A NEWLYWED when I started working the ungodly overnight shifts, including weekend duty and split days off during the week. I had to find a way to make it work. To get to work on time and also to see my husband, I would have dinner on the table when he arrived home about 5:30 p.m. By 6:45 I would leave for my night shift. On weekends Lloyd and I had our days together but I was back in the composing room at night. I was four years out of college and a world away from a segregated upbringing in Savannah and the all-female, black college I had attended. I felt out of my element working exclusively with older white men who were used to yelling across the room and felt no qualms at telling off-color jokes. Based on the increasingly boisterous behavior as the nights wore on, I was pretty sure alcohol was being consumed.

I was not yet mature enough to ask why women or African American men were not invited to this white man's club, or to understand how unions were created for craftsmen who were only white and male. In some ways, this environment was much like the white male entitlement structure in the South where I grew up, where African Americans, even some with college degrees, were locked out of certain careers. I was taught, by example, to keep my head down and not to ask questions where white people were concerned. Maybe this is why my grandmother encouraged me to take classes in education, so I would have the credentials to run and hide from what she surely knew was a world that might not be welcoming to a young black woman from the Deep South.

I knew I had to learn to understand this new world. I had to make it work. God had given me an incredible gift—to be able to work at a newspaper like the *Washington Post* considering where I came from, a foundation of Jim Crow laws that constantly told me what I could or could not do. I had regretted jumping to the *Journal* in Atlanta, but I never regretted taking the job at the *Post*. Papers like the *New York Times,* the *Wall Street Journal,* and the *Post* were every print journalist's dream. I knew that.

But I wasn't working in the newsroom, and I missed being able to edit copy, write headlines, and commiserate with reporters and other editors. I missed putting my stamp on stories on the front end before they landed in the pneumatic-tube life cycle of the daily newspaper. I missed the copy desk, and I missed spending time with my husband.

A couple of months in at the *Post* I mustered the courage to walk into Lemmon's office to request a transfer to one of the newsroom's copy desks. I reminded him that copy editing was my experience and I wanted to work with some of the best editors in the business. I had met some of them during my one-week Metro copy desk tryout a few months before, and I knew I would fit right in. I never reported the uncomfortable conversations or the physical brushes by the union men in the composing room. I never let on that I had to be mindful of what I wore, where I stood, and how I reacted to bad-boy behavior. I never reported the disparaging comments about women. In fact, in 1975, I'm pretty sure I was not even aware of the term "sexual harassment." I just knew I was working in conditions that didn't feel right.

I kept my request professional and it worked. I was reassigned to the Metro copy desk to work with an amazing group of people who helped me grow as an editor and as a person.

One of my new colleagues was Dorothy Ing Russell, a soft-spoken, kind-hearted woman of Asian descent who grew up in Canada. Dorothy was the only woman on the Metro copy desk when I got there, and I can only imagine the steps she took to break glass ceilings in journalism as a woman and as a person of color. A lover of culture and the arts, Dorothy was a divorced single mother. She dearly loved and constantly talked about her son, Matthew. I wasn't a mother yet, but I learned so much by observing how Dorothy juggled duties of motherhood by day and a career that she loved by night.

According to her *Post* obituary when Dorothy passed away in 2012, "As a young journalist, she was acting chief of the United Press bureau in Jakarta, Indonesia, and she was a stringer [freelancer] there for the *New York Times*. Later she was a writer and editor for the *Japan Times, Asahi Evening News,* and *Stars and Stripes* in Tokyo. She also was a reporter for the *American Weekly* in London and a writer-researcher for *World* magazine in New York."

Dorothy became a good friend. Even after I left the Metro copy desk for another assignment in the newsroom, we enjoyed catching up from time to time outside the paper. She had been at the *Post* a long time and knew all of the newsroom family secrets. She wasn't one to gossip, but she wanted to ensure I knew who could be supportive and who was not likely going to have my back.

THE *POST* NEWSROOM WAS a huge operation with almost a thousand reporters (some of those thousand were news assistants, clericals) and editors—each responsible for a piece of the journalistic pie. I was well aware of the *Post's* reputation. Just a few years prior, Publisher Katharine Graham, whose family owned the newspaper, and editor Bradlee had courageously led the *Post* to a Pulitzer Prize in the Watergate era. Investigative reporters Bob Woodward and Carl Bernstein were by then household names. Those two reporters alone were probably responsible for thousands of young people deciding to study journalism and seek newsroom careers—whether in newspapers or on TV. In the mid to late 1970s, the University of Missouri School of Journalism, which claims to be the world's oldest college journalism program, reported an uptick in students majoring in journalism. The school began to offer classes in investigative journalism to satisfy the needs of students who wanted to make a difference through journalism, just like Woodward and Bernstein.

The journalism rose was glamorous and sweet when I joined the *Post* in June 1975. Outside, scenes of the movie *All the President's Men*, adapted from the Bernstein-Woodward book, were being filmed on Fifteenth Street. From time to time, stars Robert Redford or Dustin Hoffman would come strolling through the newsroom with Katharine Graham to visit with editor Bradlee.

Every day as we entered the building to work, I would pass through the glass-walled entrance to the lobby and look to the right and down to the basement where the presses were often printing pre-run sections of the newspaper. This was a popular spot for touring school groups to stand and watch the humming presses and listen to narrators' tidbits, like how much ink and how many tons of newsprint were used daily. For staff members leaving late at night, there was a sense of satisfaction and pride to actually pass by this spot and look down to see the work we had just produced— pages for the next day's newspaper being printed, folded, cut, and moved along conveyor belts where bundles were strapped and sent outside to the loading dock. There trucks lined up in a long alley waiting to carry our daily miracle off to far-flung neighborhoods and news stands. There is something to be said about enjoying the smell of ink on freshly printed pages.

When there was good news to celebrate and Pulitzer Prizes were announced, Bradlee would stand in the middle of the newsroom, with hundreds of journalists surrounding him, and announce the *Post's* latest honors. Regrettably, we witnessed a sad day in 1981 when the newspaper announced that a Pulitzer Prize would be returned. Reporter Janet Cooke had written "Jimmy's World," a Sunday Page One story about an eight-year-old black boy who allegedly lived in "a world of hard drugs, fast money and the good life he believes both can bring." An attractive young African American woman, Cooke set out to write about a new strong heroin being used on the streets of Washington. She apparently attempted to find a story like the one she wrote, but when she couldn't find the exact subject she needed for her story, she created a fictional tale with her great writing ability. Cooke's story went through the normal layers of editing, and some skeptical editors did warn against running it. One was Vivian Aplin-Brownlee, editor of the District Weekly, the section of the newspaper where Cooke was assigned at the time. Aplin-Brownlee was Cooke's supervisor, but the story that ran on Sunday, September 28, 1980, was published while Aplin-Brownlee was on vacation.

The story as it ran was so compelling that Bob Woodward, then the assistant managing editor for Metro, submitted it for the Pulitzer Prize, print journalism's highest honor. In New York that year, the Pulitzer jurors in the local news category shifted the entry over to the team reading in the feature writing category, perhaps to position it for a better chance to win. When news of her Pulitzer was picked up by the Associated Press, the skeptics came forward. The *Toledo Blade,* where Cooke had previously worked, tipped a *Post* editor that some of Cooke's background information did not fit with the data on file with their newspaper. Someone from Vassar College called Bradlee to say their records showed Cooke "attended" Vassar but was not a graduate, as the press release indicated. The AP reported, from the submitted biographical information, that Cooke had earned a master's degree from the University of Toledo, but that also proved incorrect.

Several *Post* editors, including then-assistant Metro editor Milton Coleman, questioned Cooke for hours. She ultimately admitted her ruse. Her journalism career was ruined, and, for a time, the *Post's* reputation was taken down a notch.

Cooke's fate had reverberations throughout the *Post* newsroom and across the industry, because her hiring revealed cracks in the vetting process. The newspaper had the requisite resumes and background information on file. But how deeply checks on credentials or references were made was not known to those of us who had already gone through the process.

In a 2016 *Columbia Journalism Review* article by Mike Sager, a quote from economist and media contributor Julianne Malveaux may have said it best: "Janet Cooke gave white folks permission to be skeptical about black people in the newsroom."

Among African American journalists at the *Post* there were rumors and suspicions that some of our credentials were getting a second look. These suspicions may have come from our own insecurities and, yes, even anger that Cooke's fiasco would leave us in this vulnerable position. Fortunately, no African Americans were officially challenged or fired after the Cooke incident. But her story just confirmed something my grandmother used to say, that as African Americans and women we have to do better, be better, look better, smell better, study harder, work harder, and jump higher to be as successful as white people. The bar for us is higher.

A seminal moment at the *Washington Post* occurred at 4 a.m. on October 1, 1975, four months after I began working at the newspaper. I woke up to local TV news that members of the union representing the pressmen, who had come to an impasse in renegotiating their union-favorable contract, had damaged the presses to the point where the equipment was no longer operable. Subsequent stories would report that pressmen also started a fire.

Versions of that information may or not have been true. The fire department did come and put out a fire, and there was at least some "dismantling" if not damage to the presses. If burning the presses was the pressmen's goal they could have achieved it. One pressman was quoted in a story in the *New Times* magazine. "We could have burned the place down if we wanted, but we set the alarms off when we saw the fire." It was a fact that when a pressroom manager came into the area to see what was happening, he was roughed up, the beginning of several reported incidents of violence during the strike, on and off the premises.

The pressmen went out on strike and members of the local Newspaper Guild, the union that represented many newsroom and business staff members, struck in support of the pressmen. The *Post* did not publish a newspaper the following day, but in subsequent days a small version of the newspaper was printed on presses in other locations, including at some competing newspapers. That truncated twenty-page *Post* was a shadow of the hefty daily newspaper that on some days weighed a few pounds with special sections, classified ads, and advertising inserts.

I was still relatively new on staff, and I was one of those told to go home and wait for a call to see when I would be needed again. After a couple of boring weeks at home and periods of career gloom and self-doubt, I convinced myself that I would probably never work at the *Post* again. I needed to think about my future and how I would help pay the rent and other expenses in our new marriage. Lloyd and I both made decent money before the strike, but the Washington area was expensive and we were living paycheck-to-paycheck. Lloyd was often away on business trips and I was new to the area and didn't have many friends. My self-pity evolved into depression.

One day I drove down Little River Turnpike in Annandale to the main campus of Northern Virginia Community College and enrolled in a course for interior design, something that had interested me and, I thought, could become a new career. At the very least, it was a way to pass the time doing something I might enjoy.

The next day I got a phone call from the *Post*. "Come back to work tomorrow. We need you."

Over the months of the strike I continued to work on the news desk where we quickly adapted a process of editing stories from manual typewriters to IBM Selectrics in a system called scanner copy. Reporters and copy editors continued to use manual typewriters. At 5 p.m. each day, secretaries from throughout the building would report to the news desk from other departments and begin to retype every speck of copy that would go into the next day's newspaper. I was a traffic control editor, logging in stories from the copy desk and assignment editors and distributing every page to one of the fast typists who were then pulling a second shift that day. I had learned how to use this scanner system at the *Providence Evening Bulletin* and I was happy to be trusted in this role to get the *Post* out each night.

I went from working five days a week to six- or seven-day rotations, a grueling schedule of overtime that boosted our newlywed household budget. We wanted to buy a house and the extra income helped our bottom line.

A few months into the strike Katharine Graham announced that she was going to replace all pressmen who didn't come back to work. The word went out that people looking for work should apply to be trained for these jobs. When I came to work the first day of the job openings, I saw a line stretched about a block along Fifteenth Street and around the corner. The white and male union was gone, and the line of applicants included young people, women, and people of color. It was an unforgettable diversity moment.

I WORKED IN THE *Post* newsroom for eleven years, minus a few weeks away after our daughter was born in 1982. I ended up spending most of my *Post* years on the desk of the Los Angeles Times-Washington Post News Service, a jointly owned news agency that provided content from *Post* and *Times* reporters to newspapers around the world. I started as an assistant editor and moved up to deputy Washington editor. I interacted with and edited stories written by some of the best reporters in the business, reworking their copy for an audience of large media organizations and their readers. In addition to the hundreds of organizational customers in the United States, we were in direct touch with Washington correspondents for international news organizations. If not for the news service, I might not have learned about organizations like the Japanese *Yomiuri Shimbun,* which at the time had the largest newspaper circulation in the world, or *Maariv,* the Hebrew-language daily newspaper in Israel. I edited stories produced by Paris-based Agence France-Presse, because we had the rights to distribute AFP stories to clients in the United States. We talked to people every day who lived in countries that respected American journalism and who understood that news coming out of our newspapers from Washington to Los Angeles could be trusted.

16. Work-Life Balance

OUR DAUGHTER WAS BORN on August 4, 1982. She came into the world about three weeks early, which was just fine with me. I was ready to begin motherhood. That morning at home I was sitting on the side of the bed talking on the phone with my mother in Savannah. Lloyd had gone to work. All was right with the world, or so I thought.

When my mother and I said goodbye and I stood up, I realized that I had been sitting in a puddle of dampness. My water had broken. What transpired next was a series of female efficiency and stupidity on my part. I called my doctor's office to let them know what I thought was happening. I didn't want to alert Lloyd yet, just in case my assumption was wrong. A nurse told me something like "it might be a good idea to go to the hospital and get checked out. They'll call us If the baby is coming."

I still wasn't sure this was the day so I set up the ironing board and spray starched and pressed a teal blue cotton maternity dress in case the hospital sent me home on a false alarm. I wanted to be ready for a quick change and drive into the city for my afternoon-evening shift. I also ironed a couple of shirts for Lloyd so he would have them in case I didn't make it home from the hospital that day. I was a good wife.

I drove myself to Greater Southeast Community Hospital in Washington's Anacostia section, parked in the lot, and strolled through the front door like I was there for a visit. I was not feeling labor pains.

"May I help you?" the admissions staffer asked.

"I'm having a baby."

"I can see that, how may I help you? When?"

"Today, I think. My water broke."

"Who is with you?"

"Nobody, I drove myself."

That's when a nurse and two or three other people looked at me like I had no sense. I was quickly settled into a wheelchair and pushed out of the lobby area. After a pelvic exam that confirmed that my water had broken, I was asked who needed to be called. I gave them two names and two phone numbers.

"Call my husband, Willie Lloyd, at this number. And call George Eagle at this number. Tell him I won't be able to come to work today."

George was one of my editing colleagues. A nurse later chuckled that his response was, "Oh, my goodness, what do I need to do?" The nurse assured George that the hospital had things under control and he didn't need to do anything. George and I had a good laugh later about that exchange.

Lloyd arrived quickly and we kissed while I was being prepped every which way. I was still not feeling labor pains. In fact, I was more worried that we now had two cars being charged an hourly rate in the hospital's parking lot.

"That's too much money," I said. "Take my car home and get a neighbor to bring you back over here." Plus, he needed to fetch our camera and a book of baby names. From the beginning we hoped for a girl and had settled on naming her Shelby Renee. When we had a sonogram we decided that all we wanted to know was that we were carrying a healthy baby. We chose not to know the gender. So here we were, T-minus delivery, and my first thought was that maybe we should have a name for a boy just in case.

When Lloyd came back to the hospital we talked about the names we had flagged in the book and narrowed our "son" to Travis Walker Lloyd, Walker being my mother's maiden name.

After a few hours of observation, the doctor said he needed to induce labor because of fear of infection. I slept two of the four hours in labor, which was somewhat disappointing because we didn't get to use much of the breathing technique we had learned in Lamaze classes. At 4:50 p.m., Shelby Renee Lloyd, long and slender, arrived and made us a family of three.

We immediately dialed our mothers to share the good news. "Hello, Grandma," I said when Gloria picked up the phone.

THE NEXT MORNING WE got some unsettling news. First, Shelby was jaundiced and needed to stay in the hospital a few days under the bilirubin lights until she got her color. Jaundice, we learned, is a fairly common occurrence in new babies and not much cause for alarm. But another diagnosis was enough to test our faith. The expression on the doctor's face and the sad looks from the nurses around him frightened us.

"Your baby's head is elongated and we have reason to believe that the membranes around her brain are fused."

What the heck was this about? We had so many questions. What caused this? Did I do something wrong during the pregnancy? Could this be fixed? Was she going to be a slow learner? Was she ever going to walk, think, speak? Was she going to live?

The medical staff wanted to transfer Shelby by ambulance to Children's Hospital for some testing. "No," I said. "When she can be discharged I want to take my baby home for one night and then we will take her to Children's."

Reluctantly, the doctor agreed.

Right after Shelby was born I showed symptoms of fatigue and a cold coming on. I think I willed myself sick because I didn't want to leave Shelby behind. I was also nursing and wanted to spend as much time as possible with nurses to help me get the hang of feeding the baby. My doctor agreed and I was medically able to stay in the hospital about five days. So much was happening, and looking back on it, I think I was on the verge of a breakdown.

Lloyd and I had been married for seven years and I was thirty-three when Shelby was born. Maybe this was some kind of punishment for not already having a big family, for being so career-centered that I forgot to slow down and have babies in my twenties. Whatever it was, I was emotionally spent.

News about Shelby's impending "surgery" spread quickly among my colleagues in the newsroom and black journalists across the Washington area. People were genuinely concerned. But one call in particular gave me great comfort. The phone next to my hospital bed rang and the African American caller identified herself as a journalist, someone I didn't know. She said she was a member of a group called Journalists for Jesus and she wanted to pray with me over the phone. I had not heard of this group but I couldn't think of a good reason to turn her down. We prayed. She ended the call by reminding me that we had now put Shelby's care in God's hands, and that everything was going to be okay. I called Lloyd to share the experience I had just had. I hadn't had the good sense to write down the woman's name and number; as far as I know, she and I never spoke again.

My mother, by then retired, took the first flight she could get from Savannah. I think her bags had been packed for weeks. On the day we discharged from the hospital a nurse told me an appointment had been made for the next morning with the chief of neurosurgery at Children's.

We took Shelby home to sleep in her crib for at least one night. It was her room, and I was going to be sure she saw it before we faced whatever would come next.

I wanted Shelby to look up at the musical mobile dangling over her bed. I wanted her to see the pictures on the wall we received at the baby shower held at the home of my dear friend and *Washington Post* colleague, Bobbi Bowman. I wanted to change Shelby's diapers on the changing table/dresser that my mother and Aunt Catherine had gifted us. I wanted to rock Shelby to sleep in the wooden rocking chair I had placed in her room so I could read stories to her, sing "You Are My Sunshine," and nurse her to sleep. And I wanted at least one morning to reach into the closet and take out a pretty outfit and dress Shelby up like the little doll she was before we delivered her to the hospital. Those things were important to me.

The next day, with Shelby swaddled in my arms, we left my mother standing at the top of the stairs forcing a smile through tears and waving goodbye. We had no idea how long we would be gone and, frankly, I think Gloria volunteered to stay home with Angel, our cocker spaniel, because she was afraid of what we were facing at the hospital. None of us knew what to expect.

DR. BONANNO, THE NEUROSURGEON, greeted us in the exam room. She was a petite woman, maybe in her forties, sure of herself.

"Let me take a look." She gently picked up Shelby and unwrapped the hospital blanket that covered her body, naked except for a diaper.

She gently pressed her fingers around Shelby's head and mumbled "Hmmmm. Hmmmmm. Hmmmm" a few times. She weighed Shelby on the tiny scale in the exam room, and she measured her length.

Lloyd and I stood like stones, afraid to ask any questions, afraid to cry, simply afraid. A couple of times the doctor glanced at Lloyd, but still without speaking.

Then: "Go get me a tape measure," she said to a nurse.

A few seconds later she asked Lloyd "How tall are you?"

"Six-five."

"Sit down," she gently ordered.

She positioned her petite frame closely in front of him and wrapped the tape measure around his head. She paused, looking upward, obviously mentally calculating.

"Has anybody ever told you that you have a small head for your size?"

"Well, yeah. They used to call me peanut head," Lloyd replied.

"Uh-huh. I thought so. There's nothing wrong with this baby's head or her membranes," Dr. Bonanno said. "She just has a small head like her daddy. Take your baby home and have a good life."

I quickly re-dressed Shelby and we got out of there like we were running from a plague. I didn't want Dr. Bonanno to change her brilliant mind.

Today Shelby is just fine. No, she is better than fine.

WHEN I RETURNED TO work after maternity leave, I was beginning to think about my future at the *Washington Post*. I loved the work, but I was mindful that my career could stagnate if I didn't press for upward movement. Also, as a mother now, working nights and weekends was getting old for our family life. I needed a better work schedule before Shelby was ready to go to school.

In a hiring spree similar to the one I had experienced at the *Miami Herald*, by the late 1970s the *Post* was bringing in some incredible black journalists. This was one of the nation's best newspapers, able to attract outstanding talent.

When I arrived at the *Post*, Dorothy Butler Gilliam was one of the veteran black journalists who welcomed me. Dorothy got her start in the black press—the *Louisville Defender* in Kentucky and *Jet* magazine—before getting her master's degree in journalism at Columbia University. She joined the *Post* in 1961 as the newspaper's first black female reporter, left in the mid 1960s when her three daughters were very young, and returned in 1972. For much of her time at the newspaper she wrote a metro column focusing on education, politics, and race. I never met a person in Washington who did not know the name Dorothy Gilliam.

Other black journalists who came to the *Post* were Courtland Milloy and Tom Morgan, colleagues I worked with at the *Miami Herald*; Juan Williams, a reporter and columnist who later worked for Fox News and who authored *Eyes on the Prize: America's Civil Rights Years, 1954–1965*; Milton Coleman, who rose to become a deputy managing editor; reporters Gwen Ifill, who later joined the *New York Times* and then co-anchored the PBS NewsHour, and Michelle Martin, whose trajectory later took her to the *Wall Street Journal* and NPR where she hosted "Tell Me More"; *Post* Style section features reporters Jacqueline Trescott and Karen DeWitt; sports reporter Michael Wilbon, who became an analyst for ESPN; Warren Brown, who covered the automobile industry for more than thirty years; and Eugene Robinson, who covered the Patty Hearst trial for the *San Francisco Examiner* before joining the *Post* in 1980 (as city hall reporter, assistant city editor, international correspondent, editor in a host of other roles, and now as a Pulitzer Prize-winning columnist, associate editor, and regular commentator on MSNBC).

One of my favorite colleagues and friends at the *Post* was syndicated columnist William "Bill" Raspberry, who wrote insightful commentary for more than forty years. When I was editing in the news service, Bill would often wander into our part of the room and ask, "What's up in the world?" We had a wall of slots filled with newspapers from around the world and Bill would go through a few each week to get ideas for his twice-weekly column. Sometimes we would talk about a couple of column ideas, and then off he went back to his office where he would put his thoughts down in short order, sometimes as quickly as twenty or thirty minutes. His copy was always perfect and pristine.

In 1994 I was asked for the second year in a row to serve as a juror for the Pulitzer Prize. Pulitzers are curated at the Columbia School of Journalism in New York. When jurors arrive on campus for the three-day process, they learn what category they will be reading, so as not to taint the pool of jurors and put them in a position of being swayed by nominating news organizations. That year I was a juror for commentary. As we went through the voluminous books of entries over a couple of days, it became clear that Raspberry would be in the group of commentary finalists.

I was senior editor *USA Today* at the time. The other jurors on the 1994 team for commentary were Bill Kovach, curator for the Nieman Foundation at Harvard University; David B. Cooper, associate editor, *Akron Beacon Journal*; Warren Lerude, professor, Reynolds School of Journalism, University of Nevada-Reno; and Alan Sorensen, editorial page editor, *Roanoke* (Virginia) *Times & World News*.

After we whittled down our last dozen or so "best" entries (usually out of more than a hundred submissions), we settled on three finalists: Jane Daugherty of the *Detroit Free Press*, Peter H. King of the *Los Angeles Times*, and Raspberry. We divided the duties and I had the honor of writing the nominating paragraph for Raspberry's work. I realized that whatever I would write needed to be strong enough for the Pulitzer Board, which has the final vote, to understand how much we thought of Raspberry's entry. More importantly, jurors sign a pledge of secrecy. I could not call my friend Raspberry to let him know he was a finalist, but secrets get out every year so I'm sure he knew he was in the top three.

Bill Raspberry passed away in July 2012. A few months before his demise, recognizing that he was suffering from prostate cancer, his friends held a love-fest for him at the *Washington Post* building to celebrate his life while he was alive. I flew to Washington and joined the celebration.

OVER MY YEARS AT the *Post*, I tried several times to move into roles with more responsibility. I inquired about becoming an editor in Outlook, the Sunday section for long-form journalism; I applied to become editor of the Federal Page, the daily coverage of the federal government and agencies; and I inquired about working full-time on the copy desks of the national and business sections. I did not have ambitions to become an assistant managing editor. I knew that wasn't going to happen for me at the *Post*, a family-owned newspaper that did not yet have a plan to elevate women or African Americans. After several tries to move around the newsroom, I became disillusioned. When I applied, some of the top editors told me I didn't have the "depth of knowledge" or the "experience" or the "polish" or . . . well, any number of descriptors that were used to send me back to my corner of the room, the news service. At that time I did not have a mentor or an advocate, and frankly, I'm not sure I realized that's what I needed.

I was also starting to see other black journalists leave the newspaper. My friend Alice Bonner moved across the river to *USA Today* in northern Virginia to become an assignment editor; my friend Bobbi Bowman went to the *Detroit Free Press* as an assistant city editor. Gwen Ifill, Michelle Martin, and Tom Morgan left for reporting jobs at other big newspapers. The ranks were thinning, and while a few new people were coming in, the *Post* just wasn't as satisfying for me.

Black journalists were having conversations among ourselves about how to address this diversity gap. Eventually some of us started to share our concerns with management, including with editor Ben Bradlee. He was never one to take criticism well, in my opinion, but he listened politely one day when Dorothy Gilliam, assistant city editor Marcia Green, and I made an appointment to talk to him. We wanted a conversation about the discontent among African Americans in the newsroom, and we asked how we could help turn the tide. Bradlee listened patiently but made no promises and did not seem interested in our suggestions to make retention of people of color and diversity a stronger priority.

Immediately after the meeting with Bradlee, some of us huddled in Gilliam's glass-enclosed office in the middle of the newsroom. We agreed that we probably didn't make much of a dent in Bradlee's thinking. Gilliam, older and wiser, looked at me with sympathetic eyes and said, "Wanda, I think if there is a sacrificial lamb as a result of our discussion, it's probably you." Thinking back, I may have spoken up the loudest, and with the angriest tone. I knew then that I probably should start thinking about leaving the *Post*.

One person Bradlee did listen to was Milton Coleman, who was a former

Metro reporter, then city editor, then reporter on the national news staff. Coleman had Bradlee's ear and admiration. In 1985, my last full year at the *Washington Post*, as Bradlee and other top editors began to listen to voices of discontent, Coleman was asked to survey all journalists in the newsroom to gauge attitudes about affirmative action. The survey was a snapshot of employee opinions on a broad range of subjects. The underlying mission was to ascertain how African American journalists were faring, and perhaps to see if there were solutions for retaining talent.

The survey, conversations, and a fifteen-page report were completed and submitted in to the *Post* editors in February 1986. The survey team included three African Americans—Coleman, Jeanne Fox-Alston, and Eugene Robinson—and three white males—Robert Signer, Barry Sussman, and Tom Wilkinson. These six were probably there as much for their areas of expertise in the newsroom as for their race. For example, Fox-Alston was the newsroom's recruiter at the time; Sussman designed and conducted surveys and opinion polls for the newspaper.

The report was entitled *Blacks in the Newsroom of the Washington Post, Where We Are; Where We Should Be, and How Are We Going to Get There.* It described the newsroom as full of favoritism, cronyism, and snobbery, a place where "edicts" dropped from on high along the lines of "so-and-so is going to Tokyo" as a correspondent, or "so-and-so is moving to work on the national desk to work in Texas," or Chicago, or Los Angeles. A survey respondent asked, "How is it that such things are decided?"

At the time of the survey, the newspaper served a Washington metropolitan area that was about 30 percent black, Hispanic, and Asian American. The newsroom staff of 450 full-time journalists included 12.9 percent minorities, far below the representation of the metro area's minority population. The *Post* had not established goals for racial diversity. And as an indicator that diversity matters, the only newsroom department with an African American in senior leadership was photography, where Matthew Lewis was assistant managing editor. The photography staff was 28 percent black, which made it the most racially integrated of any of the newspaper's larger staffs.

On the Metro staff, twenty out of 102 (19.6 percent) were people of color, but once there, it was difficult for minorities to move across the room to work in sections like business, sports, features or national—Metro had negative moniker as the newsroom's "ghetto." Thus, many black reporters were ripe for picking by other big newspapers, and each time it happened, the *Post* lost ground with diversity.

In 1976, Harvard graduate Herbert H. Denton had become city editor, making him the highest-ranking black journalist in the room at the time. But a decade later at the time of the survey, no other African American had risen above the management level where Denton broke through.

Fortunately, the survey team reached out to other news organizations to look for diversity best-practices. The team called people in management and human resources at the *New York Times, Wall Street Journal* parent company Dow Jones, Knight-Ridder (which included newspapers in Detroit, Charlotte, and Philadelphia), the *Louisville Courier-Journal and Times,* and the *Cleveland Plain Dealer.*

The *Washington Post* also reached out to Gannett, the company that had three years earlier launched *USA Today* and would later own more newspapers than any other company in the nation. At the time, Gannett was recognized as a leader in diversity—both for staff diversity and for diversity in the content of its newspapers. Gannett's CEO and *USA Today* founder Al Neuharth used to say his company's policy "is to make sure our leadership reflects our readership."

Gannett would be my next career step.

IN RETROSPECT, AS MUCH as I had given Elsie Carper credit for being a tenacious recruiter in bringing me to the *Post* in 1975, I came to understand the driving force behind her effort. In 1972, seven African American journalists—Ivan C. Brandon, LaBarbara "Bobbi" Bowman, Leon Dash, Penny Mickelbury, Ronald A. Taylor, Richard Prince, and Michael B. Hodge, who died in 2017—took a stand against what they said was discrimination in the *Post* newsroom. They filed a complaint with the U.S. Equal Employment Opportunity Commission, alleging that the newspaper was "denying black employees an equal opportunity with respect to job assignments, promotional opportunities, including promotions to management positions and other terms and conditions of employment," according to an article by

Steven Gray in the September 2002 *NABJ Journal*, the publication of the National Association of Black Journalists.

The efforts of the Metro Seven "accelerated the hiring and promotion of scores of journalists of color," Gray wrote. I was one of those journalists who directly benefited.

At a press conference in 1972, Metro Seven member Bowman, a woman who would become my dear and lifelong friend after I was hired at the *Post*, stated that "the complaint to the EEOC represents our belief that this discrimination cannot continue to exist at a publication in a city that is 71.1 percent black. . . . [the complaint] came after very much thought, very much consideration. We're very sorry we had to take this step. There is no alternative."

The Metro Seven settled their discrimination claim against the *Post*. They did not ask for monetary compensation. They just wanted the newspaper to hire and promote more African American journalists and make it possible for those who were there to be fairly treated in assignments.

In 2019, I was pleased to sign on as one of those who benefited from the efforts of this brave group by helping to compile the nomination of the Metro Seven to NABJ's Hall of Fame—forty-seven years after the EEOC complaint. Proudly, I was present for the induction at the organization's August 2019 conference in Miami, Florida.

17. Catapult to Leadership

"Hi, Alice, this is Wanda. I was wondering if I could get those clothes for Shelby today."

"Okay, come on over," Alice Bonner said. "Let's meet in the parking lot. The clothes are in the trunk of my car."

This was the phone call that began my path to *USA Today*.

With the onset of spring in 1986, I was making arrangements with my friend Alice Bonner, a former *Washington Post* colleague who had jumped to *USA Today* to be an assignment editor at the relatively new newspaper across the Potomac River in the Rosslyn part of Arlington, Virginia. From the higher floors of the newspaper's perch in one of the twin towers leased by Gannett, *USA Today's* parent company, you could almost see the *Post* building.

Alice is mother to Destiny, who was an adorable and bright little girl a few years older than Shelby. When our girls were children, Alice generously handed down some of Destiny's things as the seasons changed. Now with Alice no longer working in the same building with me, the handoffs were a little challenging.

When I got to the *USA Today* parking lot, I didn't see Alice so I went inside and asked the guard to let her know I was there. She was on deadline and told the guard to ask me to come up and wait with her. When I walked up to her desk she was huddled with a reporter editing her last story for the day. She looked up, shrugged, and gave me a look that said, "I'm not ready, please have a seat."

"That's okay," I said. "I'll just go find my friend Ron Martin while you're finishing up."

Ron, executive editor at *USA Today*, had been managing editor at the *Miami Herald* when I worked there a decade before. He had hired me, and we parted as friends when I left the *Herald* and moved to Atlanta.

"Knock, knock," I said, lightly tapping the open door to Ron's office.

"Hey, stranger." His smile was a welcome for an old friend. "Are you ready to come to work here?"

"I don't know, Ron. What did you have in mind?"

I shared with him that my mission was to rendezvous with Alice, and after a few minutes of catching up he turned his back to me and reached for the phone on the credenza behind his desk.

"Hey, it's me," he said softly to someone on the other end of the phone line. "I have someone in my office I want you to meet."

Ron arranged for me to have lunch with Karen Jurgensen, one of the *USA Today* "founders"—staff members who were on the newspaper's launch team for the first edition on September 15, 1982. Karen (pronounced Kaa-ren) had just been promoted to managing editor for Cover Stories, the department responsible for planning and producing four enterprise stories per edition of the newspaper, one for the cover of each of four sections in the newspaper.

When Karen interviewed me over lunch at Windows, a restaurant on the entrance floor of the *USA Today* tower, we were immediately comfortable together, like we found a female kinship. We were about the same age, both raising daughters as only children and both passionate about the work we were doing. We discovered that we had worked at competing newspapers in Miami, Karen at the afternoon Cox-owned *Miami News* and me at the morning *Herald*.

One of her questions over lunch sticks in my mind today.

"Would you say you are serious most of the time or not serious?"

Wow, I had never been asked that question and I had to think fast to respond. Long-time friends and colleagues now tell me they have always considered me to be serious, studious, and matter-of-fact. But on that day, my response was as noncommittal as I could make it.

"Well, I guess I would have to say I am serious half the time and not so serious half the time," I said.

"That's good because we're never serious at *USA Today*," Karen said.

A few days later Karen offered me a position as deputy managing editor of Cover Stories. I was about to step into a management role at the self-described "Nation's Newspaper."

When I told my mother about the offer, she was not so sure about *USA Today*. I had been at the *Washington Post* for more than a decade, and I was in as secure a position as any job can be. Gloria was always glad to brag that her daughter worked for a newspaper that most people knew about and respected, especially after the *Post* became a household name publishing the Pentagon Papers and covering the Watergate scandal.

"But Wanda, you have a baby, and a mortgage," she said.

Nevertheless, I cast my lot with *USA Today*, which came onto the scene in 1982 with stories that were shorter than in most newspapers, dueling editorials, diverse content and images on Page One, color photographs, and groundbreaking informational graphics. I was leaving a very traditional newspaper with its gray headlines, long stories, and black and white images.

This would be the first time I would work for a woman. So rare were women leaders in newsrooms that I had never had that opportunity before. Karen was clearly on the fast track at *USA Today*. She had been a deputy managing editor in the Life Section and now she was a managing editor. As it turned out, she would be my supervisor only for a year before she was promoted again, to senior editor for enterprise and data journalism. She later became editorial page editor and then made history when she became the first female editor of *USA Today* (1999–2004).

Memories are short and after Karen and I were both retired from daily journalism, Joanne Lippman was named editor-in-chief and touted by *USA Today's* marketing folks as the first female top editor. The newspaper received a barrage of negative social media posts from those of us who knew better, and *USA Today* was compelled to run a correction, giving Karen her props.

ONE THING I HAVE learned over the years is to take advantage of every reasonable opportunity that comes my way, even if it seemed impossible to fit it into my life. My personal confidence and leadership came from years of participating in leadership classes and with opportunities to lead. However, one opportunity I almost passed up came in 1987, a year after I joined *USA Today*.

Executive Editor Ron Martin called me into his office one day. "I want you to consider this program," he said, pushing a brochure across his desk.

The program was MTC, the Management Training Center at Northwestern University's Kellogg Graduate School of Business. The eight-week program was an immersive course to prepare diverse (mostly racial minorities) newspaper professionals to become executives, not just in newsrooms but on the business side in departments like advertising, circulation, finance, marketing and human resources. The program, informally known as a "mini-MBA" for newspaper professionals, or "publisher's school," was created by the Maynard Institute to increase the capacity of media organizations to promote more people of color into top leadership roles. *USA Today* would pay the $5,000 fee plus all travel expenses, Martin told me.

I scanned the brochure, which indicated that training would take place five to six days a week, that participants would be required to work in cohorts to produce a case study using the instructional topics of circulation math, managing change, business ethics, conflict resolution, performance assessment, marketing and advertising, media law and antitrust, joint ventures, women and minorities in management, strategic planning, information systems, capital and operational budgeting, First Amendment issues, and production and pressroom leadership. About two-thirds of the way into the program, participants would complete a two-week internship-type visit to a newspaper and work side by side with a publisher—the CEO of a newspaper— to learn the practical applications of the concepts discussed in the program's classroom studies.

The aggressive graduate-level agenda was daunting, but that's not what made me hesitate.

"Ron, this is flattering but I can't possibly be gone for two months," I found myself telling this generous man who was showing his confidence in my ability to master this program and come back as a rising star at the newspaper. "I can't possibly leave my family and go off to school," I responded, thinking about my husband and assuming he could not take care of four-year-old Shelby without me.

He pushed the brochure back across his desk toward me. "Take this with you," he said. "Think about it overnight."

I would not be the first *USA Today* newsroom staff member to attend the Management Training Center. Reporter Dorothy Bland had attended and was later promoted to run the *USA Today* library, turning it into a revenue stream. Caesar Andrews, editor at Gannett News Service located in the building with *USA Today*, attended and then left to become executive editor at the *Detroit Free Press*.

That evening during dinner I said to Lloyd, "You'll never guess what Ron wants me to do," sharing details of my conversation about the program at Northwestern.

"And why can't you go?" Lloyd asked.

Before the night was over, Willie Lloyd, this man who has encouraged me in everything I've ever done in our marriage, had cobbled together an amazing support group that included next-door neighbors on both sides, another neighbor down the street who would deliver her son and Shelby to the same summer camp, and Lloyd's sister who would take some of the weekend duty by having Shelby stay with her family, which included Shelby's three-year-old "sister-cousin," Jessica. Weekend duty meant making sure the girls got to youth activities at our church on Saturday mornings and to worship services on Sunday.

There were no more excuses. The next morning I confidently went into Ron's office and accepted the opportunity to leave in a few weeks for the program at Northwestern. After eight weeks, Lloyd traveled to Illinois to observe and celebrate my graduation from the Management Training Center, and I returned to my work as a deputy managing editor at *USA Today*. By then, Karen Jurgensen had been promoted out of the department and Peter Prichard, another star Gannett editor, was my new boss. He greeted me warmly, welcoming me back to the Cover Stories section.

One of the first things I did my first day back was to email Ron Martin, letting him know I had returned and thanking him for the awesome opportunity.

He quickly responded and asked if I had time for lunch. We went downstairs to Windows, and he listened intently as I gave him a rundown on what I had learned at Northwestern. His few questions did not let on to what would happen next. After lunch we got on the elevator and pushed the buttons for our respective floors. When we got to the floor where I would get off and return to my desk in Cover Stories, Ron said, "Got a minute, come talk to me in my office."

I followed him up one more floor, and we walked into his office where he explained that due to a resignation he wanted to promote me to managing editor for newsroom administration. I didn't even know there was such a thing.

There wasn't. Donna Rome, the director of newsroom administration, had informed Ron that she was leaving the newspaper to work with her husband in his business. Rome's title as director fit with her business background. She was not a journalist.

Two months after Ron suggested that I step away from the newsroom and my family for training at Northwestern, I was reaping the benefit of the confidence that he and my husband had in me. This promotion became the springboard for the rest of my career in Gannett newsrooms—from deputy managing editor, to managing editor to senior editor at *USA Today*, and a top editor in two additional newsrooms. The sacrifice I made by leaving my family for eight weeks paid off financially by more than tripling my total compensation over the next few years.

Three years later, on the day of my second promotion at *USA Today*, my mother said something that at first puzzled me, and maybe even pissed me off. I was then a senior editor, reporting directly to the editor of *USA Today*, and in her way of congratulating me, Gloria said, "Wanda, I think your career is really about to take off now."

"*About* to take off?" Here I was, a woman who came out of the Jim Crow South and dared to work for mainstream daily newspapers. I was almost at the top of the newsroom organization chart for one of the largest-circulation newspapers in the nation, overseeing a staff of more than four hundred, and responsible for five budgets with annual expenditures totaling more than $40 million. And all Gloria Walker could come up with was that my career was "*about* to take off."

In the end, I had to admit that mother knew best. I could not have imagined how much farther my career would take me.

I DIDN'T RECOGNIZE THE caller ID, a number from the local 703 Virginia Area Code.

When the desk phone rang I had already risen from my office chair, standing there in my proper business suit and high-heeled pumps supporting dancing feet that were ready to race down the hall to the conference room to sit at the head of the table and lead one of the daily *USA Today* news meetings. I was always keen about getting into the room before the meeting time, aware that my leadership encouraged others to take a seat so the meeting would begin on time.

The director at my daughter's summer camp was calling me.

"Mrs. Lloyd, I need to share something that happened with Shelby today."

My heart raced, fearful that my five-year-old daughter had fallen and cracked open her skull on the Alexandria campus, or she had run off from the grounds and the police were looking for her—or worse, she had drowned in the pool, although the last fear was probably not the case because when she was two years old I had made sure to enroll Shelby in swimming lessons through her day-care program.

"By the time we called all of the kids out of the pool today, Shelby had dropped her towel in the water," this director told me. "The children take a rest and quiet down on their towels after pool time. Shelby asked one of the other little girls if she could share her dry towel. The little girl told Shelby no, because she said 'my granddaddy said I can't let black people touch me because the black might wear off on me.'"

My mind, now far away from the urgency of the news meeting going on down the hall without me, struggled to process what I just heard.

"The black might wear off?" I repeated into the phone, not just to say it to the camp director, but to myself.

Stunned, I walked around my desk and closed the office door. Someone else would lead the meeting. My silent tears were starting to fall. I was angry that I had lived through the Jim Crow years when we were told when, where, and how we could exist; had survived the humiliation of being called "nigger," of being spat at, of living a dual life of the best black this and the best black that —not just the best at something. I had grown up in the South, where we were never surprised in the 1950s and 1960s to hear some dumb stuff about what white people thought about us or said out loud to us, or denied us the right to the best education, or careers or neighborhood amenities.

Here I was more than twenty years after leaving the Jim Crow South and some white grandfather had instilled in one of his own that my child was a danger to his child because mine was black.

I was not mad at the child; it wasn't her fault. And I was not mad at the director because she told me the child, the daughter of a camp employee, was immediately sent home for the day after she was confronted with the reason my Shelby was left standing, crying by the pool because this little girl had denied sharing a towel. Shelby was not old enough to understand the racist statement "the black might wear off." Shelby was likely just not happy that someone she probably considered to be a friend had denied her the opportunity to share her towel, her space, although Shelby's lesson was clearly to be more careful with her own towel from then on.

But as my fingers swept away my own tears, I recognized that I had to go home that night and explain to my daughter—as best I could explain it—the lesson this little white girl had learned from her grandfather, someone who was probably still steeped in the racist behavior of his own ancestors.

I had not imagined that I would still be dealing with this kind of racism directed toward my own child. Now I fear that Shelby may someday have to deal with racism with her children, and her children's children. The thought angers me to this day.

A HANDWRITTEN NOTE FROM one of our editors showed up on my desk one day in 1988. I had just been promoted to senior editor for newsroom administration, where I had oversight for the team responsible for functions including staffing, performance evaluations, budgeting, supplies, and resources, staff training, internships, and the loaner program—a constantly transitioning group of dozens of journalists who came from other newsrooms in Gannett, *USA Today's* parent company, to work in ours.

Our staff was overwhelmingly young, the average age thirty-two. About half of us were women. Unlike most traditional large newsrooms made up mostly of men and more seasoned journalists, the *USA Today* newsroom was made up of men and women who were just beginning to make marriage and having children a priority.

"There seems to be an exceptional amount of miscarriages here," the note began. "Two people in News had miscarriages last week, and I know of at least six miscarriages just in the news department in the past 12–18 months. For sure there are likely other reasons involved here, but it seems that someone might want to be assured that *USA Today* isn't in any way contributing to the process."

It fell to me to help lead the effort to find out what was happening. It is difficult to express the emotions we went through as we watched colleagues suffer these losses, especially because we didn't connect the dots for more than a year, too late for many to consider that their miscarriages may have been caused not by nature but maybe by what we later came to know as Sick Building Syndrome, or SBS. The Environmental Protection Agency defines SBS as "situations in which building occupants experience acute health and comfort effects that appear to be linked to time spent in a building."

Based on a 1984 World Health Organization report, some of the causes of SBS can be attributed to chemical or biological contaminants or inadequate ventilation. In some cases, sick buildings follow on the heels of renovation of facilities. Over about a two-year period, our newsroom floors were being renovated.

To our credit, the company was transparent throughout the vetting of our building discoveries by telling the staff what we knew about the investigation. Karen Jurgensen, then a fellow senior editor, was assigned the task of speaking to each of the women identified as having had miscarriages, to ask them specific personal details of their circumstances. Most were anxious to talk to her; only one was too pained to cooperate. By January 1989 at least fifteen miscarriages were known to have occurred, yet during the same time we had eleven live births.

I recall these details mostly from my notes and a speech I was asked to deliver in June 1989 at the technology conference of the American Newspaper Publishers Association (ANPA). This group had read about our so-called "cluster" of miscarriages and wanted to hear what steps we took to investigate and prevent further losses. One thing is clear from my notes. Women leaders in the company played major roles in the investigation and solutions. The response might not have been as strong in companies with fewer women leaders than Gannett had placed at *USA Today* and elsewhere in the company. Having women as key leaders was one of the reasons I was attracted to Gannett in the first place. Now it was paying off, to ensure women overall would have confidence in an investigation of what could turn out to be a life or death situation.

Our investigation became a case study in crisis management. It was a learning experience on how to manage a large building project and how to show compassion without becoming alarmist. It gave me real-time instruction in a place that included a large workforce of women. Like with people of color, it does not do much good to build a diverse workforce that includes women if consideration and compassion for the uniqueness of these individuals is not a part of the equation.

I told the ANPA tech conference participants that we took these steps.

• A Health/Workplace Task Force of managers and other employees was formed to guide a study, to ensure that lines of communication would be open. *USA Today* Publisher Cathie Black led the task force and other members included a medical reporter and a clinical counselor from our contract employee assistance program. Employees were invited to several open meetings to help guide our thinking.

• We asked the technical staff at ANPA to come into our building and randomly test personal computers and the video display terminals used in our newsrooms. (Fortunately, they determined that radiation levels were below established safety levels.) The newspaper provided lead aprons—the kind some are given when getting dental X-rays—to all women who were pregnant or admitted they were trying to conceive.

• We informed our workforce of the availability of Material Safety Data Sheets for substances related to production of the newspaper and construction around the building. Several women asked to share these sheets with their doctors.

• We hired two independent labs to test carpet samples, wallboard, paint, glue, air quality and water. During the initial testing process, we found higher-than-acceptable lead levels in a few water fountains installed in the walls. All water fountains on twenty-two floors in the company's rented two towers were shut down and we brought in portable water fountains, which were replenished with fresh bottles weekly. When we reported the information about the water supply to our staff, we offered to pay for off-site testing of dependent infants if a mother tested positive with high blood levels of lead. None of the children tested positive for lead.

• Finally, we took a step almost unheard of in corporate responsibility at the time. Gannett contacted NIOSH, the National Institute for Occupational Safety and Health, the agency responsible for conducting research and making recommendations to prevent work-related injury and illnesses. NIOSH reacted quickly. It followed some of the private testing groups to conduct air sampling and interviews with the women who had miscarriages.

I don't recall if it was determined that we actually had a statistical cluster of miscarriages. What I do know is that having gone through this painful time we were forced to address some ancillary offshoots of workplace issues, such as stress, ergonomics, and smoking. A second task force was formed to look into establishing a company-wide smoking policy. The staff became much more open about concerns for health of all our workers, but for me there was a keener interest in the well-being of women. At the time, Mollie Jackson, one of my direct reports, was pregnant and I constantly reminded her to excuse herself from the presence of noxious fumes or stressful situations during the building renovation. I reminded her not to stretch herself beyond the seven and a half-hour workday. Every baby became precious to us, including Mollie's, who fortunately was born healthy.

My own daughter, Shelby, was six or seven at the time of our investigation. She was on my mind throughout this entire ordeal. I concluded my speech at the technology conference this way:

As a manager and a mother, I'd like to think we all learned something from this experience. The most important are two "C" words—compassion and communication. We are heartbroken for the women and men who suffered losses. But the unfortunate situation of the past eighteen months has opened the lines of communication like never before. We are all better for that.

IN GANNETT, I BENEFITED from the corporate value of diversity at all levels. I quickly moved into a position of influence in the company by helping to assess and recruit talent. I was included in a class of the Gannett Leadership Academy, a program for leaders who were targeted for promotion. Before long I found myself on the circuit to train newsroom professionals at places like the Poynter Institute in St. Petersburg, Florida, the American Press Institute in Reston, Virginia, the non-profit Freedom Forum (an outgrowth of the former Gannett Foundation), and in journalism programs on university campuses and newsrooms across the country.

One day I got a call from our corporate office telling me that Gannett CEO John Curley had selected me to be on the cover of the company's 1993 annual report, a document that would be distributed to all of the publicly traded company's shareholders and corporate executives. The sixty-eight-page report printed on slick heavy paper was also sent to Gannett's board members, who included at the time former First Lady Rosalynn Carter; African American syndicated columnist Carl T. Rowan; Stuart T. K. Ho, chairman and president of Capital Investment of Hawaii; and John J. Louis Jr., a former U.S. ambassador to Great Britain.

In my cover shot I am standing with a rolled-up copy of *USA Today* smartly placed under my arm. I was wearing a blue two-piece knit dress and it was no coincidence that I decided that day to wear a prized piece of jewelry that spoke to my African American heritage. It is a black cameo designed by African American artist Coreen Simpson, someone I met at a National Association of Black Journalists conference in Atlanta, where she came to show and sell some of her pieces.

Inside the annual report, in a story titled "Leadership in Employment Development," the report stated:

In 1993 *USA Today* Senior Editor Wanda Lloyd won the Ida B. Wells Award, named after the black pioneer publisher, for her distinguished leadership in the hiring and advancement of minorities. Lloyd was the first woman to receive the award, sponsored by the National Conference of Editorial Writers, the National Association of Black Journalists and the University of Kansas.

In accepting the Wells award, Lloyd mentioned that she had had no role models or mentors early in her career—that she was, in fact, the first black journalist she had ever met. "It's made me more driven in my work and in wanting to help young minority journalists," Lloyd says. "I see so many who don't have mentors—like I didn't—so I try to give them those under-the-table hints and advice.

"We need to value people for their differences, and not penalize them. My dream is that these differences will become something we look for rather than fear and resist."

Even though *USA Today* was considered to be the newspaper industry's leading organization for diversity in staffing and coverage, that was no panacea for one big breaking news story. In the fall of 1995 the O. J. Simpson murder trial was coming to an end. Simpson, the former college and pro football standout and actor and broadcast personality was charged with killing his ex-wife, Nicole Brown Simpson, and her friend, Ron Goldman. The lengthy and internationally publicized jury trial ended with a verdict on October 3, 1995.

Like with most big developing stories, at *USA Today* we had a plan for the end of the trial. Day after day we waited for the jury to come back. Once the verdict was in, we knew we would increase the number of pages, taking the size of the next day's paper up to the number of pages needed for the stories that were planned. Photographers were in place to get the all-important shot for Page One.

My office was on the fifteenth floor of the *USA Today* tower, where the Life and Money sections were located. News and Sports were on the fourteenth floor. As soon as word zoomed through the newsroom that the jury was coming back, some of us gathered in the News section. Instinctively, I guess, we wanted to be in the "news" part of the newsroom to experience the end of what had become known as the "trial of the century."

Dozens of journalists gathered under ceiling-mounted TV sets sprinkled around the room. I was standing near the assignment desk, the place where the editors worked. As the verdicts were handed to the judge you could almost hear a pin drop on the carpeted floors in our newsroom. Only the gentle tap-tap-tapping of a few computer users was heard around us. No one spoke, phones didn't ring. The world, it seemed, was on hold for the verdict.

"Not guilty," we heard once.

Silence in the newsroom. I didn't move, but in a few seconds I heard a sniffle. Without turning my head my eyes scanned from one side of the room to the other. A young white female editor was crying.

From the courtroom came the second verdict. "Not guilty." More sniffles. Another young white female editor was crying.

I didn't expect this. I didn't know what to do or say.

When it was over, I returned to my office a floor above, where I sat at my desk and started to read some of the first news alerts about the trial coming across from the Associated Press and other news services.

Reading the stories, I was feeling gleeful—not happy that two people were dead without justice—but happy with the verdict. Throughout the ordeal of the investigation and trial, most people were sad that two people were killed, and I shared that empathy. But in the minutes after the verdict was read I was feeling pretty good that someone with whom we identified racially had avoided going to prison. It was all about the economics that made up for some of the unjust verdicts of young black men who were given life sentences—or worse—for crimes they didn't commit, or decades-long sentences for possessing small amounts of drugs.

My back was to the door of my office. Seconds after I sat down I felt the quiet presence of someone standing behind me. I turned and saw one, then two, three—several of my African American newsroom colleagues had followed me. I was one of the few African Americans on staff with an office, with a door that could be closed for privacy. Someone else came in and shut the door.

Our emotions erupted, a pandemonium of a group high-five. It was amazing to me that even though we hadn't discussed the trial's expected outcome, we African Americans had the same feeling. O J. Simpson had plenty of money and he had beaten a system that could have been stacked against him as a black male. He had hired a dream team of lawyers led by the dapperly dressed Johnnie Cochran, the attorney who amazed us with his legal strategy and entertained us with his poetic antics.

In arguing about reasonable doubt of his client, if the glove "doesn't fit, you must acquit," Cochran told the jury in his closing remarks.

But there was a price to pay. All around us there were young white women who identified with Nicole Brown Simpson. They were in pain. A woman was killed, and no one would pay for her murder. We soon learned that the chasm of feelings was the same across the nation. African Americans were celebrating Simpson's success, and young white women were feeling like they lost a sister without justice for her murder.

To his credit, Peter Prichard, editor of *USA Today*, picked up on the divide right away. He wanted to understand what was happening around us. Prichard asked me to set up listening sessions so staff members could air their concerns. In those sessions we talked about our different emotions, and why one group didn't have a clue that the other group would react the way we did. Young white women didn't know that we could not have imagined how much they identified with Nicole, the victim. African Americans expected the court system would assume that O. J. was just another n-word and punish him as black men had been treated for generations, whether guilty or not. In these listening sessions we examined our coverage of the trial, and we assigned a story about this issue that was dividing the nation. As a staff, we did what we could to heal and come back together, although I don't think we ever totally healed.

ONE MORNING IN FEBRUARY 1995 I walked into the newsroom at about 7:30, my normal arrival time. The building was quiet and almost empty. I went into the kitchen in our suite of offices and prepared coffee and a bowl of cereal. Then I settled down at my desk and opened email. A note to the staff from Dave Mazzarella, who succeeded Peter Prichard as editor of *USA Today* in December 1994, was waiting for us. I was stunned at the internal memo.

Robert Dubill, a senior editor like me, was named executive editor.

Thomas McNamara was promoted from managing editor for News to associate editor of the newspaper.

Hal Ritter, managing editor for the Money section, became managing editor for News.

John Hillkirk was elevated from deputy managing editor for Money to managing editor for News.

Columnists Joe Urschel and Taylor Buckley were named the newspaper's first senior writers.

Mazzarella had essentially elevated and repositioned six white men in the newsroom. No women or people of color were promoted, or even discussed.

I was furious, as much with Mazzarella as with myself. When Mazz, as he was known, became editor of the newspaper we didn't start as friends. There was a distance between us and I sensed that he would not come to depend on me to help sort out staffing needs as the other top editors had since I came to the newspaper in 1986. I continued to try to do my job, even though I realized that I was being kept in the dark on many of the decisions Mazz was making about content and staffing. Mazz was different from the previous top editors. With these moves he managed to set back many of the diversity gains we proudly made under previous leadership.

"Do you realize what this looks like?" I asked Mazz as soon after he arrived in his office that morning. "You promoted six white men. Did you even *consider* women or people of color?"

"Frankly," he said, "that never occurred to me. I moved some of our best people into key positions."

Mazzarella had shuffled a deck of white men into high profile and higher leadership positions without any consideration for diversity. "Best people," to him, meant white and male. With that, I knew it would soon be time for me to move on.

18. ASNE and a Presidential Question

"I think it would be a good idea for you to join either ASNE [American Society of News Editors] or APME [Associated Press Managing Editors]," Ron Martin told me one day shortly after I returned from the Management Training Center at Northwestern. "It would be a way for you to have an impact on the industry, and as a member you'll learn a lot, too."

I knew of both organizations, but I had not considered that I was eligible to join one of the venerable organizations of top editors of newspapers from across the nation. I also knew that most of those top editors were white and male, and I just didn't see myself becoming part of a group that was so different from my own cultural experience. I had grown up and gone to schools in a segregated society and I was still carrying a lot of baggage from that part of my life. I was confident of my professional skills, but not my social skills.

At the time, my industry vision was limited to the scope of African American journalists. I had joined the National Association of Black Journalists (NABJ) in 1981 and begun to work my way through the maze of its committees, task forces, programs, and relationships. When Ron suggested that I join one of the "white" associations, I didn't have the self-confidence that would position me anywhere more than among journalists who looked like me—my African American colleagues.

Ron gave me a quick rundown on the differences in the work of the two groups: APME deals with mostly journalism content issues, and ASNE on building the capacity for newsroom leadership.

I chose ASNE, because my interest in building newsroom leaders was already emerging in NABJ. ASNE holds an important annual conference, at which the attendees participate in workshops, listen to top-level speakers, and work in committees. In the years I was active in ASNE, the conventions were mostly held in Washington, to take advantage of the proximity of speakers who were members of Congress, federal agency heads, people from political think tanks, and even presidents and vice presidents.

To say there was a lack of racial diversity in ASNE is an understatement. It may have been one reason Ron, who by then I considered a mentor, suggested that I join. He has always supported diversity in the news organizations where he worked, but he was rarely vocally on the front lines of advocacy. He encouraged me and others to do that.

Of course, diversity within ASNE and other mainstream news associations was limited by the number of women and people of color who then held top positions that qualified them for membership. By the time I joined, the organization's gender diversity was slightly better than its racial diversity. ASNE was founded in 1922, and sixty-five years later Katherine "Kay" Fanning, editor of the *Christian Science Monitor,* was elected as the first female ASNE president (1987–1988). There was a "women's caucus" at the annual conferences, and Fanning remarked that the first one was held in her hotel room because there were so few ASNE women members. As the number of female members grew, the caucus moved to small hotel hospitality rooms, then to bigger ones.

Professionally and socially, I grew up in ASNE. I plunged in by joining committees, the foundation of the organization's work. Ultimately I chaired ASNE committees of Human Resources, Floor Managers, Nominations, and Minorities (later called Diversity). I became co-editor (with Peter Bhatia, who would become ASNE's first Asian American president) of the *ASNE Bulletin,* the organization's magazine. For many years I served on the Program Committee, which honed my passion for programming, a skill I have used in many other organizations.

At various ASNE conferences I introduced speakers and participated on panels. One year I was asked to introduce Cornel West, the prolific Harvard/Princeton professor, philosopher, author, and public intellectual who was invited as the featured speaker on diversity. Someone on the Program

Committee suggested and secured him. Admittedly, he was not my choice for a speaker. This may sound petty to some, but as brilliant as West is, his rhetoric has often been an enigma to me mostly because of the style of his delivery and his stuck-in-the-seventies appearance. But getting this nationally recognized figure to ASNE was a huge deal, and I accepted the challenge to present him to our members.

The day didn't turn out well. First, I was tasked to sit with West in a hospitality room in Washington's J. W. Marriott Hotel leading up to his time on stage. Sitting in a room with Cornel West and listening to his activist rant tested my ability to focus. I listened, but I'm sure he picked up on my distraction. (Cornel West, if you read this and you happen to remember that day, please accept my apology. It was probably the mediocre level of my ability to receive your message and not any lack of brilliance of your thoughts that drove my behavior.) When we moved from the holding room to the ballroom, we took our places on stage, me standing at the podium and West seated next to a small table with a pitcher of water and two drinking glasses.

When I looked out into the audience I saw the quiet rush of the backs of hundreds of white men in suits heading for the door. The full room of editors present for the session preceding ours apparently suddenly needed to heed the call of nature, or they had to get to phones to take care of some pretty important business, even though generous program breaks were built into the conference schedule. Or maybe it was something else. Whatever the reasons, these editors chose that moment to escape.

By the time I finished the introduction, the room was sparsely populated with the few minority and female editors, ASNE Board and Program Committee members, and a small number of invited guests from minority journalism organizations who had come specifically to hear West. It was embarrassing to present him to an almost empty room. Nevertheless, West rose and presented his speech. I don't recall whether he mentioned the white flight stampede out of the room.

AFTER I WAS IN ASNE for a few years, I was nominated to run for a position on the organization's board, a prestigious group that met twice a year and charted the organization's path for impact in the industry. Newspapers were facing many issues—economic sustainability, readership and demographic changes, declining customer base, the emergence of new technology, and staff retention. We were on the cusp of change, and the ASNE board confronted these trends every year with surveys, reports, programming, and advocacy. And there were the usual fights against assaults on the First Amendment.

I didn't win election the first time I was nominated. A board member consoled me and said I should expect to be nominated again, that members needed to see me work in the organization and get to know me. I was told to keep up the committee work, which I did. The next year I was nominated and I missed again, but by only a few votes.

"I'll never do this again," I remember telling John Seigenthaler after that second loss. Seigenthaler was editor and publisher of the *Tennessean* in Nashville and the founding editorial page editor at *USA Today*, roles that kept him on airplanes as he spent part of each week in Nashville and part at *USA Today* in northern Virginia. He was a strong defender of the First Amendment, which guarantees five freedoms, including freedom of the press. In the 1960s, Seigenthaler stepped away from journalism for a while when he served as a field officer and special assistant to U.S. Attorney General Robert Kennedy. Seigenthaler was severely beaten in the head with a pipe when a mob attacked a busload of Freedom Riders in Montgomery and he tried to intervene.

Seigenthaler and I became close colleagues, and I respected his good counsel. He served as ASNE president in 1988–1989. "Don't despair," he told me about losing the ASNE board election for the second time. "It took me five times before I was elected to the board."

"John," I replied, "I can absolutely assure you that I will not humiliate myself by running five times."

The following year I was nominated for a third time and was elected to my first three-year term. I won again three years later, serving the maximum six years.

Serving on the ASNE board broadened my visibility in the newspaper industry. As one of few African American members and a board member, most of the top editors and many other journalists in the nation actually knew the name Wanda Lloyd, and they associated me with *USA Today*. I began to get calls from across the nation to be a speaker or to give my advice on minority job candidates. Editors would call me to read and weigh in on diversity in stories they were planning to run in their newspapers. Reporters from national news organizations called to ask me to be a quoted source for national stories about newsroom diversity.

ASNE opened a lot of doors for me. I was asked to serve as a juror for the Pulitzer Prize for two years (and ten years later for another two years of Pulitzer service). I served six years on the Accrediting Committee for Journalism Education (and, almost unheard of, years later I was elected to serve six more years). I was invited to become a member and a mentor for journalists in the Asian American Journalists Association's program for aspiring leaders. I wrote articles for media industry journals and magazines. Newspapers asked me to come to their cities and help them develop a diversity audit, a formal process to measure diversity content. And universities and organizations of journalism academic leaders asked me to speak on their campuses and at national conferences.

In 1993, I lectured in Germany at a conference for American students enrolled in U.S. Department of Defense high school journalism classes. (That was my second trip to Europe; I had spent a week with Shelby and her eighth-grade class touring France.) Lloyd accompanied me on the trip to Nuremberg, Germany, where a group of American journalism professionals and professors worked with the students in workshops and writing exercises. When I returned home I wrote an article for *USA Today's* international edition, where I described how we worked with students in Germany in a building called "The Berg—a centuries-old castle that serves as a *Jugendgasthaus* or youth hostel."

CNN was a relatively new national network in the 1980s. The network headed by Ted Turner followed ASNE's annual newsroom census, a data report on the number of minorities (and eventually women) in newsrooms, and I was asked at least a couple of times to appear on CNN's "Reliable Sources," the weekly talk show that focuses on the news media with the founding host Bernard Kalb. I never saw myself as a TV personality, and I had to bury my shyness to hold my own on these pre-recorded shows.

The first time I appeared on the show with seasoned guests it took about five minutes to realize that I had to jump in there and be as aggressive as the others (men) to be heard in the discussion. I revived my training with The Masquers, my high school drama group. In addition to the expertise I brought regarding media diversity, I added a dose of theatrics. After that, I was comfortable in the role. But I was so shy about seeing myself on TV that every time I was on the prerecorded weekend shows, I would go for a walk while they were being broadcast. I also appeared on "Both Sides with Jesse Jackson," the public affairs show hosted by the activist minister. Fortunately, Lloyd taped all of the shows, and eventually I would go into a quiet space alone and watch myself. My self-critique helped me get better in future TV appearances.

ASNE gave me the opportunity for quite a bit of domestic travel. Traditionally, the president of ASNE hosted each year's fall board meeting in his or her city. As part of the visits, we would tour the president's community. These board trips took me to places like Minneapolis; Sarasota, Florida; Portland, Oregon; Colorado Springs, and Austin.

The 2000 meeting in Austin was one of my favorite ASNE board trips because President Rich Oppel, then editor of the *Austin-American Statesman*, took us on a bus trip to the LBJ Ranch, the national historic park in Stonewall, Texas, where President Johnson was born, lived, died, and is buried. Lyndon and Lady Bird Johnson donated their property to the National Park Service but retained lifetime rights to use the house. After Johnson's death in 1973, Mrs. Johnson lived on there until her death in 2007.

On the day we visited, the First Lady's staff hosted the ASNE leaders and our guests with a tour of the ranch house and grounds. Then we went for a cookout on the banks of the Pedernales River, where LBJ spent a lot of his boyhood time. My husband and I were seated next to Mrs. Johnson, who was sight-impaired but still with a sharp mind and a keen memory of the past. She was a kind, patient woman who gave us a lot of insight into many aspects of her husband's presidential years, including the immediate aftermath of the assassination of President Kennedy when Johnson was quickly sworn in as president. Mrs. Johnson had a front-row seat to many events during the civil rights movement and shared some of those memories.

On the tour inside the Johnsons' house, something most visitors to the ranch don't get to do, we observed that not much had changed. It was a modest home with dated furnishings. In the family room, I asked the woman who was our tour guide, an assistant to Mrs. Johnson, about a vintage rocking chair.

"That was the president's favorite chair," she said.

"May I sit in it?"

"Sure," she said without hesitation.

I took a seat, rocked a few times, and imagined how it must have been for a president to come home from Washington to the comfort of such a cozy room and relax in his favorite chair.

The Johnsons had separate bedrooms across a hallway. On the wall near his bed, the rotary dial red phone for secure calls was still there. I had learned about these red phones at some point in school, although I doubt that a red phone exists for presidents today. In LBJ's bathroom, his vintage shaving brush and cans of shaving cream were still in the built-in medicine cabinet (yes, I opened the cabinet). His massive walk-in closet/dressing room was neatly arranged with rows of his suits and embossed leather cowboy boots—all clean and shiny—with heavy leather belts hanging from hooks and western hats on a shelf. It seemed like time stood still in that closet.

In Mrs. Johnson's bedroom, something really caught my eye. I spotted a sterling silver hand mirror on the first lady's dressing table and asked our guide about it. The mirror was exactly like one my grandmother had used every day. I used to watch as she styled her hair. She would sit in front of her own dresser mirror and hold up the silver hand mirror to check the back of her head. I was curious about Mrs. Johnson's mirror because I wanted to know about my grandmother's, which more than sixty years later I still have.

The guide didn't know, but when our group went outside and I had a chance to talk to Mrs. Johnson, I asked her about the mirror.

"Oh, I remember where I got it," she said. "It was a gift from Madame Chiang Kai-shek [Soong Mei-ling, wife of the former president of the Republic of China]."

When Lady Bird Johnson died in 2007, I wrote a Sunday column for the *Montgomery Advertiser*, where I was executive editor at the time, telling readers about my memory of the day we spent with the former first lady on the LBJ Ranch.

OVER THE YEARS, U.S. presidents have had a cordial relationship with the American Society of News Editors and have spoken at most of the national conferences when those meetings were held in Washington. As a committee chair and board member, I had the honor of sitting on the dais when presidents and vice presidents were the keynote speakers. I met George H. W. Bush, Bill Clinton, Al Gore, and George W. Bush. In every case the officials would go down the line of dais guests, shaking each person's hand and giving each of us a few seconds to exchange a quick greeting.

In 1994, President Clinton's staff made arrangements for ASNE members to visit the White House for a reception. The cursive-type invitation read:

> The President and Mrs. Clinton
> request the pleasure of your company
> at a reception to be held at
> The White House
> on Friday, April 15, 1994
> at six-thirty o'clock

So formal, yet so simple. As quickly as the invitations arrived, the ASNE staff alerted members who wanted to attend to submit information for background checks, including the name and information of a spouse or guest. When Lloyd and I arrived at the White House the night of the party, we were given a color-coded card indicating when we would go into the room with President Clinton to have a quick chat and take a photo with him.

I remember two significant conversations that night. First, as we were milling about the party with drinks in our hands, I spotted an ASNE member I didn't know. Her name tag identified her as Rexanna Keller Lester, managing editor at the *Savannah Morning News*.

"Hey, you're from Savannah?" I questioned. "I grew up in Savannah."

Rexanna, a white woman about my age, said she grew up on a farm in Oklahoma. She lived in Germany with her husband and young daughter before returning stateside and pursuing her career with Morris Communications. In Atlanta she was bureau chief for Morris News Service, with oversight for Washington and state government coverage, before transferring to Savannah to become managing editor of my hometown newspapers. The *Savannah Morning News* and *Evening Press* had not embraced the black community when I was a child. I never aspired to work for the newspapers, so forgive me if I was a bit suspicious meeting this white woman at a party at the White House. I didn't know her politics. But we quickly found our common ground—newspapers, editing, raising daughters, living in the South, and best of all an understanding that to survive and thrive newspapers would have to change by embracing diversity in content and staffing.

Rexanna and I were buddies for the rest of that evening, and we have been sister friends ever since. Growing up in an all-black restricted world in Savannah, I never imagined that I would have a white friend as close as a sister could be. When Lloyd, Shelby, and I would visit Savannah on vacation over the years, Rexanna and I hung out together, taking tours and sightseeing in the Historic District, shopping on Broughton Street at the iconic family-owned Globe Shoe Company, and exploring restaurants from the Historic District to the beach on Tybee Island. When she returned to Washington for ASNE conferences, Rexanna and I stuck to each other like glue in workshops, committee meetings, and luncheons. We always found time to steal away for a quick shopping trip.

When Rexanna's daughter, Vanessa, was married in Savannah, I was the only African American guest at the wedding, which elicited puzzling glances from Oklahoma-bred family members. "Now, *who* are you?" one of her relatives asked me at the reception. I had a great time giving as little information as possible. Rexanna would have to fill in the gaps about her only black guest later with her family.

The other person Lloyd and I spent time with at the White House party was David Gergen, a senior advisor in the Clinton administration (and before that an aide in the Nixon, Ford, and Reagan administrations; now a CNN political analyst and Harvard professor). Lloyd and I enjoyed a lengthy exchange with Gergen, who noticed that the color on our card to meet with the president had expired.

"You missed your window with the president," he said, but he assured us that he would get us into the room for our handshake and picture. We hung out with Gergen for a while, talking about politics and about the White House, and toward the end of the evening he personally escorted us into the room where we were number two or number three in line. We watched President Clinton interact with the ASNE members in front of us. As we approached the president, a door opened near where he was standing. In walked Hillary Clinton, the First Lady, who had been out of the White House for an event, returned and came into the room just as we approached the president. So we were among the few ASNE guests to get a picture with both Clintons; the picture of Wanda and Willie Lloyd and Bill and Hillary Clinton hangs in our living room.

My role in ASNE positioned me to work quietly with newspapers across the nation to consider people of color for leadership positions where they would become eligible to join ASNE. Over a few years, a handful of us built what we unofficially called the ASNE diversity "kitchen cabinet" to help build the ranks of newsroom leaders who were African American, Hispanic, Asian American, and women. My friend LaBarbara "Bobbi" Bowman, a former colleague at the *Washington Post* and *USA Today*, was director of Diversity Affairs at ASNE. She called us together from time to time when she needed support as she helped ASNE committee chairs create diverse annual conference programs. But our work went deeper.

When a person of color was promoted to assistant or deputy managing editor or higher in a daily newspaper newsroom, one of us would call the person, congratulate him or her, and urge them to join ASNE. Membership was no small commitment of time or money, though the fee was normally a cost borne by the newsroom's budget. Once these diverse editors joined, it was no accident that they quickly found themselves immersed in committee work and then nominated for board positions. After a couple of years on the ASNE board, some were elected onto the leadership path—a seven-year commitment of service—to become president of ASNE. At the same time, women were rapidly moving up newsroom leadership ladders, and they also joined ASNE.

For a while, the ASNE board was disproportionately more racially diverse than the organization's membership. As women and people of color on the board, we were the best example for how an organization can reach and exceed diversity goals, including in leadership. In the span of eight years, the following served as president:

- 2003–04, Peter K. Bhatia (Asian American), the *Oregonian*, Portland
- 2004–05, Karla Garrett Harshaw (African American), *Springfield* (Ohio) *News-Sun* and Cox Community Newspapers
- 2005–06, Rick Rodriguez (Hispanic), the *Sacramento* (California) *Bee*
- 2007–08, Gilbert Bailon (Hispanic), *Al Día*, Dallas, Texas, and the *St. Louis Post-Dispatch*
- 2010–11, Milton Coleman (African American), the *Washington Post*

Also, Kay Fanning was ASNE's first woman president in 1987–88, and ten years later Sandra Mims Rowe, then editor of the *Oregonian*, was the second woman president. Five other women (including Harshaw above) have served as president.

My participation on the ASNE board and on committees helped me overcome a great deal of the shyness I had as a young adult in what my grandmother used to call "mixed company"—conversations with black and white people in the same room. Slowly, my social confidence grew as I began to see myself on the same level as white people in the room at ASNE meetings and events. When we talked about journalism and newsroom leadership, I realized that my experiences were valuable. Race was no longer the barrier—or the issue. I soon found myself passionately leading discussions in committee meetings, sharing what I knew about newsroom culture, and advocating to make more people aware of diversity in news content.

At an ASNE conference luncheon in 2001, I helped write the next day's headlines. At the end of major speeches by high-powered guests, the ASNE president opens the floor for questions in this way: "As is our normal practice, only members of the Society may ask questions." Year after year I saw fellow ASNE members confidently rise and walk to one of the pre-positioned microphones on the floor and ask questions about national or world affairs.

I never thought I would have that much confidence, to stand and ask a question in front of hundreds of my newsroom peers. Year after year, program after program, I sat and listened to my colleagues make news by asking questions that would become the lead story on the nightly network news or on Page One in the next day's *Washington Post, New York Times,* and other papers. After the conference, the editors would go home across the nation and write columns about how they made news by pitching good questions to members of Congress or the president or vice president.

On April 5, 2001, Hillary Clinton, then the senator from New York, was the featured ASNE luncheon speaker. As Senator Clinton spoke, I started to visualize her not just as a former first lady or a current member of the U.S. Senate. I started to think about how smart she was, how confidently she spoke, how knowledgeable she was about global matters. Yet I also saw her as a wife and mother, just like me. Clinton and I are of the same generation of women who crashed through glass ceilings, served our communities, raised daughters, and consistently took on increasingly more challenging roles.

A question was forming in my mind. Before I knew what was happening, my feet were following my head to the microphone. As I stood, I still wasn't sure if I was about to embarrass myself by asking the question in the way it was coming together in my mind. There I was, standing in the middle of that big space, with network television cameras linked to the microphone with my voice and pointing at me from the back of the room. When I was recognized, I said this:

"Senator Clinton, you and I have something in common in that we are both the mothers and role models for college-age young women. And so, on behalf of Chelsea Clinton, Shelby Lloyd, and all young women who look up to us, please tell us if you will ever consider running to become the first female president of the United States."

Oh. My. God.

I said that?

First, silence in the room. Had I just made the biggest career mistake of *any* ASNE member? Then slight laughter, then rapt silence as she stumbled over her response to a question that apparently caught her by surprise.

Of course, her answer was "no."

"Thank you for your question," she responded. "That's not something I'm going to be doing. Right now I'm just planning to be the best senator I can be to represent the people of New York."

That pretty much wrote the next day's headlines. In a design that took up the majority of the tabloid front page of the April 6, 2001, *New York Post*, the headline appeared in big bold letters over a photo of the senator standing behind the microphone.

"HILL NO! Clinton says she'll NEVER run for prez"

On page three the *Post* ran what they labeled "New York Post Exclusive," a sixteen-inch story by Vincent Morris, under the all-caps headline: "HILL RULES OUT A PREZ RUN—EVER." Out of all of the issues the senator discussed in her speech, Morris's story followed up on my question.

Ironically, as we all know, Hillary Clinton did eventually run for president, twice, and her defeat under controversial circumstances in 2016 was a loss deeply felt by women across the nation.

19. From Big to Small

Sometimes having a seat at the table can be a clash of culture for working women who are raising families. It can mean having to make choices in life—between having power at work, power at home, or no power. In my case, the choice was to have it all.

In *The Making of McPaper: The Inside Story of USA Today*, Peter Prichard wrote about the chaotic 1982 launch and early life of the national Gannett newspaper. "McPaper" was the nickname given to *USA Today* in the beginning, because it reminded many journalists of the cookie-cutter ubiquity of McDonald's, the fast-food pioneer. *USA Today* gave readers quick reads with short stories, infographics, and color photos. I was not one of the pioneering journalists who worked at *USA Today* on Day One in 1982. I arrived three years later, but the launch-period stories are legendary.

In an early chapter, Prichard wrote about Nancy Woodhull, the founding managing editor of the A Section, where national and international news stories appeared. Like many *USA Today* "founders," Woodhull was a young wife and mother who found herself working from early in the morning until 11 p.m. many nights, making it difficult to spend quality time with her eighteen-month-old daughter, Tennie.

Woodhull's maternal dilemma was like that of many women in the newspaper business, with long workdays that sometimes blend one into the next. Some, like me, were fortunate to have supportive mates. Yet many of my female journalist friends never married, never had children, and in many cases didn't have much of a social life outside the network of colleagues. Many of us have moved from newspaper to newspaper, or changed markets for television news jobs. So much so that when we get together at conferences or industry meetings, our conversations often begin by figuring out our linkages: What do you do? Where have you worked? Who do you know? Where do you want to go next?

As the number of women in newsrooms was rising in the 1970s– 1990s, we newsroom managers were feeling intense pressure about work-life balance. Women saw the need to prove that we were cut from the same cloth as men who rarely, it seemed, had guilt about not seeing their families news day after news day, especially when big stories were breaking. At *USA Today*, according to Prichard's book and stories I heard firsthand from colleagues when I started working there, women were hired, promoted, and valued. At *USA Today's* beginning, there was little difference between the schedules kept by the hard-working men and the hard-working women who were managers and editors. Not that there should be much difference, but I heard from some men that they ultimately wished they had cut back on their hours instead of being the overworked and overwhelmed role models for women.

Prichard wrote of Woodhull's dilemma:

> Finally she would arrange to have her daughter, Tennie, brought each evening to the *USA Today* building about 6 p.m. She would spend forty-five minutes with her baby in the Great Eatery, the restaurant on the mall level of the building. Woodhull was afraid to tell (Executive Editor) Ron Martin what she was doing, so she always left an assistant on standby who was supposed to run down and fetch Woodhull if Martin wanted anything."

Over time I have heard women express angst about the amount of time they took to nurture their babies, but I don't think males in the newsroom would have recognized then that they, too, should have stepped away from work to take part in raising their children. It would take years for men to recognize their family shortfalls and the impact their drive may have had on women in the workplace.

I BATTLED MY OWN mothering dilemmas. Here's one.

There were three daily meetings at the big table in the conference room at the *Greenville News,* a daily newspaper in upstate South Carolina. I had left *USA Today* in June 1996, transferring within Gannett to Greenville, because I found conditions of diversity had become untenable and I was also ready to return to the South.

I created my own reverse migration after more than two decades in the hustle and bustle of the busy, expensive, crime-ridden nation's capital. To me, this was not a step down from a big newspaper to a smaller newsroom, but a step up in quality of life in a place that had a sense of community, a more affordable lifestyle, and tolerable winter weather.

Some former colleagues told me they were envious of our move. New colleagues in Greenville were skeptical, some asking if I was placed there to change things at the newspaper that Gannett had purchased just a few months before. I repeatedly said I accepted an opportunity that my husband and I thought was good for our family and my career. And that was the truth. In hindsight, I suppose it did look suspicious since I was the first Gannett journalist to invade the newspaper formerly owned by a local company. Outside the newsroom, Joyce Ray, a Gannett human resources director, preceded me in Greenville by a few months.

I had been a key player in the *USA Today* newsroom and in Gannett's corporate news division, and I saw the same opportunities in Greenville. I still had a seat at the table, just a table in a different state, a different newsroom.

As one of two managing editors—Chris Weston, a long-time *Greenville News* staff member was the other one—I often sat at one end of the table and ran the news meetings.

Shelby had attended Browne Academy, a small private school in Alexandria, Virginia, until her eighth-grade graduation. In Greenville, we enrolled her at Christ Church Episcopal School. During her ninth-grade year at Christ Church, I faced what I called the Tuesday afternoon challenge. Tuesday was the day I had a conflict between running the afternoon news meeting and getting Shelby to a math tutor who worked one-on-one with students at her house. It was one of those work-life balance challenges I had to figure out.

On those Tuesdays I wore an outfit with pockets, and when I parked in the garage under the newspaper's building, I would lock my handbag and driver's license inside the car and put my keys in my pocket. Then at about 2:30 when the afternoon news meeting was about to begin, I would go into the conference room, take my seat at one end of the table and get the meeting started. Those meetings often began with chit-chat while we waited for the section editors to file into the room. After the few informal pleasantries, we would get down to business:

"Sports," I would say, and the sports editor or representative would share that section's lineup for the next day's newspaper, pointing out any stories that might be important enough to be considered for Page One.

"Features," and the features department's lineup was shared. "Business." "Metro," and so on.

About fifteen minutes into the meeting I would excuse myself, and Chris or another editor would take the lead, calling on any department editors who hadn't yet shared their lineup. While the meeting continued, I would dash for the stairwell just outside the main second floor newsroom door and to my car in the garage. Quickly but safely, I drove the short distance to Christ Church school, where Shelby would be waiting out front. She got in the car and we made small talk about her day while I drove to the tutor's house and dropped her off with a smile and a hug. Lloyd would be there an hour later to pick her up. Then I drove back to the newspaper, returned to the newsroom conference room, and took my seat while the meeting was still underway and, frankly, I hadn't missed much of the discussion.

The only person I am sure who knew about my Tuesday afternoon routine was Gwen Shipman, the newsroom's administrative assistant. A mother herself, she understood that sometimes one has to do what's necessary to balance work and life, and I knew that—like Nancy Woodhull's lookout at *USA Today*—Gwen would keep my confidence unless in an emergency. I'm happy to say that the Tuesday trips to the tutor paid off. Today Shelby is in a business that requires her to do math all day every day. She likes it and is good at it.

BY THE TIME OUR family moved to Greenville, many people had seen my picture and the story about my impending arrival as managing editor. I was the first African American top editor in Greenville, and many people in the community quickly reached out to welcome us.

First, let me put this out there. Shelby was angry and combative when we told her over the summer that we were going to move her away from her friends to a place she never heard of. None of us had visited Greenville until I started talking to Gannett about the transfer. I flew down first to meet with John Pittman, the paper's long-time executive editor, and Steve Brandt, the publisher and CEO. A few weeks after that, Lloyd and I visited Greenville so he could see the community and we could look for a house.

Shelby spent summers in Savannah with my mother so she was clueless that her life was about to change. When she found out, there was much sobbing over the phone. She was almost thirteen, and she was convinced that her life was about to end. She would be leaving her house, her friends, her church, and members of her extended paternal family. It was a lot for her to process. I have to admit that, for a time, it made me feel like the worst mother in the world to be forcing this change on her.

Gloria said Shelby cried for a few hours that night, but the next day she called and made some demands. "Okay, if I have to move I want three things. I want a dog, a pool, and a basketball hoop in the driveway."

We found a house with a community pool, which Shelby hardly ever used, and we had a basketball hoop installed in the driveway. There was never a dog.

Shortly after the move, four welcome-to-Greenville parties were hosted in our honor. Four and a half years later when my job changed again, friends hosted seven going-away parties for us. Greenville embraced us.

Over the decades we spent moving from place to place, newspaper to newspaper, I was fortunate to be able to connect with organizations that are staples in my life. By extension, these groups were connections for our family. Joining a black sorority or fraternity is a lifetime commitment to service and sisterhood or brotherhood. The Greenville Alumnae Chapter of Delta Sigma Theta Sorority, Inc., became a family of sisters, and social events meant we had automatic invitations to service projects, fundraisers, and parties. I became very close to my sorority sisters in Greenville, and we spent family time in some of their homes. I connected with the local alumnae chapter of Spelman College, and we worked on behalf of Spelman by recruiting young Greenville ladies from local high schools.

Lloyd was a serious golfer and quickly joined a club of black golfers. He was also invited to join an investment club of black men. The club hosted a fancy Christmas party every year in honor of their wives with praise and gifts.

Shelby was not happy in her private school.

In northern Virginia, Browne Academy was a small school with a diverse population, and it supported her attention deficit diagnosis that public schools were not able to support. By the time she graduated in the eighth grade at Browne (its highest grade), Shelby's classroom of eighteen students looked like a little United Nations. Her classmates had heritages from Japan, Brazil, Iran, and Nigeria, and they were African American, Jewish, Asian and white. Her classmate Betsy was a white girl whose parents worked at the Episcopal School in Alexandria, and they lived in a house on the sprawling campus. Once when Shelby went to Savannah to spend spring break with her grandmother, Betsy's parents let their daughter go along and enjoy the week in the South.

When we explored private schools in Greenville and I inquired as to the "best" private school in town, Christ Church Episcopal came highly recommended. My frame of reference for Episcopal schools was Betsy's family and the diverse faculty and student body we knew in Alexandria.

Christ Church was not like that. When we went to the first meeting of parents and students at the start of the school year, we were told there would be a bonding out-of-town trip for the ninth graders. The destination was supposed to be a surprise for the students, but parents were told because we had to pack for them accordingly. When the destination was finally revealed to the students, cheers went up at the news that these kids from South Carolina were getting on an Amtrak train to spend a few days in—wait for it—Washington, D.C.

Shelby shrugged. She was going "home."

We raised Shelby in a very diverse environment, but life at Christ Church was everything but diverse. It was indeed a good school academically, a place where ample resources were available for learning, but the students were almost all white. There were two other black girls in the "upper school" with Shelby, but no black boys. As parents, Lloyd and I were comfortable with Shelby's middle school friends at Browne, where everything they did included the entire group of boys and girls. But we had not anticipated the quick change that would take place in high school. Shelby was now in a community where she knew almost no one and she certainly didn't see any black boys in her school to invite her to school dances or other social events. She was unhappy.

I dipped into my network of African American friends in Greenville, to let them know that Shelby was available for any social opportunities outside of school. Emma Barksdale, who co-hosted one of the welcome parties for us at her home, called to ask if Shelby would like to participate in the Beautillion, a coming-out event for boys sponsored by the Greenville chapter of Jack and Jill of America, the organization of black mothers and their children who grow up together from preschool through high school. In the Beautillion, the girls would wear long white dresses and the boys would dress formally in tails. Shelby would be paired as an "accompanier" with a young African American male. As far as I can remember, this would be Shelby's first real "date." Later in high school Shelby participated in the cotillion sponsored by Alpha Kappa Alpha, another black sorority.

The years in Greenville turned out to be a coming of age era for Shelby. Unhappy with the lack of diversity at Christ Church, she asked and we agreed to let her transfer in tenth grade to the public Mauldin High School near our neighborhood.

In ninth grade at Christ Church, Shelby had made the basketball team and showed great potential under a very good (and African American) coach. When word got out that we were going to let her change schools for tenth grade, one of the basketball team dads, a successful businessman, hinted that he would pay Shelby's tuition the following year. We made it clear to this father that Shelby was not leaving for reasons of money, but because she needed a more diverse environment.

To their credit, the Christ Church Episcopal School website now has this statement as the first line in the mission statement: "Students will develop an appreciation of diverse cultures."

WHEN IT WAS TIME for Shelby to consider college, I had to listen to her rationale when she told me she would not uphold the family tradition and become the fourth generation of women in our family to enroll at Spelman College. "You raised me in this diverse lifestyle," she said. "That's where I'm most comfortable."

An HBCU was not in the cards for Shelby, and I came to accept her decision. She applied for early decision and was accepted at Winthrop University, a small, diverse state school in Rock Hill, South Carolina, about twenty miles from Charlotte, North Carolina. To appease me, I'm sure, she maintained a good GPA and kept her South Carolina Lottery-funded tuition scholarship. And, she pledged in Delta Sigma Theta, my sorority. She made me proud.

ONE OF MY NIGHTLY tasks in Greenville was to work with the copy desk on preparing the mix of Page One stories, photos and headlines. To do this we set up a system where I would get a facsimile copy of the front page at 11 every night. Then I would get on the phone with the night news editor to discuss changes. One thing I was starting to see was an abundance of mug shots of young black men who were suspects or arrested in local crimes. I inquired as to why and I was told, "Well, we've always done it this way."

That wasn't good enough. I knew that consistent portrayals of young black men who were in trouble was fostering a stereotype that made readers think all young black men are bad.

I knew the routine. I knew about the old habits that were hard to break. I complained one night about the use of a mug shot of a young black male suspect, and a white editor on the copy desk said: "Do you know how hard we had to work to get the police to release that photo to us?"

The editor missed my point and I knew I had to do something to get his attention and the attention of others who were mired in a tradition that needed to change. I called one of my husband's friends, a man named Willie Johnson, who at the time was a major on the Greenville Police Department. He later became chief.

Johnson and my husband were in a loosely organized group called "The Lunch Bunch," professional black men who got together at a local hotel buffet restaurant for lunch every Thursday. These men were police officers, businessmen, entrepreneurs, and ministers. They wore business suits to work every day and were as successful as they looked—not rich men, but economically comfortable in satisfying careers.

I asked Johnson to attend a meeting of editors and talk about the outcome of consistently having the faces of young black men on Page One as crime suspects. Major Johnson told the group of editors just what I expected him to say:

"I hear from your readers all the time. Black readers think you are intentionally putting the pictures out there (on Page One) to enforce the stereotype that black men are dangerous and bad. White readers see the faces of black men and it tells them that all black men should be feared."

Together, Johnson and I talked about how some white women fear black men, crossing the street when they see a black man coming their way, clutching their handbags tightly under their arms when a black man is nearby, being fearful on elevators and in small spaces when black men are present.

Johnson admitted that proportionate to population, more black men *are* suspected of or arrested for crimes than white men. But that still does not mean the majority of black men are bad. He shared that the police got calls from citizens who complain that a "black man is in my neighborhood," even though sometimes the black men are neighbors—middle- or working-class citizens.

After Johnson left, I gave the editors my new rule: "From now on, we will no longer run mug shots of any suspects or arrested people on Page One. Their race does not matter. Not white people or black people, nor men or women."

It just didn't make sense to run mug shots of people who were already arrested and in jail. The exception was that if a dangerous suspect was at large and a threat to the community, we would run the photo because readers needed to know what the suspect looked like.

The police were grateful for the change, and I have to think this rule made a difference in breaking down stereotypes so people don't think the worst things about black men when they see them doing everyday normal things in public.

Years later when I became executive editor at another newspaper in the South, I applied the no-mug shot rule there as well.

20. On Becoming a Diversity Guru

Life was great in Greenville, so great we that didn't see ourselves leaving anytime soon. Greenville's diverse community grounded us, with its dozens of international corporations headquartered nearby. The city had a well-educated community of African Americans who held important positions in government, education, corporate, health care, law enforcement, manufacturing, and other areas.

Soon after we moved there I participated in Leadership Greenville, which helped me navigate the majority-white infrastructure and get to know people who owned businesses, ran for office, and were involved in revitalization of the most divine little downtown we had ever seen. We were in love with Greenville. So it is no wonder that a new job opportunity in Nashville was not appealing to me at first.

The first call came in mid 1999 from Mary Kay Blake, a former news executive who led Gannett's recruiting office. When we worked in the same complex of offices, Mary Kay and I were more than colleagues. We bonded as friends. When she left Gannett she became one of the corporate executives who moved across the street to the Freedom Forum, the foundation that former Gannett Chairman Al Neuharth set up to do some incredible work on behalf of journalism, especially programs to highlight the First Amendment and newsroom diversity.

In addition to the Freedom Forum's offices in northern Virginia, there were also Freedom Forum programs in New York City; at the University of South Dakota, Neuharth's alma mater; and at Vanderbilt University in Nashville, Tennessee, where John Seigenthaler was then emeritus editor and publisher of the *Tennessean*. In his post-Gannett years, Seigenthaler established the First Amendment Center on Vanderbilt's Peabody Campus.

"Charles Overby asked me to invite you to come to Nashville to have a conversation about a new project the Freedom Forum is planning," Mary Kay Blake said when she called me. "He wants to take you to dinner." Overby, a former Gannett top editor, was CEO of the Freedom Forum. I knew him, but not well.

I don't remember that Blake got very deep on the call about exactly what the project would be. She did say it was about newsroom diversity and Overby needed to "pick my brain" about their idea before they moved forward. We compared calendars and came up with a date a few weeks later. On the day of our meeting, Blake and I arrived at the Freedom Forum offices at Vanderbilt in the late afternoon, and we went to Seigenthaler's office. Overby joined us there.

There was a brief conversation about a new program and a new building. They spread architectural drawings on a coffee table and peppered me with questions about the state of newsroom diversity. Then we went to dinner, where slowly details of the plans emerged.

They knew I had worked in the Sumner Program for Minority Journalists at Columbia in the early 1970s, in a program that was successful in training nontraditional students—people of color—for professional newsroom roles.

"That's what this program will do," Overby said, "only bigger" because it would operate year-round, not just in the summer. The program would target mid-career African Americans, Native Americans, Asian Americans, and Hispanics. This was not a course for people who were just out of high school or even just out of college, but for adults who were brave enough to step out of the box and begin a second career. The students would ultimately range in age from late twenties to sixties.

The evening was long, but each hour brought more clarity. They said they valued my drive and experience for making newsrooms more diverse. They knew I was a founding member and former national chair of NAMME—the National Association of Minority Media Executives. They knew I had directed the study *Muted Voices: Frustration and Fear in the Newsroom* for the National Association of Black Journalists. They knew I was the current chair of the ASNE Minorities (later Diversity) Committee. They knew I was a frequent speaker on media diversity all over the country, that I was a diversity trainer inside newsrooms, at universities, and at media training institutes. They knew I was the first female recipient of the Ida B. Wells Award for newsroom diversity, and that I was respected by my peers for diversity advocacy by writing articles in media trade publications. And probably most of all, they knew I had managed resources in the large *USA Today* newsroom with its staff of more than four hundred people with budgets totaling tens of millions of dollars.

At the end of the four-hour dinner meeting, a job offer was put before me. I was being invited to become the founding executive director for what would later be known as the Freedom Forum Diversity Institute at Vanderbilt University.

"We believe Wanda Lloyd is the only person who can do this job," Overby said, giving it his most convincing shot.

Seigenthaler, a life-long Nashvillian, was there to encourage me to move to the city he loved, where he had met his beautiful wife, Dolores, and with her raised John Michael, a son who would follow his father into journalism, albeit in broadcast.

I was flattered by the offer, but I was also torn. Greenville was our home and we were happy there. Lloyd had a great job as director of safety and security with Goodwill Industries and he had a good group of friends. I was happy in the newsroom and comfortable with Gannett, remembering my mother's concerns when I left the *Washington Post*, giving up a secure position to move to a new entity. *USA Today*, it turned out, was a good move. But this new institute—I wasn't convinced yet.

I returned home to Greenville and shared the offer with my family. There was no rush to make the decision, I was told by the Freedom Forum leaders. They hadn't even broken ground on the building in Nashville yet.

Weeks went by and I stayed in touch with Blake. Each time we spoke I got a better sense of what this new program could become. I would almost be like a CEO of this one part of the Freedom Forum. I would get to help design the interior of the new 32,000-square-foot, $7 million facility to be built next door to the First Amendment Center. I would travel to training institutes around the country, see how they are set up, and learn techniques for training nontraditional students who almost all already had college (and some graduate) degrees. I would oversee curriculum for the twelve-week intensive course and find students in communities across the country using my contacts with editors I worked with in Gannett and in ASNE. I would market the program by writing articles and encouraging media organizations to use our space for their own meetings and training.

The more I thought about the opportunity the better I felt about stepping away from daily journalism. This project could help newspapers and journalism by placing well-trained people of color in newsrooms where diverse voices were badly needed. The Freedom Forum could have a big impact ensuring that newspapers provided better coverage by having more diverse journalists bring their life experiences and perspectives to story ideas and writing or photography.

I knew I could do this. I had been an administrative editor at *USA Today*. In Gannett I had even been a project manager for newsroom redesigns.

The only thing I did not like was leaving Greenville. Eventually, a call from Charles Overby made me feel better about the move. "I have a foundation worth a billion and a half dollars," he said. "Come help us spend some of this money."

I knew he was not just concerned about spending money; Overby was not a frivolous man. But he wanted me to know that the Freedom Forum was a solid, well-run organization with the ability to put funds behind the commitment to make newsrooms more diverse.

The Freedom Forum already had several diversity programs in place. Since 1991 the Chips Quinn Scholars program trained more than 1,400 young men and women through 2018. The annual Al Neuharth Free Spirit and Journalism Conference is a diverse program designed to inspire and encourage high school students who are interested in journalism careers by sending them to Washington from every state for a conference and giving them $1,000 scholarships. The former APME Fellows Program, supported financially by the Freedom Forum, put new college graduates in newsrooms and subsidized their salaries and mentored them for two years, with hopes that they would become full-time permanent journalists in their initial newsrooms or somewhere in journalism at the end of the fellowship. The Freedom Forum program in South Dakota trained Native American students for journalism careers. Of all the journalism-focused foundations in the nation at that time, the Freedom Forum was making the biggest impact on increasing the numbers of people of color and other groups of marginalized populations in newsrooms.

I ACCEPTED OVERBY'S OFFER and went to work at the Freedom Forum in January 2001, initially taking an office in the First Amendment Center while the new building was under construction. It became the best job I ever had.

Shortly after I arrived in Nashville, I spent most of my time hiring staff and cold-calling editors across the nation, telling them about our new program as a way of educating them about how to find potential candidates for the Diversity Institute, assuring them that we were paying 100 percent of the cost for training. I worked with the Freedom Forum's technical staff to develop a website and other materials so I had a place on the Internet to send editors for more information. I told editors we wanted to find people with talent for writing, or who might be trained for copy editing, photography, or graphic design. I helped editors think about how to find candidates, telling them to look at people who were already working in their newspaper building but maybe not in the newsroom. Some might be people in the community who were sources in stories, or community activists, or they might be prolific writers of letters to the editor, or frequent critics of the newspaper's coverage of people of color. I asked editors to write about our program in their weekly columns, putting out the invitation to readers to volunteer or suggest candidates for the Diversity Institute.

In an effort to reach editors who were not necessarily in my own circle of colleagues, I wrote articles that appeared in trade publications, in blogs, and on websites.

Shortly after we released information about plans to open the Diversity Institute, I took a call from an attorney who identified himself as someone working at the Montgomery, Alabama-based Southern Poverty Law Center (SPLC), a nonprofit advocacy organization that specializes in civil rights

litigation. I would come to know SPLC and its staff of attorneys and publications very well after I moved to Montgomery a few years later. But I was
not aware of the work of SPLC the day I took the call.

The attorney congratulated us for plans to launch the Diversity Institute.
He noted that our press release said we would be training only people of
color and he asked me if we had been rebuffed by any organizations challenging the work we were about to launch. I told him that at the time we
had received nothing but praise for the program.

Years later, after meeting Ken Mullinax (more about him later), I called
the Freedom Forum and asked if they would consider adding a white man
to the program. After all, being white is also diversity, I reminded them.
The answer was yes, and as far as I know, Kenneth Mullinax from Alabama
was the first and only white Diversity Institute participant.

IN NASHVILLE I HIRED Robbie Morganfield, a talented journalist and
teacher with the reputation of being a good mentor, to be the lead faculty
member for the Diversity Institute. Robbie had a distinguished career at
several newspapers as a reporter and as an editor. We worked side-by-side
training dozens of nontraditional people of color for newsroom positions.

The Institute's participants came from diverse professional backgrounds.
They were educators, professors, news assistants, an attorney, government
workers, military veterans, community activists, and tradesmen in manufacturing and construction. Our challenge was to train them in an environment
that mirrored a real newsroom, inviting working journalists to lecture, and
having the students' work published in the *Tennessean*, John Siegenthaler's
former newspaper.

Our building had one large classroom with the latest technology and
seating for up to twenty students, the maximum number we would train
at one time. A round conference room was used for guest lectures, and we
invited newspaper groups from across the nation to have some of their own
meetings in our building, thus exposing our students to top-level newspaper executives. We invited a top editor from the newspaper represented by
each student to spend a week in our program, to develop a lecture for the
students, and to help edit their stories. We built a 125-seat lecture hall,

brought in well-known speakers, and invited people from the community to attend enlightening special events.

We provided our students with subscriptions to the *New York Times, USA Today,* and the *Tennessean,* expecting them to have read all of the newspapers before our 8:30 a.m. class start, a daily discussion called "Today's News." Robbie and I asked the students to talk about which stories in that day's newspapers caught their attention. We would dissect the stories not just for content and accuracy, but also talk about some of the stories' ethical issues and how the newspapers might have better approached diversity. Did the reporter ask enough questions? Did the editor hold the reporter accountable for including diverse sources? How could the writing have been improved? Did the headline help tell the story? Was there offensive content and how should that have been handled?

Then Robbie and visiting editors went to work with lectures, writing exercises, and editing stories. It was amazing how quickly we turned people with no journalism experience into fully functional reporters, ready to go home and tackle real community coverage.

We formed a partnership with the *Tennessean* to publish the students' stories and to provide short internships. The *Tennessean* sent some of its newsroom staff members to the Diversity Institute as lecturers and mentors.

As I LOOK BACK over my career, I believe the work we did in Nashville may have been the most important and best use of my passion to drive and advocate for journalism and newsroom diversity. We tried to buck the odds of the numbers of women and people of color in newsrooms and defy the 1968 Kerner Commission report that, in part, blamed the media for causing some of the urban unrest across the nation.

As executive director, I used the platform to advocate for diversity on many levels, speaking before journalism organizations, at universities, and in newsrooms. For a year, the venerable *Tennessean* editor and columnist Dwight Lewis and I co-hosted *Behind the Headlines*, a weekly public affairs show on WSFK, the Fisk University radio station. Through that platform I was building a presence in Nashville and I tried to make the Diversity Institute a known part of the community. Lewis and I interviewed local public officials and (by phone) members of the Tennessee congressional delegation. Listeners were able to call in and have a dialogue about issues each week.

The greatest and most satisfied feeling came from the graduation ceremonies that took place twelve weeks after each cohort began their studies at the Diversity Institute. I felt like the mother duck sending her ducklings out into the waters because they were ready to swim on their own.

The hardest part of the job was filling the pipeline of potential candidates while keeping the program going at the same time. That was a never-ending challenge. After our third class graduated I took a two-week trip by car and plane to visit the newsrooms of all of our graduates to date and to touch base with their editors. I wanted to see what worked and what didn't work for them. I also needed to persuade the editors to send us more students, or at least to appeal to some of their top-editor colleagues at other newspapers to participate in our program.

Our facility was the site of one of the newspaper industry's milestone events, a 2001 roundtable discussion about the status of diversity and how to move the annual census of newsroom diversity toward the goal of parity in newsrooms. At the roundtable—literally at the table in our round conference room—were representatives from all of the minority journalism associations—the Asian American Journalists Association, the National Association of Hispanic Journalists, the Native American Journalists Association, the National Association of Black Journalists, the American Society of News Editors, the National Association of Minority Media Executives, several news industry foundation leaders, and other foot soldiers in the fight for newsroom diversity. We invited Princeton University researcher Lawrence T. McGill to join the discussion and he followed up with a meta-analysis of thirteen studies looking at the retention of journalists of color between the years 1989 and 2000. All of these studies cited the absence of opportunity for career advancement and the lack of professional opportunities as two of the main reasons journalists of color make the decision to leave their newsrooms.

Dori Maynard, daughter of the late Robert C. Maynard, the first African American publisher of a mainstream daily newspaper and president of the Robert C. Maynard Institute for Journalism Education, identified some of the reasons for the failures of newsroom diversity in an article "Why Jour-nalists Can't Talk Across Race," published in *Nieman Reports* in September 2003. She wrote:

> There is one often overlooked reason why the industry continues to struggle to retain journalists of color. It is because the news organizations that essentially serve as moderators of the nation's conversations have yet to learn how to talk about and across their own racial fault lines. What makes this conversation more difficult is that we have yet to acknowledge and understand the role that race and gender play in shaping our percep-tions of news and events around us. Just as journalists of color and their white peers experience industry opportunities very differently, they also often view news events through very different lenses.

This challenge of having conversations about race and gender across fault lines, and providing resources for diverse news media is what we were tasked with addressing. The challenge continues to this day.

IN 2003 CHARLES OVERBY asked me to join the 2012 Task Force, a group of staff members who were tasked to envision how the Freedom Forum would continue to have an impact in journalism and what the Freedom Forum might look like in 2012. By the time I came aboard the group was well into visioning and brainstorming; its members were getting close to writing a report of their findings.

The task force came back with a bulleted list of projections for the fu-ture. One bullet read something like this: "The Freedom Forum Diversity Institute will remain a viable entity if the newspaper industry supports the program financially."

When I read that bulleted item I was stunned. I had spent more than three years traveling across the nation, helping editors understand the concept of media diversity, helping them screen candidates and imagining how our graduates in their newsroom would enhance their newspapers' value in the communities they served. I made hundreds of phone calls, begging, plead-ing with editors and publishers to send us candidates, and teaching them how to find candidates in their communities. I spent nights, weekends, and much of my personal time composing emails to editors, communicating with candidates, writing blog and magazine articles, and thinking about how to make the Diversity Institute a success.

Many of my conversations with editors centered on the hardships that newspapers were experiencing, with company revenue being spent more on technology upgrades and less on developing newsroom talent. Even though the Freedom Forum was paying 100 percent of the cost for training—valued at $7,500 per student, not including fixed costs like salaries, utilities and upkeep of facilities—publishers pushed back on the prospect of holding open job slots for several months while we trained people to fill them; editors were frustrated because they needed to fill every open slot immediately, for fear of losing the openings through staff downsizing.

The bullet point about newspapers someday footing the bill for training was not a viable business model. I knew it would never happen. I could see that this program could not be sustained without the continued full financial support of the Freedom Forum, which by then was starting to put hundreds of millions of dollars into building another project, the Newseum, an interactive museum of news memorabilia in Washington on Pennsylvania Avenue between the Capital and the White House. I could not foresee a long-term future for the Diversity Institute, and no one had conversations with me about how I might fit in at the Freedom Forum if the Institute was shut down.

Maybe it was time to go home, I thought, home to Gannett.

When I left the Greenville newspaper and the Gannett Company in 2000, one of the letters lamenting my departure came from Phil Currie, Gannett's senior VP for news. His November 14, 2000, letter read in part:

> Dear Wanda,
>
> My heart is broken.
>
> I knew, of course, of your decision to go to the Freedom Forum, but when I see it in black and white as a 'done deal,' it is painful, indeed. You have brought a very personal and persuasive character to the company,

especially as we work in matters of diversity. You have been both a mentor and a role model to many, many young journalists. You have been a good adviser in helping to move programs ahead. You have been a counselor to old white guys like me. And you have been a friend.

I thank you so much for all of that—and for your good work in Greenville and *USA Today*.

With highest regards, Phil

After I digested and thought about the Freedom Forum's task force report and the impact it would have on the Diversity Institute, I called Currie one morning at 7 o'clock, remembering that he, like a lot of top executives would be working in his office early when things are quiet. There would not even be a secretary to screen calls at that hour. As expected, Currie picked up the phone, surprised but pleased to hear from me.

"Phil, I think it's time for me to go back into a newsroom."

I reminded him I wanted to remain in the South, not ever wanting to live in a cold climate again. "I know Montgomery has an opening for executive editor. What about Montgomery?" I asked.

"That's a great idea for a lot of reasons, but let me make a quick call and get back to you."

Currie called me back about an hour later.

"How soon can you get down to Montgomery to interview with the publisher? Scott Brown wants to meet you."

21. The Final Newsroom

The first time I ever traveled to Montgomery, Alabama, was as a college student in 1970. I went there with a fellow student to represent our college at a student media conference. We were young and either naive or forgiving about race relations in the South.

One evening we walked into a diner and took two seats at the counter, waiting to be served. All I remember is that a white female server threw some loose silverware across the counter at us, apparently not wanting to get too close to two young black college students who wanted nothing more than to eat dinner. That was my first experience in Montgomery, a memory I repressed for good reason.

When I drove from Nashville into Montgomery on a Sunday afternoon in June 2004, thirty-four years after that student media conference, the city's downtown was like a ghost town, hollowed out, I would learn, by several decades of urban renewal and white flight. I had arrived to begin my new position as executive editor of the *Montgomery Advertiser*, the Alabama capital city's Gannett-owned daily newspaper. I was moving to the city known as the Cradle of the Confederacy and the birthplace of the civil rights movement.

There were no open businesses, no traffic on the streets, and not even an open restaurant except inside the hotel across from the newspaper's offices. Before going to my temporary corporate housing that the publisher's office had set up for me, I drove up and down Montgomery's famous Dexter Avenue, the location of so many important moments in history. I drove around the Court Square Fountain, with its historic marker that describes Montgomery's Slave Trade Market. I drove past the famous Dexter

Avenue King Memorial Baptist Church, where the young Reverend Dr. Martin Luther King Jr. pastored and led the Montgomery Bus Boycott. I drove up to the state capitol, where Governor George Wallace gave his "Segregation now, segregation forever" speech in 1963 and where in 1965 Dr. King spoke at the end of the five-day Selma to Montgomery march for voting rights. "How long, not long," King told the crowd of tens of thousands. Doubling back down Dexter Avenue that Sunday afternoon, I turned onto Montgomery Street and drove past the Rosa Parks Museum, located on the corner where Mrs. Parks was arrested on the Cleveland Avenue bus after a long day working as a seamstress at the Montgomery Fair department store.

I was hired by the *Advertiser's* Publisher Scott Brown to succeed Paula Moore, the executive editor who passed away a few months before I inquired about taking the top newsroom job in Montgomery. I knew Paula; we worked together from a distance when she was managing editor at Gannett's *El Paso Times* in Texas and I was senior editor at *USA Today* in charge of the loaner program, which invited people from other Gannett papers to work at *USA Today* for ninety days. Paula and I frequently discussed the staff members she would send to *USA Today*, and we joked about whether she would send her best people because of the good training they would get at *USA Today*. Or, she would ask, should she send someone who was not one of her top reporters to ensure *USA Today* would return them to her staff in Texas rather than hire them away from her? In Montgomery, Paula was beloved by the newsroom staff. Now I was about to follow the good work she had done as executive editor.

Before I left Nashville, the Freedom Forum gave me a nice send-off party. It was a bittersweet departure because I really believed in the work we were doing at the Diversity Institute at Vanderbilt. Yet, I knew the industry was not in a position to help financially support the participants we were training, and also, I always had the goal of becoming an executive editor. This was a great next step for me.

Charles Overby, the Freedom Forum's CEO told me privately at the send-off party, "Why Wanda, being executive editor of the paper in Montgomery is like being the governor." It was his way of emphasizing the importance of being the top editor in the Alabama capital city that was known for racial tension.

IN MONTGOMERY, HOWEVER, I did not forget the significance of the diversity work. As executive editor of the *Advertiser*, I wrote a column calling for community people to let me know if they were interested in the program I had previously directed in Nashville. Even though I was no longer at the Institute, I wanted to continue to be involved by sending people from Montgomery. Of the people who contacted me, we sent two to the Diversity Institute.

One was Topher Sanders, a young African American man, a military veteran who had written a few freelance stories for the newspaper before I got there. We sent Topher to the program in Nashville and he came back to us as a well-trained reporter, ready to cover local stories. Shortly after he got his feet wet with experience in the newsroom, I capitalized on his military experience and added to his duties the assignment to cover military affairs at Maxwell Air Force Base, located just down the street from the newspaper.

The other person who stood out as a candidate for the Diversity Institute was Kenneth Mullinax, a middle-aged white man who had held several important jobs in government, including being a congressional aide in Washington. Mullinax wrote me a passionate letter after he read my column inviting readers to consider applying for the Diversity Institute. I called Mullinax in for a meeting and of course, the topic of his race came up.

"The Diversity Institute is for people of color," I told him, "but let's see how far we can go with this before making a decision."

I asked Mullinax to take a few days and develop some ideas for stories that he might want to report and write if he was working for the newspaper. He came back with almost two dozen story ideas, most of them quite appealing and some, I told him, we would assign to some of our reporters already on staff.

We selected one idea from his list that I asked him to go out and report, do his best to write the story, and then we would gauge his potential. Mullinax blew us away with his reporting aptitude. He had pitched a story about twenty-six-year-old Jimmie Lee Jackson, an African American civil rights activist who died February 26, 1965, after he was brutally beaten and shot by an Alabama state trooper during a peaceful voting rights march. Jackson's death sparked the previously mentioned Selma-to-Montgomery March. Mullinax knew that former trooper James Bonard Fowler was accused of causing the injuries that led to Jackson's death, but Fowler was never brought to justice.

Mullinax, the rookie and not-yet reporter for the *Montgomery Advertiser*, found the rural Geneva County, Alabama, address for Fowler and drove to his house, knocked on the door, and asked, "Are you James Bonard Fowler?"

Mullinax returned to the newspaper with a story that had great details but needed massaging into journalistic style. His story included his interview with Fowler and also with Michael Jackson, the African American district attorney in Perry County, Alabama, who subsequently reopened the case as a murder investigation in 2005. We edited Mullinax's story, putting it into the third person and adhering to Associated Press style, and published it in the newspaper. After the story ran, Alabama Governor Bob Riley offered a $5,000 reward for information leading to the arrest and conviction in the case of Jimmie Lee Jackson.

In 2010, nearly forty-five years after Jackson's death, Fowler was indicted and he pled guilty to misdemeanor manslaughter. He received a six-month prison sentence.

As I SETTLED IN Montgomery I accepted invitations to attend events and meetings with elected officials, business owners, and chamber of commerce leaders; and requests to speak at Rotary, Lions, Civitan and other civic clubs, universities, churches, and social organizations. Ken Hare, the editorial page editor, set up a roster of local and state public officials who would come in to meet with us. These would include U.S. senators Richard Shelby and Jeff Sessions.

My first meeting with Governor Bob Riley was in his office in the capitol. Riley, a Republican from rural Clay County, was the sixth generation in a family of farmers and ranchers. He invited Hare and me to have lunch with him. We made it clear, of course, that, based on the ethical standards of journalism, whatever expense was incurred for our meals would be paid by the newspaper. We arrived in Riley's large office and I immediately noticed the conference table with leather placemats embellished with the embroidered seal of the governor. I thought to myself this might be a pretty fancy meal.

A few minutes into our conversation, Riley told us one of his aides would be coming in soon with lunch—"He went to Chick-fil-A." I assumed this was a joke but sure enough, the aide came into the room with a paper bag full of grilled chicken sandwiches and waffle fries.

One of the first friendship phone calls I received in Montgomery came from a fellow journalist. Eileen Jones was a seasoned reporter at the local NBC affiliate, WSFA. An African American woman who grew up in Montgomery and graduated from Tuskegee University (an HBCU), she left Alabama for a time to begin her career and for graduate study. She returned when her parents were aging and ailing, and after they passed away she stayed. Eileen Jones is a household name in Montgomery, so I knew who she was when she called to invite me to dinner with a couple of other women.

At the dinner they told me they were a part of a larger group of accomplished African American women who met regularly for dinner. The group included lawyers, judges, journalists, doctors and other medical professionals, businesswomen, and educators. As the top person in the newsroom, I had no professional African American peers inside the newspaper or anywhere else in the state. The dinner group, which still meets today, doesn't have a formal name. It has no officers, bylaws, or social media sites. I doubt that most of the powerful people in Montgomery know that these women get together bimonthly for dinner and conversation. Collectively, they are some of the most knowledgeable and connected people in Alabama business and politics. They are world travelers and leaders in national professional organizations, much like I was with journalism organizations. This group opened their arms and their hearts to me while I was in Montgomery, a support system I needed. They were often my eyes and ears when big stories were about to erupt, and they broke down the backgrounds of Alabama history, politics, and people for me as a newcomer editing the newspaper. They had my back and I had theirs.

Sometimes when I was out and about at community events where one or two of them were present, we would speak—not a long conversation, just a hug in passing. My colleagues at the newspaper would say, "You know her?" If they only knew.

OF ALL THE SPEECHES I made in Montgomery, the one I recall the most was at the Dexter Avenue King Memorial Baptist Church. Some of our new Montgomery friends who were members had invited us to worship there as soon as we moved to the city, and I recall thinking that, like a lot of churches in city centers where neighborhoods were displaced by suburban growth, the church must be in decline because the sanctuary was never full on the Sundays when we visited. So I wasn't too worried about speaking there to what I thought would be a small congregation.

The service on Sunday, September 26, 2004, was Women's Leadership Day, and I was asked to share insights about my experience, with hopes of inspiring women as leaders. The church made it widely known in the community that the new black female editor of the *Montgomery Advertiser* would be making her first public speech at Dexter Church. All week long my face was becoming recognized through stories about my arrival, and people who saw me in the grocery store, at events around town, or even in our building at work said, "I hear you're speaking at Dexter Church. I'm planning to come."

Really?

When Lloyd and I arrived at the church that Sunday morning we were led downstairs to the pastor's office. I was invited to sit at an antique wooden desk and was informed that this was the desk where Dr. King wrote his sermons. It was an overwhelming feeling to think about the sermons and speeches that came to him sitting in the same space I was occupying. A few members who arrived at the church early trickled in to offer me good wishes, a drink of water, and a corsage to wear.

When we went upstairs to the sanctuary, I wasn't prepared for what I saw as the service began. The church was packed; every pew was full. I mean packed with people standing and filling the back wall packed. A multiracial crowd had come to hear me speak. Now I was beginning to understand what Freedom Forum CEO Charles Overby told me as I was about to leave Nashville. Being editor of Montgomery's capital city newspaper *and* black and female was a pretty darn big deal.

I began by reading my prepared remarks, but looking out over the crowded sanctuary, I realized that people wanted to know more about me. They were present to celebrate this new face in Montgomery—a face that was female and African American. As I started to feel the emotions of where I had come from and where I was in my career and in life, I felt the need to change course. Though the crowd was large, the sanctuary suddenly felt small and cozy, like a good place to have a conversation, not a speech. I closed the pages of my prepared speech and announced that I would not be reading what I had written. The emotional significance of that day and that place—the same podium that Dr. King used to preach the Gospel of God's love and civil rights overcame me. I was choking up and I had to get my composure. When I finally began to speak again the words came strictly from my heart. No notes, no prepared text. I just talked.

I told the group about my upbringing in Savannah under the restrictive Jim Crow laws, something those who grew up in Montgomery could identify with. I shared my passion for journalism and why I wanted to be executive editor in Montgomery. I gave them an overview of every newspaper and every university where I had worked—why I stayed and why I left each one. I talked about why it was important for newspapers and all media to reflect the communities they serve. I talked about what I hoped to accomplish in Montgomery, to use the newspaper to bring the community closer together and to inform them through stories not about just the big things happening in the community, but also to highlight people and organizations that don't normally rise to the level of coverage in a daily newspaper. I told them about my passion for mentoring young people to help them skip over some of the land mines I had encountered. I mentioned Shelby and promised that many of them would get to meet our daughter when she visited, and I introduced Lloyd and told the group how much I hoped they would embrace us as new citizens of the community.

By the time I finished and sat down every person in that church who could stand was on their feet. The applause went on for a minute or two. I was spent, yet exhilarated and feeling like I had introduced myself to Montgomery in a good and proper way. I rose again and waved my right hand, a symbol of thanks for the approval.

Then, right after I sat down a final time, something weird happened. Someone, maybe the pastor, was standing at the podium thanking me, or maybe the choir was beginning to sing. I just recall the image of an elderly woman walking down the center aisle toward the pulpit. She climbed the steps and pressed something wrapped in a piece of paper into my hands, then she left the sanctuary through a side door. I slipped the folded paper into the folder that held my prepared remarks, not bothering to look at it right away.

When we got home, Lloyd asked me about the woman who ascended the steps. I opened my folder and there I found a brief letter with a hand-printed blessing for success in Montgomery and a five-dollar bill. I never saw that woman again and I don't know why she gave me the money. Was she paying me for speaking? Or was it some kind of voodoo to keep me safe in my role as editor of the newspaper. I'll never know. At home, I slipped the letter and the five-dollar bill into a zippered sandwich bag and put it in a place of safekeeping. I still have that little bag and the same five-dollar bill. Perhaps the woman's gesture protected me from hurt or danger in Montgomery.

We remained in Montgomery for almost nine years, and every year I continued to meet or run into people who told me, "I was at Dexter Church when you spoke." "I remember you said" this or that. "I remember how you described your childhood in Savannah." Clearly that day at Dexter Church was memorable.

WE WERE IN MONTGOMERY for some pretty important events. I was present in May 2005 when car manufacturer Hyundai officially opened the company's North American headquarters and invited 20,000 people to the plant for tours, speeches, and lunch. The newspaper published a special section to recognize this big economic event.

I observed the development of the city's downtown from a place where the sidewalks rolled up at 5 o'clock every day to having new hotels, a performing arts center, and a burgeoning entertainment and restaurant district. Our staff covered the new downtown Alley district and the city's installation at its entrance of what some thought was an ugly water tank but turned out to be an iconic landmark. "Meet me at the water tower" became a common refrain.

Soon people were sitting on restaurant patios, walking the open-cup district with beer and wine, joining family members to grab a quick dinner after work before walking over to the baseball stadium to take in a Montgomery Biscuits (yes, Biscuits) AA baseball game. As downtown development continued we were soon listening to live music at outdoor bars, walking to the riverfront for concerts at a new amphitheater, and boarding a riverboat for dinner cruises. Instead of one nice hotel downtown, Montgomery was suddenly flush with luxury hotel rooms in renovated historic buildings that retained interesting architectural features.

Shortly after I arrived in 2004, I became aware that the following year would be the fiftieth anniversary of the Montgomery Bus Boycott that was sparked by the December 1, 1955, arrest of Rosa Parks for refusing to give up her seat on a segregated city bus. Dr. King, then a young pastor at the church on Dexter Avenue, was drafted to lead the year-long historic protest, which is generally viewed as the start of the twentieth century civil rights movement.

When I became editor I soon learned that one of the projects in process was a book that would tell the story of the bus boycott, largely using the resources of the newspaper's own files of stories, photographs, and staff members. The newspaper asked people in the community to search for documents they might have at home—items saved in Bibles or cedar chests in attics by relatives who had passed on. The resulting book, *They Walked to Freedom, 1955–1956: The Story of the Montgomery Bus Boycott*, was written by Editorial Page Editor Ken Hare, with a significant contribution by Assistant Editorial Page Editor Jim Earnhardt. I had the pleasure of editing the book.

We also produced "Voices of the Boycott," a massive special section that included interviews with some of the unsung foot soldiers of the boycott—blacks and whites, many of whom have since passed on—people who were there and people who were too young to participate but heard stories from their family members. The interviews included conversations with Inez Baskin, a black woman who wrote stories about the Boycott for *Jet* magazine; Urelee Gordon, the man who shined Dr. King's shoes and said his role in the movement was to be sure the boycott leader was stepping through the marches with shoes that looked good; the Reverend Robert Graetz, the white Lutheran pastor of an all-black congregation whose home was bombed because he was an active supporter of the boycott; and Patricia Posey Jones, a musician who provided organ and piano music for the boycott's mass meetings.

The special section included eight historic newspaper front pages so readers could look back and see how the boycott was covered in 1955, and we launched a website full of video interviews with people profiled in the print special section. The *Advertiser* worked with a group of teachers to develop a curriculum guide to go along with the special section for classroom use.

As if that wasn't enough, then something miraculous happened. Our advertising department was contacted by someone from the retail company Target, which asked us to print an additional 900,000 copies of our special section, plus 30,000 of our teacher guides, and also to rebrand the website with Target as sponsor. Target wanted to use our boycott sections as their annual Black History Month partnership donation to 30,000 schools across the nation. They paid the newspaper almost $1 million for this partnership, a very good sum for a department of our company that some teased was a non-revenue-producing part of the operation. In the months following the boycott anniversary, our collective work—the book, the special section, and the website—won more than a dozen state and national awards.

One was the Special Judges' Award from the Institute for Advanced Journalism Studies at North Carolina A&T University (an HBCU). A letter from DeWayne Wickham, on behalf of the Institute, wrote, "It is the opinion of the judges that your 'Voices of the Boycott' deserves a special honor and recognition because 'it is the absolute model of what community journalism is about. It's historic, fresh, interactive, education and poignant.' It is also damn good journalism."

A FEW WEEKS BEFORE the December 2005 boycott anniversary, I was burning some vacation time before the end of the year and I spent Monday, October 24, 2005, at home cleaning out a closet, separating items to donate and bagging things to be trashed. It was a project I had been putting off for a while. At about 8 p.m. I was standing in the closet admiring my work when the phone rang. Someone from the newsroom called to say Rosa Parks had just passed away.

I immediately put on my shoes and headed to the kitchen to pick up my keys, and as I rushed out the door I shouted to Lloyd, who was watching Monday Night Football, "Rosa Parks just died. Bye." I slammed the door behind me. We had been married long enough for him to know that with a big story like that, I would be gone for the better part of the night. No questions asked.

We had known for some time that the ninety-two-year-old Mrs. Parks was ill, and we had already prepared several pages to be published upon her passing, a journalistic practice common with regard to prominent people. The section was ready except for the details of how and when she died. Plus, we would update the newspaper's news website and rearrange Page One to accommodate a story with reaction to her death from people in the community and throughout the state.

Mrs. Parks's body was sent from Detroit to Montgomery for viewing and services at two churches, including the Dexter Avenue King Memorial Baptist Church that was so pivotal in the Montgomery Bus Boycott. Then her remains were taken to Washington, D.C., to lie in honor in the U.S. Capitol, where fifty thousand people filed by to pay respects.

WE SHARED SOME GOOD experiences in Montgomery. Beyond diversity, we launched, redesigned, and relaunched several websites. The newspaper covered some of the best college football teams in the nation with Auburn University and the University of Alabama winning several SEC and national championships. I budgeted each year under the assumption that we would need to send reporters and photographers to the big games. We produced special sections overnight after football championships and also instant books touting the winning teams.

We launched a few magazines. One was a publication called *Montgomery's Elite*, a slick bi-monthly publication targeted to upscale families, especially women. In *Elite*, we published profiles of prominent people in the community who gave service and money to worthy causes. We ran stories featuring decor in upscale homes and tips for shopping in boutiques. One of the most popular sections was "Elite Scene," which reported on local high society events like charity fundraisers, symphony and ballet openings, and the masked balls which were a long-standing tradition in the "Old Montgomery" white community. The latter balls were similar to and sometimes themed like Mardi Gras mystic society events (though Montgomery's Catholic influence was not nearly as prominent as in cities like Mobile and New Orleans). The well-to-do families would spend a lot of energy creating elaborate decorations and staging tableaus for these events, for which the attendees dressed to the nines, especially the "queen" who presided over them. The daughters of the prominent white families were also "presented" to society at these balls.

Publisher Scott Brown and I worked closely on the concept. It was no secret in Montgomery that many white people in this target group resented how their newspaper had changed when Gannett purchased it in the mid-1990s and started holding editors accountable for diversity in content. With Gannett's ownership of the Montgomery paper and many other Gannett papers in communities like Montgomery, there came an emphasis on equitable coverage, and less emphasis on negative stories about young black men. Like all Gannett editors, I was held accountable to a measure of diversity and inclusion by hiring more women and people of color and including a wide spectrum of the community in content.

Many of the *Advertiser's* traditional readers had canceled their subscriptions. Brown saw *Elite* magazine as a way of getting back some of those historically traditional readers through different publications. The definition of "traditional" in this case meant white, well-educated, high-income, and philanthropic. These were the blue-blood readers who belonged to the local golf and business clubs, who supported the local art museum and the Alabama Shakespeare Festival (a first-class theater in east Montgomery, the growing upscale part of town where gated communities were popping up), who sent their children to expensive private schools, and who held debutante balls for presenting their daughters to society.

One day Brown and I had a conversation about how to give credit to those who worked on *Montgomery's Elite*, that is, who would appear in what's called the masthead, a publication's roster of editors, writers, and photographers. Brown suggested that he didn't want my name on the masthead as editor or executive editor, even though I was doing the work as the magazine's editor. His message was clear to me, that having the name of a black editor, a name that was common knowledge in Montgomery by then, might deter people from agreeing to be profiled in the magazine or subscribing to it. That's why the first few editions did not list the name of an editor. I wrote a monthly column that appeared in the magazine and signed it "The editor."

Brown left the newspaper after a few issues of *Montgomery's Elite* were published, and I proudly inserted my name in the masthead as editor in all subsequent editions. I never had a conversation with the publisher who succeeded Brown, a woman. I just did it. There were no complaints from readers and no erosion of revenue because I was listed as the top editor.

ANOTHER NON-SECRET WAS THAT white supremacist groups and the KKK were alive and well in the South, even into the 2000s. Various Klan groups saw Montgomery as a place to hold their national conferences and rallies. Once a white supremacist group announced that they would hold a Saturday rally in front of the building that houses the Southern Poverty Law Center (SPLC), a liberal organization that does great work around the topics of hate and tolerance.

The Klan group put out a release inviting the media to a press conference. They wanted us there. In the *Advertiser's* weekend reporter rotation, it just so happened that African American reporter Topher Sanders was scheduled to work that Saturday. Topher came back and told us that not only had he been there representing the newspaper, but coincidentally all of the local television stations sent black staff members to cover the press conference. I'm sure the Kluxers must have asked themselves, "What happened here?" The racial makeup of the media that day was a coincidence, but it gave me great pleasure to know that whatever racial or racist spewing that group did was reported through the eyes and professional perspective of African American journalists.

One KKK encounter startled me. I spent a Saturday morning in my office at the newspaper catching up on paperwork. I decided to walk down the street to have lunch at the Renaissance Hotel, one of the new gems of Montgomery's landscape. As I was walking toward the hotel's side door, the one nearest the restaurant, I noticed walking toward me a group of people wearing long white robes and pointed hoods, including a couple of children, presumably going to a Klan event. Even though I wanted to disbelieve my eyes, I remember pulling out my cell phone to take a picture. The white-robed crew passed me with no recognition that I was standing on the steps of the hotel just six feet away from where they were walking. They clearly did not disapprove of me taking pictures.

AND THEN THERE WAS the most bizarre racial event of my career. One morning I woke up to an email on my phone that had arrived overnight from a Mr. Kingston. He criticized the newspaper as being racist against white people and the newsroom being run by an N-word woman. His email spewed hate toward the newspaper and some of our black staff members, but especially at me. The next day, a similar email came. I took printed copies to Publisher Scott Brown, and he seemed genuinely concerned about the racist rants. He said he would turn the email copies over to our IT department because I told him I thought the emails might be coming from someone inside our building. Some of the language was technical enough that it seemed to me it might have come from someone who understood newsroom jargon.

I was told that all computers in the building would be checked to see if the machines' history showed creation of the emails. I trust that happened late at night, when most staff members were gone. In the next day or two, more emails from the same person were there for me to wake up to and read on my phone the first thing in the morning. I had worked in six previous newsrooms, and I had seen or encountered such overt racism and sexism. I remember the day someone mailed a dead rat to the home of one of our African American *USA Today* managers in a spate of racist emails or notes to her. I had not encountered anything like the emails in Montgomery—someone attacking me personally. One day one of our top editors in the Montgomery newsroom came into my office to make a comment about Mr. Kingston's email. He was appalled.

"How did you know about this?" I asked.

"Well, I think all black people in the newsroom are getting the emails," he said.

More evidence, I thought, that Mr. Kingston might have been an insider, or a former insider. I was furious! Embarrassed! Angry!

I went into Brown's office to let him know that many people on the newsroom staff were reading those racist emails. I also let him know that my husband was out of town, visiting his ailing brother in California, and that I was going home that week to an empty house. Brown said he would alert the police and bring them in on the investigation. I was told the police offered to send a patrol car by our house frequently at night, sometimes parking out front just to be visible.

In one email, Mr. Kingston mentioned "I know where you go to church." I alerted our pastor that someone was sending me threatening messages so he could watch the door from where he sat in the pulpit on Sunday mornings.

One day after a meeting with Brown about the emails, I was headed to my office when tears of rage started to flow. I knew I couldn't go back into the newsroom; I didn't want the staff to see me affected this way. I took the stairwell and headed downstairs to Human Resources. I was looking for the HR director but she wasn't in her office. I stepped into the office of Debra Freisleben, a supervisor in the department. I closed the door and slumped into a chair. For the first time in my career, I absolutely lost it. I sobbed uncontrollably; my body shook and the rage came out in the form of screams.

"I can't do this, I can't do this," I screamed over and over. I found it difficult to breathe through the crying. I wept and I screamed until my body went limp. Debra sat in a chair next to me and held me through the sobs. She had no idea what had happened, and I was in no condition to tell her.

When she finally calmed me, and after I probably used half of her box of tissues to wipe away tears, she suggested that I go home. She asked again what had happened, but I was still too weary to have a conversation.

"Ask Scott Brown. He knows all about it," I said.

When she felt it was safe to leave me alone in her office, Debra quietly went into my office upstairs and retrieved my handbag. When she returned, she walked with me through the back door to the parking lot, hoping no one was paying attention that the editor of the newspaper was leaving in the middle of the day. A few hours later after resting at home, I returned to the newspaper, determined to press on. I first went into Brown's office. Debra had told him about my breakdown. Brown and I talked about next steps—the investigation and protection for me. By about 5:30 p.m., a time when the newsroom staff was at its peak staffing before deadline, Brown and I walked into the roomful of journalists, and he called everybody to gather around him. He told them he would not tolerate the racist behavior that someone was sending, and that I had his full support as executive editor. I don't remember if there were any questions. By then my head was in a fog and we all went back to work. Eventually, the nasty emails stopped coming, but as far as I know, the source remained unsolved.

SOMETIMES GOOD CAN COME out of bad. I picked up the phone one day and was greeted by Karen Sellers, executive director of Montgomery's Family Sunshine Center, a place where battered families can get help. She was calling to thank us for running a story about a woman who was newly married and was killed, apparently at the hands of her husband.

"This woman wasn't on our radar." Sellers told me, an indication that the victim didn't reach out for help.

Sellers asked if there was anything the newspaper could do to bring more attention to the fact that there were resources in the community to help women like this victim. They just needed to call and ask for help. In our conversation I suggested that we arrange for a summit, a roundtable discussion with local stakeholders in the effort to reduce domestic abuse. We would invite representatives from all local media organizations—weekly newspapers, television and radio stations, cable companies, and advertising agencies.

I volunteered to host the meeting in the *Advertiser's* community room, including serving boxed lunches so we could work through a full day.

Every media organization sent someone, plus we had representatives from law enforcement, hospitals, the family court system and the district attorney, herself a strong proponent for reducing domestic abuse.

On the day of the roundtable, after presentations from Sellers and other stakeholders, there was agreement that each media organization would take a week in October—Domestic Abuse Month—to run a series of stories, ads, videos, editorials, commentary pieces or billboard campaigns to bring attention to the problem and the many local solutions to reduce domestic abuse.

The *Advertiser's* first story in a week-long series ran in a Sunday edition in October. On Page One, we revisited the case of the woman whose husband was accused of killing her. We told her story through the eyes of members of her family, most of whom were aware of the abuse and had urged their relative to get away, to get help. The story was anchored with a strong photograph of the woman's young adult daughter somberly holding a photo of her deceased mother.

On Monday, Sellers called to thank me for kicking off our series. She said calls to the center's domestic abuse hotline went up more than 25 percent, largely because our newspaper and other media organizations were getting out the word about available help. We will never know how many lives we saved, how much pain we reduced with this series, but this was a case where we were able to say the newspaper made a difference in the community.

THE RECESSION OF 2008 devastated news organizations; in many ways the industry has never recovered. The Pew Research Center has documented that newsroom employment in all media sectors—newspapers, radio, cable, broadcast television and other (presumably digital)—across the nation had a nearly decade-long decline from 2008 to 2017. Pew found a 45 percent drop in newspaper newsroom employment, no doubt the largest staff reduction in all news media because newspapers generally make up the largest number of total employees in all five areas. The largest losses were in the number of reporters.

From the beginning of the recession we spent years brainstorming ideas to replace lost advertisers, lost readers, and lost circulation. A lot of effort was placed on creating digital platforms to replace the lost print audience, but even that has been slow to reap rewards at traditional media companies. Gannett and other big media organizations began to make cuts by first looking at small trims: Do we need as many batteries for cameras? Can production teams reduce waste of paper or ink? Can we fine-tune typefaces and trim the size of the pages to save paper? Can we make do with fewer assistants, letting executives and managers book their own travel and schedule their own calendars, not to mention many other important things administrative people do every day? Can we save on travel expenses by sending two sports reporters to a bowl game instead of three? Even the ceiling lights were replaced with more modern fixtures that used less power. Electronic archiving systems were created and newsroom librarians were eliminated. Open jobs were transitioned into savings, never to be filled again.

These trims were not enough as the impact of the recession and the revenue declines continued. Then came cuts of entire sections of the newspaper. Book review sections, Sunday magazines, some of the comics and game pages, syndicated columns, and weather pages were on the chopping block. At the *Montgomery Advertiser* before the recession, for example, after discussions with readers about what really mattered in their lives, we created a daily page of school news and reached out to each local school to have a contact person send us news. We shifted a copyeditor to be the newsroom's point of contact and editor of the page. The new page was successful with schools but failed to generate enough revenue to support itself. Naturally, when we cut the page, we upset readers and may have lost subscribers.

Then came the big cuts—people. We did layoffs first in certain departments and to part-time and low-salaried staff, many of whom were recently out of college. But the biggest results would come from cuts of long-time, seasoned staff members because their salaries were bigger. Why lose the manpower of two $30,000 positions when one $70,000 salary could be cut? The problem was that the veterans were the most skilled and held the institutional memory. The layoffs also left fewer people to do the same amount of work. Layoffs left behind a building full of people who were grateful to have jobs but unhappy with the increased expectations. Many felt the quality of our work suffered because we were working faster, not smarter.

The layoffs were hardest on the people—especially older staffers who would have the most trouble finding new employment—and their families who were directly affected, but they also took a toll on me. In every case I knew weeks in advance who would lose their jobs. A lot of preparation from the corporate to the local level happened before a human resources professional and I took individuals into a room, closed the door, and sadly slid a letter across the table. The letter spelled out the employee's severance benefits and provided a support phone number. In all cases, the employees were let go that very day, that very hour. Many would have health insurance only for another month or so. They were understandably devastated, and I was sickened to have to go through this process time after time after time. Some of the laid-off staffers got emotional, but I had to hold it together.

Throughout my career if I felt I needed to change jobs I always knew I could just work at another newspaper. This was no longer the case. In the name of cutting costs, newspapers were slicing themselves to death.

In 2012 after a particularly deep and painful round of layoffs of colleagues who had done the work of two or three people while staffs were shrinking, I was sickened to see what was happening in my newsroom. By then, the publisher overseeing these layoffs in Montgomery was Sam Martin, an African American with deep experience as an advertising executive at newspapers in Boston, New Jersey, Ohio, and Delaware.

After a sad period of saying goodbye to friends who no longer had jobs, health insurance, or prospects for future employment, I told Martin I was probably nearing the end of my own newsroom career.

"If Gannett ever requires me to make more newsroom staff cuts," I said, "you can have my salary. I can't do this anymore."

A year later I retired from Gannett. I had reached all of my goals in daily newspaper journalism.

I wanted to be a copy editor. Check.

I wanted to design pages and become a section editor. Check.

I wanted to be a mid-level supervising editor. Check.

I wanted to be a managing editor. Check.

I wanted to make a difference in the industry as an advocate for newsroom diversity. Check.

I wanted to be an executive editor and run my own newsroom. Check, check.

I had a good run. It was time to move on, time to figure out the next chapter in my life.

22. Full Circle

A call came in December 2012 from a long-time friend at Savannah State University. I had recently announced my retirement from Gannett as executive editor of the *Montgomery Advertiser*. A story about my retirement plans had run in the newspaper, on the Associated Press feed, and on industry websites. I assumed my friend had heard about my career change.

Charles Elmore, the long-time professor and chair of the mass communications program at Savannah State had retired but was called back into service when his successor did not stay in the position long. The program was up for re-accreditation, and the university's leadership knew Elmore could get the job done—again—because he had previously led the team through initial accreditation with the Accrediting Council on Education in Journalism and Mass Communications. "Wanda, you should consider applying to be chair of this department," Elmore said. "I promised my wife that as soon as this accreditation is done, I'm going home again for good."

I had known Elmore a long time, perhaps as far back as high school when we attended the Southern Regional Press Institute (SRPI), Savannah State's annual two-day media training conference. I attended SRPI when I was editor of my high school newspaper and again when I was editor of the *Spelman Spotlight*. SRPI directors subsequently called on me to be a trainer, consultant, and mentor across my entire career, and they have given me awards seven times since 1976 to honor my path in newsrooms. In 2019, I was inducted into the SRPI Hall of Fame.

"Charles, did you hear that I'm planning to retire early next year?" I replied. "My retirement was announced in Montgomery last month. Is that why you're calling me?"

Elmore said he didn't know I was already planning to retire from daily journalism, but he thought of me when he was asked to suggest candidates for the university's search. I reminded him, as he well knew, that I had never gotten around to the advanced degrees required of university professors. I did not have a master's degree, and my one "terminal" degree was honorary, bestowed on me in 1999 by Briarwood College, a small school in Connecticut that invited me to be their graduation speaker.

He said he knew that, but that I had the equivalent of a PhD in experience. "Think about it," he urged.

I did think about it. I was already looking around to see what I might do after retirement from daily journalism. In fact, I had already had conversations with a couple of universities in Alabama, and I was also looking into nonprofit leadership positions in a difficult and discreet search that I began before publicly announcing that I was going to step down as executive editor of the *Montgomery Advertiser*. My mother, the businesswoman, always told me to "look for a job while you have a job." My search was well underway when Elmore called.

My last few years at the newspaper were painful with all of the budget cuts and staff layoffs I had to oversee. I knew the time had come for me to remove myself from this kind of stress. Lloyd and I had prepared for retirement. Gannett had been generous with my salaries, stock options, 401(k) contributions, and retirement payout. I was disciplined with saving for retirement, careful not to blow our available cash, as so many others had to do to make ends meet after layoffs. Lloyd, five years my senior, had already retired.

AFTER AN INTERVIEW TRIP to Savannah, I accepted the position as associate professor and chair of the Department of Mass Communications at Savannah State University. Even though my mother and Aunt Catherine had passed away years before and we had no relatives in Savannah, it felt good to be going home, yet to a place that was remarkably different than when I left forty-six years before. I was desperate then to get away from the oppressive life under Jim Crow laws and being treated as a second-class citizen.

I returned in 2013 able to enjoy one of the most beautiful cities in the nation. Especially in spring, my favorite season, I enjoy driving around looking at the beauty the city has to offer, or riding out to Tybee Island to sit on the pier and watch the surf. It is hard to believe that the beach in Savannah was once forbidden fruit for African Americans. I had to get past the bitterness of remembering institutionalized racism from my childhood. I've never been one to like getting in the ocean, but I enjoy the calmness it brings to my spirit. Tybee Island is now one of my favorite spots.

In Savannah I drive past places I could not go as a child, such as libraries, parks, churches, or the front entrances to certain buildings. I have to remind myself that the buildings or parks are the same, but times—and people—have changed.

Journalists are bound by ethics that forbid political or advocacy work, or donating money to certain kinds of causes. After more than forty years working in newsrooms, I now relish the ability to volunteer my time and talent with a few nonprofit organizations, unrestricted by the rules of journalism. Doing this helps me truly feel like a part of the community.

In 2014, as a department head on the same campus where as a high school student I participated in a summer journalism workshop, I launched a summer program to train high school students in digital storytelling. I engaged transplant Tina A. Brown, a long-time journalist, herself the victim of newsroom downsizing at her newspaper in Connecticut, to direct the program, which we named SSU Media High. With the help of other staff and faculty members, we started an annual film festival and produced a magazine for long-form journalism.

At Savannah State I enjoyed the collegial and scholarly atmosphere, attending seminars and programs with interesting speakers, bringing to campus people from newsrooms and other universities to share their research with students, and helping to motivate a new generation of aspiring journalists and communications professionals.

One thing I realized was that despite the courses in the fundamentals of journalism, many of the students were not committed to the ethics and standards of journalism. Some of this may have been the disassociation of pure journalism, because the curriculum also included courses in film production, documentaries, and audio production. At a faculty and staff retreat,

I took the team through a process that led to a change in the name of our program from the Department of Mass Communications to the Department of Journalism and Mass Communications. Adding "Journalism" helped us emphasize to students the foundational aspects of reporting, writing, and editing, including in digital media coursework. The change was applauded by the university's administration.

I used my network of professional journalists and expanded the list of role models available to students. I brought to campus Belmont University Professor Sybril "Dr. Syb" Brown when she published her book, *Innovate: Lessons from the Underground Railroad.* Bobbi Bowman, my former colleague at the *Washington Post* and *USA Today,* helped set up an annual student job fair where she would don a white lab coat with the embroidered title "Resume Doctor" to help students improve their resumes. Sheila Brooks, CEO of SRB Communications, came from Washington, D.C., as a keynote speaker for the Southern Regional Press Institute. Angela Robinson, a former TV news anchor in two top-ten markets, came from Atlanta to work one-on-one with students who had dreams of becoming broadcast journalists, and later anchors themselves. Rene Marsh, the CNN correspondent who covers government regulation and transportation, was a speaker at the Press Institute. Jason Miccolo Johnson, the Washington, D.C., photojournalist with whom I worked at *USA Today,* brought his exhibition, *Yours Naturally: Beauty That Grows on You,* to the campus, and he later returned as a visiting professor. Pulitzer Prize-winning journalist Isabel Wilkerson, author of the best-selling *The Warmth of Other Suns,* and novelist and journalist Tina McElroy Ansa, author of five novels and my Spelman College friend, came to talk about writing and their books.

I took students to regional and national conferences of the National Association of Black Journalists and showed them how to pick the appropriate workshops and how to work a conference for networking opportunities. I sent students to journalism conferences on other campuses and helped prepare students for study abroad.

WORKING WITH TODAY'S YOUNG people is always rewarding but can be eye-opening. In conversations with friends and colleagues who teach in other programs, we commiserate that current students—many of them very bright—were either not challenged in high school or they did not challenge themselves. Could it have been the lack of dedicated teachers—like those we had at Beach High School—who cared deeply about making sure they prepared black students for a still-imperfect world?

As a professor, I found that many students were not good writers. They had not benefited from the lessons given us on diagramming sentences, writing and orally presenting book reports—discussions that forced us to develop critical thinking skills. The millennial students called themselves communications majors, but many rarely kept abreast of current events. I get that young people don't read print newspapers these days. They were born digital. But news is available on platforms that this YouTube generation seems to enjoy—Twitter, Facebook, and notifications on their phones. They walk around campus with buds in their ears, listening to God knows what, but probably not to news, audio books, or podcasts.

Many of the millennials I encountered seem to have left high school with poor reading and comprehension skills, often not caring about what they don't know. Many don't take notes in class lectures, don't read text-books—sometimes they don't even buy the books—and don't seem seriously concerned about project deadlines. Unfortunately, in some cases the system is set up to pass students even with these education gaps. And they are the lucky ones. Others are not even encouraged to stick it out.

Some who use the excuse of not having money to buy books must think I just stepped off a spaceship from Mars. I see the wardrobes of $150 sneakers, the elaborate manicures, and expensive hairstyles. When students convinced me they truly could not afford a textbook, I bought books myself and loaned them for the semester. If many of the students I encountered would put as much effort into school as they put into finding ways to avoid excelling, they could become millionaires and offer me a job someday.

The day I told my family I wanted to become a journalist I was in the eleventh grade, living in a city not necessarily known for outstanding ac-complishments in journalism. As an African American female growing up in the segregated South, I don't recall the name of a single woman who worked for our local daily newspapers or television stations. One may assume women were working behind the scenes, but I recall none that had bylines or on-air television news presence in Savannah.

So there I was, standing in the family kitchen announcing to my grandmother and anyone else who would listen that I wanted to work for a daily newspaper. My grandmother asked how I thought I would accomplish this, because, she said, "Negro girls don't work for newspapers." Good point, but I was too naive or too obstinate to think I could not overcome those odds.

Her advice was this: "Take some education classes so you'll have something to fall back on. Then you can always get a job as a teacher" like other women in our family. I rejected her advice. I was determined to head down a different path. My path took me to newspaper journalism, albeit with a few detours as an educator along the way. In the long run, perhaps my grandmother knew best.

I TELL YOUNG PEOPLE that they never know how networking and relationships can be useful years later. My reach as a media diversity advocate took me to some unlikely places, and one brought me full circle in Savannah.

In the early 1990s, I was invited to speak at the Defense Equal Opportunity Management Institution at Patrick Air Force Base in Cocoa Beach, Florida. I arrived in the middle of the night and was taken to a spartan military motel. My escort, a female officer, took me to the room door and handed me the key, with instructions to be ready at 0700. It was pitch dark and I didn't know exactly where I was. The next morning I was awakened by the sound of crashing waves. When I looked out the window, I realized that I had spent the night just a few yards from the Atlantic Ocean.

I received a briefing about DEOMI, an education and training program "in human relations and equal opportunity." Then after a tour and lunch I began my presentation about *USA Today's* diversity principle that the newspaper accurately reflect the nation in staffing and content. I described our strategic recruiting practices of identifying and tracking women and people of color, sometimes keeping in touch with candidates for years before hiring them; about how we recruited at conferences that people of color attended in great numbers; and how we would have a presence in public areas like job fairs but would also book a private hospitality space for conversations away from the peering eyes of candidates' colleagues supervisors. I shared how we consistently had leadership training in the Gannett Company, and I made it clear that executives were accountable through evaluations and bonuses for maintaining and increasing diversity numbers.

I shared that supervisors were trained to understand cultural differences to help diverse teams work well together. I talked about *USA Today's* mandate to have content diversity throughout each day's newspaper, and especially on Page One where every day there was the image of a woman and at least one person of color as sources in stories, and that a crime story with a black face did not count.

I told them about the Gannett concept of mainstreaming—the inclusion of women and people of color in stories as expert sources, not necessarily in stories about race, gender or ethnicity. Our newsrooms created what we called minority source guides—lists and contact information for people of color who could be future story sources. Source guides might include politicians, business owners, educators and professors, government agency workers, religious leaders, scientists, lawyers, doctors, and community advocates. The primary reason for source guides was to take away last-minute excuses that "we can't find any" experts who are women or people of color.

Many years after my visit to DEOMI, I was asked to speak to a master's program class at Armstrong State University in Savannah. Will Martin, a student in the course who also worked on my team at Savannah State, asked me to participate as part of his cohort's class project. The evening of the class I slipped into the classroom and took a seat while another group was completing its presentation. The professor kept looking at me with a puzzled glance, and on the break between presentations, she asked, "Did you ever work at *USA Today*?"

"Why, yes I did," I responded.

It turns out the professor, then a young Air Force public affairs officer, is now *Dr.* Elizabeth Desnoyers-Colas, the very same young officer who squired me around Patrick Air Force Base in the early 1990s. It was one of those times when I saw how my career and my life had truly come full circle.

Epilogue: Life Lessons
and a Seat for Women

In early 2013, nearing retirement from daily journalism, I was thinking my professional life couldn't get much better. I had come from a Jim Crow childhood, through the civil rights movement, to editing roles at seven daily newspapers. Then a call came from Crystal Williams Chancellor, director of communications for the Washington-based Women's Media Center. Crystal and I have known each other through the years working in various journalism associations, including the American Society of News Editors and the National Association of Black Journalists. She was part of the team at the *Akron* (Ohio) *Beacon Journal* that won a Pulitzer Prize Gold Medal for public service for a year-long series focusing on local race relations.

The Media Center's mission was to provoke discussion and accountability for change, bringing more diverse options to media in content and staffing. Crystal related that the Center was reviewing a survey of the conditions of women in media that "detailed persistent gender disparity in a range of media business(es) . . . that rank among the greatest influencers in society." Among the key findings of the 2013 report were:

> . . . [A]t its current pace, it will take until 2085 for women to reach parity with men in leadership roles in government/politics, business, entrepreneurship and nonprofits.
>
> By a nearly three-to-one margin, male front-page bylines at top newspapers outnumbered female bylines in coverage of the 2012 presidential

election. Men were far more likely to be quoted than women in election stories. Ironically, that was also the case in typical women's issues such as coverage of abortion, birth control, Planned Parenthood, and women's rights.

On Sunday TV talk shows, only 25 percent of expert guests were female, leaving a dearth of voices and little insight from women.

The report summary went on for dozens of bullet points, documenting how women were being stereotyped in jobs and in the kinds of stories written about them. One result that struck me: "Obituaries about men far outnumber those of women in top national and regional newspapers."

Even in death, it seems, women are not recognized as good media subjects.

On the younger end of the gender media spectrum, the report cited that girls as young as age six are starting to see themselves as sex objects, based on a combination of media influence, a mother's parenting, and religion. Girls were already being objectified, making it difficult for women to overcome disparities in later years.

Crystal asked me to join a group of women media leaders—in newsrooms, film, advertising, and public relations—to attend the March 2013 forum of the White House Council on Women and Girls. This initiative was formed by President Barack Obama's executive order to establish a coordinated response to issues that impact the lives of women and girls and to ensure that federal programs and policies would address distinctive concerns for this population, including women of color and women with disabilities.

The discussion, led by Valerie Jarrett, a senior advisor to President Obama, would advise the White House on policy making to rectify the disparities.

Walking into the meeting room, I found the White House-branded tent card with my name, which indicated my seat at the table (I still have that tent card, the only one I've ever saved). I was almost breathless when I saw some of the other participants. One was my friend Carole Simpson, who at ABC News was the first African American woman to anchor a major network newscast and the first woman of color to moderate a presidential debate (in 1992, between George H. W. Bush, Bill Clinton, and Ross Perot). When I was directing the Diversity Institute at Vanderbilt, Carole graciously accepted my invitation speak at one of our class graduations. Bad weather in the Northeast forced her to hang out with us in Nashville for a few extra days, and we became even closer. Across the room I saw Gloria Steinem, feminist leader since the 1960s and co-founder and editor of *Ms.* magazine, which became the bible of the women's liberation movement. When I introduced myself to Steinem before the meeting began I told her she had the first *and* middle names of my mother, Gloria Marie, who was also a self-described feminist. You get the idea; the room was packed with high-achieving women leaders who had taken their rightful seats at the table. Jarrett herself was another example.

The White House forum got me thinking about other such women, especially in journalism, and of my own career in that regard. Years after I had broken barriers as a woman and an African American, I proudly joined a team to produce a book about the contributions of women in journalism. *The Edge of Change: Women in the 21st Century Press,* published in 2009, was co-edited by journalists and journalism educators June Nicholson, Pamela Creedon, Pamela Johnson, and me. It was Johnson, formerly executive editor of the *Arizona Republic* and at the time on the Leadership Faculty of the Poynter Institute for Media Studies in St. Petersburg, Florida, who asked me to join the team. Poynter is one of the industry's premier programs for training journalists and a think tank for the industry.

We gathered small groups of women to talk generally about common issues relating to the industry and specifically about some of their own experiences. We brainstormed for chapter themes and people who should write their own stories. From roundtable discussions came a list of topics like "How Women are Shaping Newsrooms and Companies," "Women as Op-Ed Columnists and Editors of Editorial Pages," "Women Making Choices," and "The Future: Shifting Paradigms."

In the end, a star-studded array of women contributed to the book, including *Washington Post* columnist Dorothy Butler Gilliam; syndicated columnist Ellen Goodman; multiple Pulitzer-winning photographer Carol Guzy; Geneva Overholser, former editor of the *Des Moines Register* and also a Pulitzer Prize winner; Catalina Camia, former politics and White House editor at *USA Today* and a president of the Asian American Journalists

Association; and Deb Price, who while at the *Detroit News* wrote the first nationally syndicated column on gay and lesbian issues.

In my quest to make a difference and tell stories in journalism, *The Edge of Change* may have been one of my most significant steps. Over the years I have written chapters for books edited by other journalists and journalism professors, and I've been interviewed or profiled in more books than I can count.

In 2019, part of my journey was included in a chapter in Kristen Grady Gilger and Julia Wallace's *There's No Crying in Newsrooms: What Women Have Learned about What It Takes to Lead.* (Wallace was my former colleague at *USA Today*.) The authors anchored the chapter with my story with this quote from me: "If you're not covering the entire community, you're not accurate."

As women began to move into leadership positions in media and in other industries, one thing we had to figure out was how to think and work like men but still act like the ladies we were. In corporate-speak, I am what we call a two-fer—black and female. I have been asked frequently which status challenged me the most. Just as I had to learn to become racially bicultural when I graduated from Spelman College and entered a mostly white work world, I had to learn how to play a man's game in business. I wasn't always comfortable in the transition from quiet personality to forthright businesswoman, but that had to change.

My changes included speaking up and sometimes speaking out over the voices of others in the room, accepting leadership on challenging projects, speaking before large groups, and touting my own accomplishments and abilities. I saw men do this time after time, and I realized that I had to become my own best advocate.

I recall too well times in meetings when I would make a suggestion about a story or policy change much in the way that any man would make the case. Yet my suggestion would fall flat and the conversation would move on. A few times, my male supervisor or perhaps another woman would jump back in, forcing my suggestion back onto the table by saying something like, "Isn't that what Wanda just said?" I give credit to Peter Prichard when he was editor of *USA Today* for doing this many times, supporting my ideas when he thought they deserved further discussion.

USA Today Executive Editor Ron Martin sent me to a workshop for new women managers. The two-day training was conducted by Deborah Tannen, a professor who published *You Just Don't Understand: Women and Men in Conversation* in 1990. The book was one of the first on gender differences in conversation styles. Tannen wrote about why women and men were able to walk away from the same conversation with completely different impressions of what was said.

In the workshop, she taught us how to give a firm business handshake while looking the other person in the eye. We learned that when a woman enters a man's office for a meeting, he might point toward a low-profile sofa, but *he* is likely to sit in a comfortable straight chair, seated on a higher plane. Tannen told us to politely refuse the sofa and ask for a seat similar to the man's, putting us on an equal level. Tannen taught us how to work a room at a reception and to always have a business card ready when someone hands you their card. In mentoring relationships, I've passed along these and similar lessons.

I have had so many opportunities to serve in seats at industry tables, especially in newsrooms as the top editor with a group of others making decisions about positioning the best stories for each day's newspaper. I had the obligation to lead the discussion not just for the news content of stories, but also to ask questions and give direction on whether stories accurately reflected our community of readers.

But there were other tables. I sat at the table of the Dow Jones Newspaper Fund's Board of Directors to help the foundation create opportunities for journalism education and newsroom internships. For several years I sat at the elegant and historic dining room table of Mrs. Jean Friendly in Washington's ritzy Georgetown community as a member of the Advisory Board of the Alfred Friendly Press Foundation. (I'll never forget the day I nervously knocked over and broke one of Mrs. Friendly's antique demitasse cups, in which her house staff served us coffee. She was so gracious about it.) The Friendly board was charged with charged with selecting journalists from countries that did not have a free press to work in the United States for six months.

I sat at the table of the Accrediting Committee of the Accrediting Council on Education in Journalism and Mass Communications (ACEJMC) with a group of industry professionals to review the site team reports for universities seeking initial accreditation or reaccreditation.

In Alabama I sat at the table as a member of the board for two press associations, and for four years I sat at the table at Columbia University as a juror for the Pulitzer Prize. And I sat at the table of committees deciding other journalism writing awards, for large media companies like Cox, Gannett, Hearst, and for the Society for Professional Journalists.

I sat at the table at a White House council, and at the table of advisory boards for university programs. I sat at the table as a member of the board of the American Society of News Editors. In several cities I sat at the tables of local nonprofit organizations whose missions were to aid those in need of educational, social, or financial support. As a person of color, I have sat at the tables of project teams to help improve newsroom diversity for young and aspiring African American, Asian American, Hispanic, Native American, and women journalists.

I do this not only for my generation and my industry, but for the generations to come. I do this for those who take seriously the five freedoms guaranteed in the First Amendment—especially freedom of the press. And I do this for young women who are rising through the ranks in corporations, law firms, government, universities—anywhere there are opportunities for professional growth. I try to inspire women and young people who are starting their own businesses because self-employment is self-determination.

I try to make all of this possible for young women like my daughter, Shelby, whom I have brought along on my journey. I want Shelby, as a buyer for some of the nation's largest retail companies, and her peers to know that when they understand how to optimize life's best opportunities, they can demand a seat at the table so that their influence is appreciated and impactful. They must understand that when they get a seat at the table, they are obligated to mentor—to pull up a chair and invite another hard-working and deserving woman or person of color to take her or his own seat at the table.

A HAND REACHED DOWN to help me ascend the portable steps of the stage in a hotel ballroom in Miami on August 2, 2019. The hand belonged to Craig Melvin, NBC/MSNBC anchor and correspondent. He handed me off to actress Alfre Woodard, his co-presenter. The questions in my heart and in my head at that moment: Was this a dream? Was I stepping up into heaven?

Almost.

I was being inducted into the National Association of Black Journalists Hall of Fame, a prestigious honor bestowed by an organization that I have worked in for four decades. In 1993, I was the first woman to be given the eleventh Ida B. Wells Award for my work and advocacy for media diversity. NABJ was one of the presenting organizations. Also in 1993, I directed a landmark survey and report for NABJ—*Muted Voices: Frustration and Fear in the Newsroom*, the first of many industry studies of people of color and women working in the media. I was a member of NABJ's Print Task Force which commissioned the study, and *USA Today*, my newspaper at the time, sponsored its production.

As I approached the podium for brief acceptance remarks in 2019, in one of the happiest moments in my life, my peers rose to their feet across the massive ballroom, applauding me with praise and respect. Standing before me were people in my generation and millennials who were there to see what a journalism hall of famer would have to say to them. My husband, Willie, and our daughter, Shelby, were in the audience, beaming with pride.

"My heart is about to explode," Shelby posted on Facebook before I returned to my seat in the ballroom. It was a proud moment for all of us.

I began my prepared remarks, for the first time in my life as a print journalist using a teleprompter. I wanted to make eye contact with this audience so I accepted the challenge to use unfamiliar technology to help me say exactly what was in my heart that day.

"Ever since I attended my first NABJ conference in Louisville in the early 1980s [1981, my friend and Louisville journalist Betty Baye blurted out across the room to make it more specific], this organization has been a part of my personal and professional life. I'm honored to be inducted with this cohort of great journalists and to join this club of outstanding colleagues. Thank you NABJ, not just for this honor, but for being my rock, my enabler, my supportive professional family."

When NABJ sent out a press release with news of my upcoming induction, hundreds of journalists reached out to congratulate me. I wanted to give the audience some advice that came as a result of so many people telling me that they learned how to become better journalists and better leaders simply by watching me.

"The message I want to leave you with today is that people are watching," I said. "Whether you are making your way around the halls at this conference, or back in your newsroom or on the job in your digital space, people are watching *you*. When you are building a campaign for your best clients, or leading a meeting, conducting an interview, shooting a story or editing a package, people are watching. And most of all, for those who are now leaders or aspire to become leaders, people are definitely watching you, as they were watching and then emulating me. That's the greatest praise I could receive.

"For those of you who desire to be a leader, promise me this. Go grab yourself a mentor and learn how to lead with compassion and authority. And then, when you become a leader, I want you to make it your business to bring someone else along. Whether you are a college student or a seasoned journalist, you have a responsibility to mentor others, especially your brothers and sisters in NABJ."

When I finished, after a quick paparazzi moment to visually document the event, actress Woodard took both of my hands with a big smile to congratulate me.

"You have an amazing story," she told me. "I want a copy of your book," referring to this memoir which was mentioned twice on stage that day.

She added, "I want an *autographed* copy of your book."

I assured her that would happen.

Index